Trust in the Lord with all your heart and
lean not on your own understanding;
in all your ways submit to him,
and he will make your paths straight.

—Proverbs 3:5–6 (niv)

MYSTERIES OF COBBLE HILL FARM

Digging Up Secrets

MYSTERIES OF COBBLE HILL FARM

Digging Up Secrets

ELIZABETH PENNEY

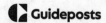

MYSTERIES OF COBBLE HILL FARM

Digging Up Secrets

GLOSSARY OF UK TERMS

brown sauce • a British condiment, main ingredients are tomatoes and tamarind extract

chancer • an unscrupulous person who will resort to just about anything to get what they want

cheeky • boldly rude or impudent in usually a playful or amusing way

chivy • to tease or annoy

dooryard • a yard next to the door of a house

elevenses • midmorning tea break

fit • British term for very attractive

good sort • a kind and likable person

growler • a small, round pork pie

hoggs • Yorkshire term for lambs born the previous spring

lay-by • an area at the side of a road for vehicles to pull off and stop

nibs • an important or self-important person—used in the phrase *his nibs* or *her nibs* as if to say *his highness* or *her highness*

tat • something cheap and of bad quality

CHAPTER ONE

A s Dr. Harriet Bailey unlocked the door that connected her new residence to the veterinary office, a canine symphony rose from the kennels in the back. On this Tuesday morning in June, she felt like pinching herself. How did an animal doctor from Connecticut find herself practicing in a remote yet charming English village at age thirty-three? The short answer was that a failed romance and an unexpected inheritance had added up to a life-changing opportunity.

Harriet was the new vet at Cobble Hill Farm in White Church Bay, Yorkshire, attempting to fill the shoes of her beloved grandfather, Dr. Harold Bailey. Thankfully, her aunt Jinny, a local physician and fount of wisdom, lived next door. That helped keep homesickness for her stateside family and friends at bay.

Inside the cheerful clinic, a row of patients and their owners waited.

"Cobble Hill Vet Clinic. How may I help you?" Receptionist Polly Thatcher, her ponytail swinging, held the phone receiver in place with her shoulder while tapping on the computer keyboard. She greeted Harriet with a grin and mouthed, "Miss Birtwhistle, Room One."

Harriet found the file in the day's stack and skimmed it as she hurried down the short hall. The blood test results confirmed exactly what she'd thought.

"Good morning, Miss Birtwhistle." Harriet greeted the retired schoolteacher, who was seated in the examination room clutching a black-and-white cat to her chest. "How are you today?" She set the chart on the counter, suppressing the treat-and-go training she'd received at her former job, where high daily volume was the metric for success. In White Church Bay, she was learning that veterinary practice included the whole family, both human and animal members, and she could show genuine concern for all involved, which was her natural desire anyway.

"I'm doing pretty well," Jane Birtwhistle said. "This dry weather means my joints don't ache so much."

"I'm glad to hear that. How's Mittens? Let's weigh him." Harriet reached for the cat, likely named for his white paws. He really was adorable.

Jane surrendered him reluctantly then hovered near the counter as Harriet set the cat in the weighing bucket. "Usually, sick cats go off their feed," Jane said. "But he's a greedy old brute. He's been stealing food from the others." She owned a dozen or so cats at last count.

"And still losing weight." Harriet made a note. He was down an ounce from the last visit. Another sign that her diagnosis was correct. She gently lifted Mittens out of the bucket and onto the counter, where she listened to his heart and checked his vitals, murmuring soothing words to him.

"Is he going to be all right?" Jane's pale blue eyes filled with tears. "He's my favorite. I've had him twelve years, ever since he was a wee mite."

"I have good news for you." Harriet stroked Mittens under the chin, eliciting a purr. "His diagnosis is treatable. It's hyperthyroidism, a disorder of the thyroid gland."

Jane sniffled. "Are you sure? I thought maybe it was cancer." Her voice lowered to a whisper on the dreaded word.

"No, there's no cancer. We checked for that too, just in case. Like with people, it's common for older cats' bodies to start to work differently as they age. Hyperthyroidism is common. It's characterized by rapid weight loss even though the cat is still eating." Harriet showed her the printout. "See? The blood test confirmed it. His levels are out of optimal range, but as I said earlier, it's treatable."

Hope transformed the elderly woman's face, pinking her cheeks. "So he'll be all right?"

"He'll be fine if you give him this medicine as directed." Harriet gave her a tube of cream to rub inside the cat's ears, along with instructions and things to watch for. "Ear cream is easier than giving him pills, and there are fewer side effects."

Jane laughed in relief. "He doesn't like taking pills, do you, my love?" She picked up her cat and put him inside the carrier. "Thank you, Doctor."

"I'm happy to help. Polly will schedule a follow-up visit so we can make sure everything is going okay. But please call if there are any problems."

Harriet led the pair out and then picked up the next folder. It was for a patient she hadn't seen before—a retriever mix named Jolly with a mysterious lump, according to his owner, a Mr. Terry Leaper.

"Jolly?" she called in the reception area.

A stout middle-aged man dressed in a blue work shirt and jeans got to his feet, tugging on a leash attached to a dog with silky golden fur. Moving forward, Mr. Leaper eyed Harriet up and down. "So, you're the new Doc Bailey."

"I am. And this handsome creature must be Jolly. Right this way, please, Mr. Leaper."

As they walked to the exam room, Mr. Leaper said, "Please, call me Terry."

With cancer on her mind after Jane Birtwhistle's worry, Harriet was relieved to diagnose a common problem. "It's called a lipoma," she told Terry. "A soft growth in the tissue under the skin."

Terry eyed the lump dubiously. "What's to be done about it? I'm worried that it might keep growing."

With its position on Jolly's ribs, the growth was already impeding the movement of his front leg. "I recommend removing it. It's a simple operation. He'll be in and out in hours." While the clinic didn't have facilities for long and complicated surgeries, it was perfectly adequate for simple procedures like this one.

Terry gripped the edge of the counter, his face going white. "Sorry. I don't like the idea of my poor dog going under the knife."

Harriet helped Terry to a chair. "That's understandable. *Operation* is always a scary word. And our pets are like family to us, aren't they?"

"They are," Terry agreed gruffly. "Lost my wife a few years ago, and Jolly has brought me a lot of comfort. He even goes to work with me. I'm a plumber, you see, so I travel all over with Jolly in my van."

"We'll take good care of him," Harriet said. "I promise. Like you take good care of him. Why don't we schedule this for next week?

Say on Monday morning?" She returned to the dog, giving his head and neck a thorough scratching. "You'll feel much better, won't you, boy?" Jolly wagged his tail as if he understood her words.

Terry nodded. "Monday. Thanks, Doc. It's nice to know what that is and how to fix it."

By midmorning the place cleared out, the first group of patients handled. "Should I pop through and put the kettle on for elevenses?" Polly asked, rolling her chair back. They usually took a break at this time.

"Thank you," Harriet said. "I'm ready for a cup of tea." While she started each day with coffee dispensed from her beloved machine, she'd learned to enjoy the tea breaks built into her new routine. People in England made a point of sitting and relaxing instead of grabbing food and drink on the go.

While waiting for the kettle to boil, she finished up notes on the charts and stacked them to be filed. Polly was very particular about her filing system, and Harriet wouldn't dream of disturbing it. When she'd arrived a month ago to take over the practice, she'd been relieved to find Polly, age twenty-four and local, already on board. Not only did she know all the patients, but she had made it her mission to help Harriet navigate the inevitable potholes and pitfalls.

"Tea is on the terrace," Polly sang, inclining her head around the door. "It's such a nice day, I thought we might as well enjoy the sun on our faces."

"I'll be right there." Harriet made sure the answering machine was on and followed Polly out to the slate patio, accessed by French doors from the kitchen. Her grandfather had added the surprisingly modern touch to the stone Georgian-style house, which had been built around 1820. The plumbing, electrical, and heating systems had been updated to comply with safety regulations, but many things were beginning to show their age. Otherwise, the house had kept its considerable charm.

The garden itself was an enchanted fairyland on this brilliant June morning. A low stone wall enclosed the area, with a green wooden gate on one side leading to Grandad's art gallery, and another that led to a barn with extra kennel space. Bees buzzed among the sweet-scented riot of rose, delphinium, foxglove, and lavender, and birds twittered in the crab apple and cherry trees.

Harriet's heart soared with joy as she chose a teak chair at the table. Good work, new friends, and a beautiful place to live. *Thank You*, she breathed in a silent prayer. *I am truly blessed.* What a reversal from the bitter despair of several months ago, when her world had imploded with her grandfather's death on top of her broken engagement to a colleague.

As was their habit, the clinic cat, Charlie, a scruffy female calico, and Maxwell, a long-haired dachshund with wheeled rear legs due to an injury, joined them. Maxwell, as always, lurked near the table, hoping for crumbs, and Charlie jumped onto the wall to bask in the sunshine. Harriet chuckled again at the thought of her grandfather naming every single one of his office cats Charlie, regardless of their gender. He said it kept things simpler that way. One less thing to keep straight.

Polly handed her a mug of tea then pushed a plate of scones toward her.

"What flavor do we have today?" Harriet asked. A neighbor brought them home-baked goods every morning, something she'd always done for Old Doc Bailey, as he was known.

"Her famous apricot. She added almonds to this batch and topped them with toasted oats as well." Polly took a bite of one and hummed in approval. "Very good," she muttered with her mouth full.

Harriet bit into a scone and enjoyed how the pastry melted in her mouth. Plenty of butter and fresh eggs made all the difference. Doreen Danby and her husband, Tom, owned a nearby farm, where they raised sheep, chickens, and five long-legged children. When things calmed down, Harriet really should pay Doreen a visit and thank her for her kindness—and the delectable baked goods.

Polly's cell phone rang. She looked at the screen and frowned.

"Who is it this time?" Harriet asked. To say Polly had an active dating life was putting it mildly. Harriet could barely keep up with her young assistant's active social life and roster of friends, who had a constant calendar of picnics, movies, concerts, and dancing keeping Polly busy.

"It's Van. It's not like him to call when he's on duty. Maybe I'd better take this." She answered the phone and listened intently. Then she handed it to Harriet. "It's for you. It's an emergency."

Harriet pressed the clutch and changed gears, her sweaty palm sliding on the shift. It was bad enough that she had to drive on the wrong side of the road. Operating a tricky manual transmission at the same time was too much. The clinic's Land Rover was a beast of a vehicle, and as soon as she could afford it, she would replace it with a sleek new automatic. Maybe then she could get used to driving on the left side of the—*whoops*. She'd started to drift over the center again.

She rattled to a stop in the dooryard of Primrose Cottage, parking next to the police car and ambulance already there. Beside the kitchen door, two men watched as EMTs guided a gurney through the narrow opening. She ran to join Detective Constable Van Worthington and Pastor Fitzwilliam "Will" Knight, the minister of the village church.

"How is she?" Harriet asked, fearing the answer. Elderly Meredith Bennett was unconscious, an oxygen mask over her nose and a terrible gray tinge to her thin cheeks.

"We're praying she'll be all right," Pastor Will said in the same deep voice that brought his flock comfort during sermons. "I found her lying on her kitchen floor when I came to visit." His soft brown eyes were somber with concern.

"What happened? Did she fall?" Harriet pictured Meredith taking a tumble and breaking a hip. But she had a head injury, judging by the bandage.

"Someone knocked her on the head," Van said. "I'll be interviewing the neighbors to find out if they saw anyone here before the reverend came to call." Despite his assertive words, the young policeman appeared worried. Deadly assaults didn't occur very often in White Church Bay. Or so she'd been told.

A chill went down Harriet's spine. Who would hurt sweet Meredith? Although her tiny cottage was well furnished, she wasn't wealthy.

"We're also trying to locate her granddaughter, Stacey," the detective constable went on. "She'll need to know about this."

Pastor Will nodded. "Good thinking, Van. She may need to stay with Meredith for a bit, until she's fully mended."

A howl reached them from inside the house. Meredith's dog, Huntley, was the reason Harriet had been called to the scene. He'd need to be boarded while his mistress was in the hospital unless the granddaughter was willing to take him.

"That's my cue," she said. After retrieving a leash from the Land Rover, she went into the house. Huntley, an aged springer spaniel with brown and white spots, was still howling. She approached him cautiously, speaking gentle words. "It's all right, boy. I'm here to help. Your mistress will be fine, I promise."

I hope.

CHAPTER TWO

The howl diminished to snuffling as Huntley explored his new acquaintance. Harriet realized the poor thing was practically blind. But he could smell well enough to gobble down the treat she offered him. While he was distracted, she clipped on the leash.

"Everything all set in here?" Van asked. "Pastor Will went to the hospital. I've got to lock up once you're done."

"I think so, yes." Harriet glanced around the kitchen, noticing an old blanket behind the Aga stove alongside food and water dishes. "Think you could grab those for me? He'll sleep better with his own blanket."

The detective constable obliged and carried the dog's belongings out to Harriet's vehicle. After Harriet stowed them along with Huntley in the back, he stood there, shifting his weight.

"Is there something else I can help you with, Van?" Harriet prompted as she closed the rear door of the vehicle.

He pulled at the collar of his uniform. "Do you think Polly would go to the tractor fest with me?" His fair skin flushed, making him appear younger than the midtwenties Harriet guessed him to be. He wasn't bad looking with his blond hair and hazel eyes, but he was a bit awkward and gangly.

"I can't speak for Polly, I'm afraid. You'll have to ask her your-self." Harriet climbed into the Land Rover. "I'm sorry, but I've got patients waiting for me."

"Put in a good word for me?" Van called as she started the Land Rover.

She managed to turn the vehicle around without stalling then gave him a wave, hoping that would suffice as an answer.

Back at Cobble Hill Farm, she stowed Huntley in a boarding kennel along with his blanket and dishes. With fresh food and water, he was all set. Each kennel opened to a large, enclosed area, perfect for exercise.

Inside the clinic, Polly greeted her with relief. "People are get-ting antsy. What took you so long?"

Harriet gave her a teasing smile. "DC Worthington wanted to discuss his hope to take you to the tractor festival."

"Really?" Polly looked taken aback. "I didn't know he was inter-ested. But maybe he means as friends. He could have texted me about that." She shook her head and then said, "It's so sad about Meredith. Poor duck. I hope she'll be all right."

"Me too." Harriet changed into fresh scrubs and began to work through the list. A busy couple of hours lay ahead. Apparently, people didn't care if she was the new "Old" Doc Bailey, or perhaps they were simply curious about her. Either way, she'd take the business.

After a long afternoon engrossed in appointments and patient notes, Harriet locked the front door of the clinic and trudged into the house, drooping with weariness and eager to get into the shower. She was too tired to even think about cooking dinner. Her cell phone rang when she was halfway up the stairs, on the landing where a portrait of her great-great-grandfather—another Harold—glowered.

"Aunt Jinny. How are you?" Harriet was glad to hear from Dr. Genevieve Garrett, her father's sister and a general practitioner. Aunt Jinny lived and saw patients next door, in the dower cottage that had once belonged to Cobble Hill Farm.

"The bigger question is, how are you?" Aunt Jinny asked with a laugh. "I remember the early days in my practice. Should I bring supper over?"

"I'd love that. Thanks." Harriet's step lightened as she climbed the rest of the stairs. Missing her parents the way she did, it was wonderful to have family close by. Her aunt was great company and a wonderful cook.

In the upper hall, she paused at a rear window to gaze out over the property. From the second story, she could see fields extending west to where they met the moors, reminding her she hadn't had time to explore the countryside yet. The mysterious moors, inspiration for the Brontë sisters—how they captured the imagination.

Closer at hand stood the small building that held her grandfather's art studio and gallery, which had sold prints of his famous oil paintings. It had been closed since Grandad's death, and Harriet hadn't worked out the details to reopen it yet. The busy veterinary practice was taking up most of her time and energy thus far. She'd get into the swing of things soon, and then she'd address the gallery.

A high-pitched barking rose to her ears from somewhere outside, and she recognized Huntley's distinctive voice. Was he hurt? Forgetting her shower for the moment, she hurried downstairs and out to the kennel.

In the far corner of the yard, the dog dashed back and forth, barking. Harriet hurried toward Huntley, noticing that he'd dug a hole in the soil. A rather deep hole, judging by the mound he'd created.

Was something buried there? A dead animal or something? Feeling slightly squeamish, Harriet crossed the run to the spot and peered into the hole.

A rusty metal chest about the size of a large toolbox sat at the bottom.

Naturally, Harriet's first thought was of treasure. Gold coins from a pirate's hoard, perhaps. *What else would be buried in an old chest, right?* Laughing at the notion, she stared into the hole, noticing that the object was firmly lodged in the soil. More digging would be required before she could investigate its contents.

Huntley sat at her feet, staring up at her as if he waited for a response. "Good boy," Harriet said, patting his head. "You found something."

He stood, hindquarters wagging, and trotted away to flop down in a corner, where a large and ancient tree shaded the pen. *My job is done*, his actions seemed to say. *Next move is yours.*

Harriet had seen garden tools in the barn, lined up along one wall. There was likely a shovel among them. "I'll be back," she told Huntley, striding through the yard to the gate. She let herself out, made sure the gate was latched behind her, and continued into the barn.

Like the house and other outbuildings, the rectangular barn was made of local stone. Harriet entered through an arched entrance, leaving the door open. The barn had very few windows, and the interior was wreathed in gloom. A lone light bulb provided little illumination. Even though there hadn't been cows or sheep housed in there for years, the air still held a pleasant farmyard aroma.

Harriet found the tools stored neatly near a wheelbarrow and a riding lawnmower and cart used by the hired groundskeeper. She selected a long-handled shovel and a hand trowel then returned to the dog yard.

Nothing like a mystery to provide a shot of energy, she reflected. It was hard to believe that she'd been exhausted and ready to collapse mere minutes before.

Using the long shovel, she began to dig, her intention to free the chest so it could be removed from the hole. Mindful of her back, she removed small slices of the heavy soil at a time.

Who had buried the chest in the first place? Had it been her grandfather, or was it from before his time? One of her biggest questions was *why*. Why would someone bury a chest in a dog yard? Of course, there might not have been kennels here at the time. It could have been put here centuries ago and forgotten.

Once the chest latch was revealed, Harriet pushed the shovel upright into the ground and crouched to examine it. A small padlock held the chest shut, and it didn't appear all that old. She rubbed her fingers over the metal, wiping away the dirt. The lock was too shiny to be an antique. In contrast, the chest itself was rusty and darkened with age.

"Harriet? Harriet, where are you?"

A familiar voice drifted from the direction of the house, and Harriet suddenly remembered that Aunt Jinny was bringing dinner over.

She stood and hurried across the dog yard and let herself out. A few steps brought her into view of the back patio, where Aunt Jinny stood. She waved when she spotted Harriet, a smile breaking across her attractive features.

"There you are," Aunt Jinny said. Tall and slender like all the Baileys, she wore her blond hair pinned up, bangs framing her face. Always casual yet stylish, she wore loose black linen slacks and a white blouse with sleeves rolled to the elbow.

Instead of moving forward, Harriet motioned. "Come with me. There's something you need to see."

Folding her arms, Aunt Jinny tilted her head. "Really? What is it?"

Harriet laughed, knowing how absurd the truth would sound. "Believe it or not, a treasure chest. Huntley—Meredith Bennett's dog—dug it up in the dog yard."

Aunt Jinny's mouth fell open. "Are you putting me on?"

"Not at all." Harriet grinned. "I know it sounds crazy, but you'll have to trust me."

Aunt Jinny extended a leg, glancing down at her sandals. "I'm not exactly dressed for traipsing around."

"You'll be fine," Harriet promised. "I'll do the dirty work. Do you have any idea how to get a padlock off?"

"Dad kept bolt cutters in the barn. They might do the trick."

After a detour to the barn for the bolt cutters, Harriet led her aunt to the chest.

"You weren't joking," Aunt Jinny said as she stared into the hole. "What on earth?"

"I was shocked too," Harriet said. "This was the last thing I expected to find out here when Huntley alerted me. Old toys or a bone, I would have understood. But this is weird." She wondered if she should pull the chest out first or go ahead and open it. Her curiosity won, and she applied the cutters to the padlock.

"Open it," Aunt Jinny urged. From the eager expression on her face, she'd caught the treasure-hunting fever as well.

Harriet's pulse thrummed in her throat as she removed the broken padlock and undid the hasp. At first, the lid was stuck, but after a couple of tugs, it finally lifted free. Harriet was using so much force, it thunked backward into the earth behind the chest.

Caught by the trunk's contents, she barely noticed.

The wink and shine of jewelry glinted from the chest's dark depths, necklaces and bracelets, earrings, even a tiara, all tangled up together as if they had been tossed inside.

Aunt Jinny gasped and knelt next to Harriet. "You weren't kidding," she said. "You did find buried treasure."

CHAPTER THREE

Harriet pointed at Huntley, still lounging in the shade. "Well, actually, he did." Reaching into the trunk, she gently picked up a diamond necklace, its cut stones flaring fire in the late afternoon sun. Although Harriet wasn't an expert by any means, she would guess that this wasn't costume jewelry. "Any rumors of lost jewels in our family that you know of?" She relished the idea of how much good she could do with this find. The animals she could help, even adopt.

"Afraid not," Aunt Jinny said. She pressed her lips together as she pulled her phone from her pocket. "We need to call the police. They'll want to know about this."

Van Worthington promised he would be along shortly, much to Harriet's relief. Although the dog yard wasn't the most comfortable place to wait, she was reluctant to leave the jewels alone with only Huntley to guard them. Plus, they seemed so fabulously ephemeral, as if she'd imagined them and they'd disappear the moment she looked away. *Diamonds and emeralds and rubies, oh my.* Buried where dogs roamed and played on her grandfather's property, no less.

She quickly decided there was no way Grandad could have known about the jewels. For one thing, he wouldn't have left them there, because there wasn't any honorable reason to do that. Her grandfather had been honest and upright, a man of his word, and entirely trustworthy. She'd seen the respect people felt for him when they shared stories with her. She hoped to earn the same trust as she tried to follow in his footsteps.

Her mind whirling with speculation, Harriet fed Huntley and refreshed his water dish. Then she tidied the other kennels, whose occupants had left at various times during the day.

Meanwhile, Aunt Jinny stood by the fence and gazed toward the road to the village, which was visible across a stretch of pasture. She was clearly lost in thought.

Harriet had visited England several times over the years, and she loved Aunt Jinny. After the move, her aunt had welcomed Harriet and been generous with her support. Still, Harriet had to admit she didn't know her aunt all that well. Although she could tell something was bothering her—she was far too quiet, for one thing— she had no idea what it was.

She joined Aunt Jinny at the fence and gestured toward the chest. "Are you as puzzled as I am?" she ventured. "This is like something out of a novel." She attempted a laugh. "*The Mystery of the Hidden Jewels at Cobble Hill Farm.*"

Her aunt turned to face her, and Harriet saw something unexpected in her eyes. Was it worry?

"Don't say that, Harriet," she said in a low, almost stern tone. "Not even in jest." She looked back toward the road, where a couple of cars rumbled by. "You don't need to feed the rumor mill. It operates fine on its own. One of the best things about White Church Bay is that everyone knows each other. Sometimes it's also one of the worst."

"It was the same in Connecticut," Harriet said. An ocean might separate the two places, but the people weren't all that different, really. A discovery as startling as a chest full of jewels would definitely spark speculation and gossip in her hometown, so it made sense that her aunt anticipated a similar response here.

"Here he comes," Aunt Jinny murmured.

Harriet glanced toward the road. Instead of the familiar police car, she saw—and heard—a noisy little sedan rocketing along. "Is that the detective constable?" Maybe he drove a different vehicle when he was off duty.

Aunt Jinny scoffed. "No. It's a young man who likes to drive far too fast. He annoys me several times a day blasting past here. He lives up the way, I'm guessing."

As the low-slung vehicle roared past, Harriet understood her point. Did that car even have a muffler?

A few moments later, the police vehicle did appear, DC Worthington driving at a sedate speed appropriate to the narrow road edged with stone walls and hedges. He slowed to a crawl as he approached the farm, and Aunt Jinny waved. "Now he'll know where to find us."

Soon Harriet heard the crunch of gravel and the slam of a car door. "Hello." Van hailed them as he came through the stable yard. "Got here soon as I could."

"We appreciate that, Van," Aunt Jinny said, letting him in through the gate. "Harriet's boarder dug up something very interesting."

"Boarder?" Van glanced around until his gaze fell on Huntley, who sprawled on the ground near the hole. "Oh, right. Meredith's dog. Wouldn't think the old codger had it in him."

"How is Meredith?" Harriet asked. She'd been praying that the older woman would recover fully with no aftereffects.

Van's face creased with concern. "As far as I know, she's stable. She regained consciousness quite quickly, thank goodness. Unfortunately, she can't recall who hit her or what happened."

"Head injuries can cause memory loss," Aunt Jinny said. "Hopefully it will be temporary, although recall of the actual incident might never return."

Van made a disgruntled sound. "That would be a shame. We need to find whoever it was—and fast. Imagine attacking a woman that way, in her own home. Whoever it was won't get away with it on my watch."

Harriet shivered at the thought of being harmed by an intruder. As women who lived alone, she and Aunt Jinny would need to be extra vigilant until the assailant was caught.

"What was the motive?" Aunt Jinny asked. "Robbery?"

"We're not sure yet," Van said. "If they did break in to steal, it wasn't obvious to me. The cottage seemed undisturbed."

Harriet thought back to when she'd picked up Huntley. "It did to me as well."

"Meredith will need to tell us if something is missing," Van noted. "I'll follow up with her when she returns home."

The trio reached the hole where the chest still rested. "Here it is," Harriet said. "As you can tell, I went ahead and opened it to see what was inside. We figured we should let you do the actual removal."

Van's eyes widened as he took in the glittering contents of the chest. "It won't be me." Before Harriet could ask him to clarify his cryptic comment, he knelt to get a closer look. "Have you heard of the Ravenglen Manor heist in July of '83? Huntley may have solved it for us." He began taking stock of the chest's contents.

Over forty years before. Had the chest really been here that long? And why had it been buried here in the first place? She recognized the name Ravenglen Manor. Polly had scheduled her for a stable tour there tomorrow. Her grandfather had been the veterinarian of record for the property, and she was taking over.

"I haven't heard about the heist," Harriet said. "How about you, Aunt Jinny?"

Her aunt nodded. "It was the talk of the county for years, and it's still revisited in the papers now and again. Someone broke into the manor while the owner was away, and stole the Montcliff jewelry collection. Although there were several suspects, no one was ever charged, and the jewels were never found. Until now, perhaps."

The distant expression had returned to Aunt Jinny's face, and if the detective constable hadn't been there, Harriet would have asked what she was thinking. She had the sense Aunt Jinny was holding something back. She would ask her about it later.

"It's one of North Yorkshire's biggest unsolved crimes," Van went on. "Maybe we're finally making progress." He rose to his feet and brushed off his knees. "I need to call the district office. This situation is above my pay grade."

"What do you mean?" Harriet asked.

The detective constable pointed at the chest. "Any major crimes are handled by officers of higher rank called in from county headquarters. In this case, it will be Detective Inspector Kerry McCormick. Don't worry. She's a good sort."

Harriet hadn't been worried, but now she wondered if she should be. Would she and Aunt Jinny be considered suspects? Or Grandad? Harriet's chest tightened at the idea that suspicion would shadow her beloved grandfather.

Aunt Jinny sighed. "If we have to wait for the DI, I'd better go put the kettle on."

"Oh, dear. Our supper." Harriet finally remembered the meal Aunt Jinny had brought over.

"I'll put it in the fridge," Aunt Jinny said. "We won't be eating for a while."

Harriet had lost her appetite anyway. "Do you need me to wait here, Van?"

"Go ahead back to the house. I'll stand guard until DI McCormick gets here." Van smiled at the dog, lying nearby with his head on his paws. "With Huntley's help, of course." Huntley thumped his tail on the ground a few times at the sound of his name.

Neither Harriet nor Aunt Jinny spoke as they crossed the property toward the kitchen entrance. Harriet, bursting with curiosity, tried to decide which question to ask first.

Something rustled in a nearby copse of trees thick with undergrowth. Harriet glanced over, hoping to see a red squirrel. She'd just learned they were endangered in England, unlike Connecticut, where they were common. But whatever it was remained out of sight.

Inside the house, Aunt Jinny picked up a covered casserole dish resting on the counter and placed it in the refrigerator. "Shepherd's pie. We can reheat it later."

"One of my favorites," Harriet said. She pulled mugs from a cupboard while Aunt Jinny filled the kettle and set it on the stove. "Think the officers will want tea?"

"Probably," Aunt Jinny said. "Do you have any biscuits?"

Harriet opened a large round tin, revealing golden squares of shortbread. "From Doreen Danby. She spoils me."

Aunt Jinny laughed as she took the tin from Harriet and set it on the table. "She used to spoil Dad too. She often brings me treats when their children have appointments."

"A great neighbor to have." Harriet placed a small pitcher of fresh farm milk on the table next to the sugar bowl.

The kettle whistled, signaling that the water had boiled. Aunt Jinny filled a teapot with steaming water and then settled a cozy over it. She brought the teapot to the table, joining Harriet.

A silence fell, broken only by the tick of the wall clock and Maxwell's nails clicking on the kitchen floor as he scouted for crumbs. Pressure built in Harriet's chest as thoughts crowded her lips, urging her to speak. She had so many questions.

"Aunt Jinny—" she began.

At the same time, her aunt said, "Harriet—"

"You first," Harriet said. She found herself clasping her hands in her lap, both nervous and eager to hear what Aunt Jinny had to say.

Aunt Jinny removed the teapot lid and stirred the tea, checking to see if it had steeped enough. Then she filled two mugs. "I'm trying to get my head around it all. Yes, it was forty years ago, but right now it feels like yesterday."

Harriet realized that her aunt was more closely connected to the crime than she could have guessed. Afraid to interrupt and change

Aunt Jinny's mind about sharing, she kept quiet as she added milk to her tea.

"Your uncle Dominick and I were quite close to Julian Montcliff at that time," Aunt Jinny said.

Harriet nearly choked on a sip of tea. She hadn't expected to hear that her relatives were friends with the wealthy estate owner.

"We were newly married and building our practices, but we'd let our hair down on the weekends," Aunt Jinny said, a reminiscent smile on her face. Her late husband, Dominick, had been an attorney. "Julian was the center of our little circle, and he often suggested the next fun thing to do. Plays, concerts, dinner parties—even scavenger hunts and costume balls. Ravenglen Manor was *the* place to be."

"Sounds wonderful," Harriet murmured, picturing her aunt and uncle socializing at the elegant old house.

Aunt Jinny sighed. "Then Julian was robbed, and it all came to a screeching halt. It happened a few days after his midsummer gala, you see, so the trust between us was broken."

"Did many people know about the jewels?" Harriet asked.

"Everyone." Aunt Jinny added milk to her mug and stirred. "Julian kept them in a safe, of course, but he wasn't averse to showing off a necklace or tiara now and then, especially from the Lady Amelia Montcliff collection." Aunt Jinny's eyes glowed with recollection. "She was related to Queen Victoria, which gave her jewelry extra cachet. Not that it wasn't beautiful on its own."

And now that royal collection was in a chest in her dog yard, and apparently had been for forty years. Harriet could barely wrap her mind around it.

A sharp, insistent rapping at the front door made Harriet jump. She and Aunt Jinny gaped at each other until Harriet remembered who they were expecting. She pushed back her chair. "That must be the police."

Heart in her throat, Harriet hurried to answer. Despite her ignorance and innocence regarding the chest, she couldn't deny that she felt off-balance. Friendly, approachable young Van was one thing. These were major crime officers. What if they didn't believe her or Aunt Jinny? What if they thought a Bailey had committed the theft? It wasn't that big a leap, considering the loot was found on their property.

Before opening the door, Harriet took a deep breath and rubbed her perspiring hands down her pant legs then smoothed her hair in the hall mirror.

But instead of the officers she'd expected—dreaded—an older man with thick gray hair and handsome chiseled features stood on the front steps. His blue eyes twinkled as he held out a well-manicured hand.

"Dr. Bailey?" he inquired, his voice deep and charmingly accented. "Julian Montcliff. I understand you have something that belongs to me."

CHAPTER FOUR

"How did you find out about the chest?" The words burst from Harriet's lips before she could stop them.

"So, it is true," Julian said, triumph flashing in his eyes. When Harriet took an involuntary step backward, he edged past her, glancing around the hall. "To think the jewels were at Cobble Hill all along. I never would have guessed Old Doc Bailey was sitting on them the whole time."

A quick defense rose to Harriet's lips, but before she could speak, Aunt Jinny's brisk footsteps interrupted. "Julian. What are you doing here?" Her eyes were sharp, her lips pressed tight.

Outside the open door, tires crunched, and a yellow-and-blue police cruiser halted in front of the steps. After Julian's arrival, Harriet was now glad to see the officers. Hopefully they could corral him before he started making unfounded accusations.

Leaving Julian to her aunt, she hurried out the front door and hovered on the porch. Two officers emerged from the cruiser—an attractive woman with sleek russet hair that contrasted sharply with her pale complexion, and a handsome young man with dark hair and eyes.

"Dr. Bailey?" The woman assessed Harriet with sharp green eyes and held out her hand. "Detective Inspector Kerry McCormick. How are you?"

"I'm fine, I think." Harriet shook hands with the inspector and then with the other officer, who introduced himself as Sergeant Adam Oduba. "Thanks for coming."

The DI glanced around. "Where is the dog yard? I understand that's where the discovery was made."

"Next to the old stables," Harriet said. "Before we go out there, I'd like your help with a…situation." She could clearly hear the voices of Aunt Jinny and Julian behind her.

So could Sergeant Oduba, judging by his raised eyebrow toward the open door. "What's going on in there?"

"Julian Montcliff showed up." Harriet noticed a sleek green Jaguar parked in the drive behind Van's cruiser. Julian's car, she supposed.

The officers exchanged glances. "Sounds like we'd better get a handle on it," the DI said.

Harriet let them enter the house first.

"What's all this?" DI McCormick's voice cut cleanly through the argument.

Aunt Jinny and Julian moved apart. Aunt Jinny folded her arms and scowled while Julian threw the officers a megawatt smile. He moved forward, hand extended. "I haven't had the pleasure, though I've spoken to your predecessors many times over the years. Julian Montcliff, owner of the stolen jewelry. I'm so relieved that it's finally been located."

Instead of shaking his hand, DI McCormick held up her own. "Hold on, Mr. Montcliff. One thing at a time." She looked around the hallway. "Is there a place where we can talk privately, Dr. Bailey?"

"How about the study?" Harriet went to the nearby door and opened it.

DI McCormick peeked inside. "This will do. Mr. Montcliff, take a seat somewhere, and we'll call you in when we're ready for you." She looked from Harriet to Aunt Jinny. "Which of you made the actual discovery?"

"I did," Harriet said. "A dog I'm boarding here dug up the chest."

"Smart dog," Oduba murmured. "Why don't I go out and touch base with DC Worthington? Let him know we're here."

The inspector nodded in approval. When Julian tried to tag along, she said in a stern voice, "Wait here, if you would, Mr. Montcliff." She waved Harriet toward the study. "After you."

The officer closed the door behind them. "Do you mind?" she asked, moving to the chair behind the desk.

"Not at all," Harriet said. She chose a chair across from the inspector, reflecting on all the times she'd sat there, waiting for her grandfather to finish a task. Then they'd be off in the Land Rover, much newer then, to pay a call at one farm or another. Such precious memories, experiences that had shaped her life.

Like the rest of the house, the study still held the imprint of Harold Bailey. That was his large desk, covered with a blotter, stacks of paperwork, and a few books. A wall of bookcases stood behind it, filled mostly with medical tomes, although other subjects were shelved among them—history, novels, nonfiction concerning various Yorkshire topics, and art books of all types. Art had been his second passion after his vet practice, and his interest was reflected in the antique oil painting and porcelain figurines decorating the mantel.

DI McCormick settled into the desk chair that rocked and swiveled. "How did Julian Montcliff find out about your discovery?"

The blunt question took Harriet by surprise, and she stammered for a moment. "I—I don't know," she finally managed to say. "I only found out about the Ravenglen Manor heist today, after Van—DC Worthington showed up."

"I assume he filled you in." The inspector took out her phone.

"A little." Harriet shared what Van had said. "Aunt Jinny told me more over tea—which reminds me. I was going to offer you tea and biscuits. I can't imagine how I forgot about that."

"It's fine," DI McCormick assured her. "We're here on official business, not a social call."

"Right. Anyway, my aunt Jinny lived here then and remembers the incident." She deliberately left it at that, to allow Aunt Jinny to speak for herself. Besides, didn't the police need to hear from her directly?

"Did Dr. Garrett call Mr. Montcliff?"

"No," Harriet protested. "Why would she? Plus, she couldn't have. We were together the entire time."

DI McCormick tilted her head, studying Harriet for a long moment. "You're not in trouble, Dr. Bailey. Neither is your aunt. I'm trying to put together an accurate picture of what happened today."

"I see." Harriet settled back in the chair, which was polished wood and not very comfortable. "Should I start at the beginning?"

"Please do." DI McCormick tapped at her screen. "With your permission, I'm going to record this interview."

"That's fine with me." After the inspector recorded introductory notes, Harriet gave her the overview of why Huntley was boarding and then took the officer through the discovery, including how she had snipped the padlock and opened the chest.

"No one else had access after you opened it?" the inspector clarified.

"We stayed to guard it until the detective constable arrived," Harriet said, glad they had been so cautious. "He released us to come to the house and wait. Then Julian arrived." They were back where they had started.

Someone knocked softly on the door. "Yes?" DI McCormick called.

Sergeant Oduba opened the door and put his head around the jamb. "The team is here to retrieve. Standing by."

DI McCormick gestured for him to come in and switched off the recording. "I have a couple more questions for Dr. Bailey, and then we need to interview Dr. Garrett and Mr. Montcliff before we get to that. Maybe you'd like to sit in."

"I would. Thank you." He took the chair adjacent to Harriet's.

The inspector started the recording again. "Dr. Bailey, were you aware of the chest's presence before the dog dug it up?"

Harriet rocked back against the chair, startled by this shift. Not only was the question more pointed, but both officers watched her like hawks.

She licked suddenly dry lips. "I had no idea. None."

"How long have you lived in England?"

"For about a month, but I used to visit my grandfather here before he passed."

"I'm sorry for your loss," the inspector said. "Did anyone, including relatives, ever talk about the Ravenglen Manor heist and the missing jewelry? Did anyone ever hint at knowledge concerning the burglary?"

"No," Harriet squeaked. "I had zero idea about the whole thing until today." She suddenly thought of a point in her—and Aunt Jinny's—favor. "If we knew about the jewelry and wanted to keep it, we wouldn't have called DC Worthington. Right?"

DI McCormick gave a grudging nod. "All right, Dr. Bailey. You're free to go. Please send in Dr. Garrett, will you?"

Harriet didn't give her time to change her mind. On the way to the kitchen, where she guessed Aunt Jinny was waiting, she noticed Julian in the living room, browsing through the bookshelves.

He tipped a book back into place. "Is the DI ready for me?"

"Not yet. Aunt Jinny is next."

His shoulders slumped. "Seriously? The jewelry belongs to me, you know, and it's been missing a long time."

Harriet felt a pang of sympathy for the man, even if he had pushed his way into her home while making assertions of her family's involvement in the crime.

"They need to do everything in an orderly way," she said. "That's how it was explained to me."

"I suppose." With a curl of his lip, he turned back to the books.

Harriet recalled another issue she had to raise. "Do you still want to keep the appointment tomorrow? I'm scheduled for a stable tour in the afternoon."

His eyes widened in surprise. "Why wouldn't I? You're fully qualified, aren't you? And you weren't even alive when the theft took place. No need to change vets midstream."

"I'll be there." Harriet continued into the kitchen, where Aunt Jinny was filling a dish with kibble for Charlie. Maxwell was already eating. Harriet froze, realizing that their dinners were late. "Thank you. I totally forgot."

Aunt Jinny shrugged. "You were a little busy. How did it go?"

"I honestly have no idea. The DI wants to talk to you next." Feeling the teapot, Harriet discovered it was still warm. She dumped her cold tea and refilled the mug. "Brace yourself. They gave me quite a grilling."

Her aunt almost dropped the sack of cat kibble. "What do you mean?"

Harriet focused on her tea, not wanting Aunt Jinny to see the tears stinging her eyes. "The DI wanted to know if anyone from Cobble Hill had mentioned the stolen jewelry. She asked me if I knew it was in the dog yard."

Aunt Jinny slipped an arm around her shoulders and squeezed. "She's simply doing her job, love. Of course you didn't know anything. I didn't either, and you'd think over forty years' time, I would have had a clue."

Harriet forced a laugh. "I told her we wouldn't have called Van if we'd dug them up on purpose. She couldn't argue with that."

"That's the spirit." Aunt Jinny straightened. "The sooner I get in there, the sooner this will be over. Wish me luck."

Harriet thought of a question regarding the stolen collection. "Aunt Jinny? Was the collection insured?"

Aunt Jinny paused in the kitchen doorway and thoughtfully smoothed her linen pants. "I believe so. Yes, I remember Julian talking about the insurance adjuster coming."

Interesting. Harriet wasn't quite sure how that worked, but if so, wouldn't Julian have been reimbursed for at least part of the value?

What would the insurance company do now that the jewelry had apparently been recovered? Would Julian have to reimburse the payout?

Harriet added the questions to her growing list.

After the interviews, they were allowed to accompany the officers out to the dog yard. As the sergeant had said, two additional constables had arrived to take the chest into custody, and they waited with Van in the dog yard.

Sergeant Oduba opened the gate for everyone to enter.

Julian practically ran into the yard, causing one of the constables to step forward. "Steady on, mate."

Ignoring him, Julian knelt on the ground, heedless of his fine trousers, and began to sift through the contents of the chest.

The constable threw DI McCormick a concerned look.

"Leave him be," she told him. "He's not taking anything tonight."

That caught Julian's ear. "Why on earth not?" He held up a sapphire bracelet that winked and twinkled. "I recognize this. It belonged to my great-great-grandmother."

"We discussed that inside," DI McCormick replied coolly. "We need to conclude our investigation before we can release any of the evidence. Which is what that jewelry is. Not to mention whatever you're obscuring with your fingerprints."

Julian wasn't one to take no for an answer, Harriet guessed.

"So you are certain it is the Ravenglen Manor collection?" DI McCormick asked. "The jewelry that was stolen in 1983?"

"What else would it be?" Julian demanded as he continued to sort through the chest. "There are not many collections of this value in North Yorkshire."

Harriet bit her lip, astounded that he would speak to the DI that way.

After a few more seconds, he sat back on his heels. "We have a problem. A lot of pieces are still missing." His angry gaze bore into Harriet and Aunt Jinny, standing together nearby. "I wonder where they went."

CHAPTER FIVE

The implication struck Harriet immediately. Julian was saying that only part of the collection was in the chest. Had the rest of it ever been there, or had it been removed piece by piece over the years? Or was Julian accusing Harriet and Aunt Jinny of stealing the jewelry before informing the authorities about their find?

"Don't look at us," Harriet told him. "We had no idea the chest was here, nor did anyone at Cobble Hill raid it, now or in the past." Not to mention that the storage spot wasn't easily accessible.

A crafty expression slid over Julian's face. "Maybe the remainder was never here. The pieces might have been taken apart and sold." He turned to DI McCormick. "Don't thieves do that? Sell the stones without the settings so that they're harder to trace?"

Van, who had been fairly quiet, answered for the inspector. "It would be almost a worse crime if they did. Such beautiful and historic pieces."

"Take the chest into custody," DI McCormick ordered the constables. "Mr. Montcliff, come with us to the local station. We'll compare what's here to the list of stolen items. We need to figure out which pieces are still missing."

Julian stood, brushing off his trousers, and the constables got to work. Van closed the lid before helping another officer lift the chest from the cavity.

"We'll be in touch," DI McCormick told Harriet and Aunt Jinny. "Please call if you think of anything you want to add to your interviews."

"Or if you find something else," Julian chimed in. "A diamond ring under a bush, perhaps."

Harriet was careful to address the lead officer. "We certainly will. You have our full cooperation." She smiled around the circle. "Thank you for your prompt assistance." Even under the glare of suspicion, she would maintain her manners and composure. That was what Harold Bailey would have done.

"They're gone," Harriet called to Aunt Jinny, who was in the kitchen. She moved away from the front window, where she'd been watching the procession of vehicles ease down the drive, taillights bobbing in the dusk.

"Good," Aunt Jinny called back. "Come eat some dinner."

"I'll try." Harriet still didn't have much of an appetite, although she had to admit the aroma of the warming shepherd's pie was tempting.

"You need to keep your strength up." Aunt Jinny cut a fresh loaf of bread and arranged slices on a plate. Creamery butter was already on the table, in a crystal dish.

Harriet filled two glasses with water and brought them to the table. "Don't get me wrong. This all looks great." She took a chair then scooped out a serving of succulent meat, veggies, and gravy topped with golden-brown whipped potatoes.

Aunt Jinny joined her at the table. After she said grace, they picked up their forks. Harriet's hunger returned with the first bite, and she cleared her plate in no time, mopping up gravy with buttered bread.

"Totally delicious." Harriet reached for the serving spoon. "Mind if I take a little more?"

"Help yourself." Aunt Jinny finished her last few bites. "I'll make tea."

As Harriet polished off her second helping, Aunt Jinny carried her plate to the sink. "Leave the dishes," Harriet told her. "I'll do them later. You cooked, so I clean."

Aunt Jinny smiled. "All right." She emptied the teapot and made a fresh pot while Harriet cleared the rest of the dishes.

Harriet turned on the hot water tap and waited. And waited. The water remained icy, refusing to get warm.

"That's odd," she said. "I don't have any hot water."

"The heater *is* a bit wonky. Dad had trouble with it sometimes." Aunt Jinny went into the pantry, where the heater was tucked inside a closet. A moment or two later, she returned. "I can't get it to light. You'll have to call someone."

Harriet groaned. "I guess I'll be boiling water for the dishes." Then she recalled the shower she'd never taken. "And to wash up before bed. Is there an old tin bath around?" When Aunt Jinny's mouth dropped open, she added quickly, "I'm joking. I desperately need a shower though."

"Come take one at my house," Aunt Jinny offered. "If you need a plumber, I recommend Terry Leaper. He knows this old house well."

"Terry's a client at the clinic. I'll call him in the morning." Harriet returned to the table for tea. "One thing I know for sure. If Grandad had stolen that jewelry, this old house wouldn't have so many issues."

Aunt Jinny laughed. "Mine either." Her eyes sparkled with mischief. "Perhaps we should make that point to DI McCormick."

"On it," Harriet said. Then the seriousness of the situation crashed over her like a wave. "Are we really under suspicion? Is Grandad?"

Aunt Jinny took her time answering. "On the surface, it seems suspect, doesn't it? The jewelry was found on Dad's property. I was in Julian's social circle, and Dad was his vet. We both had access to Ravenglen Manor."

"That doesn't help," Harriet protested.

"I'm not done yet," Aunt Jinny told her. "We're innocent, as was Dad, and we need to stand on that with confidence. Besides, something doesn't quite add up about the dog yard."

"What about it?" Harriet asked.

"It wasn't always that large. Dad extended it years ago to give the dogs more room to roam and stretch their legs." Her brow furrowed. "Something else was in that spot, but I don't remember what it was."

"How can we find out?" Harriet asked eagerly.

"Dad's journals, maybe. We can also check old photographs in the albums he put together. He liked to keep a record of everything going on around here."

"I didn't know Grandad kept journals. Or photo albums. I can't wait to go through those. Do you know where they are?" Harriet's pulse leaped with excitement. Beyond helping with their concerns regarding the heist, they might contain a wealth of veterinary knowledge and wisdom.

"They should be in the study," Aunt Jinny said. "The albums are in the cabinets below the shelves, but I'm not sure about the journals."

A huge yawn surprised Harriet. What a long day it had been, from Meredith Bennett's attack to discovering treasure in her own backyard, on top of a full day of appointments. "I'll check it out tomorrow." Despite her eagerness to learn more, she was too tired to start the search. "I'd better take that shower before I fall asleep."

"Come over when you're ready," Aunt Jinny said.

An hour later, Harriet returned from Aunt Jinny's, freshly showered and dressed in flannel pants, a T-shirt, and flip-flops. A cloth bag held her used clothing and the toiletries she'd taken with her.

At this hour, the countryside was quiet. Halfway between the houses, Harriet paused to absorb the beauty of the night. Overhead, a thin crescent moon gleamed among twinkling stars, and all around her, thick trees rustled in a brisk and briny breeze. Harriet was still getting to know her new home, its moods and atmospheres in varied weather and at different times of day.

Something snapped and cracked in the bushes nearby.

That's enough lingering in the dark. Harriet lurched into movement, eager to reach the safety of her home.

In the dog yard, Huntley whined. The note of distress in his voice tore at Harriet's heart, and her vet instincts clamored at her to make sure he was okay.

Diverting in that direction, she discovered that Huntley still lay in the shelter of the tree instead of inside the kennel on his blanket. When he heard Harriet approach, he lifted his nose and gave a tiny yip, his tail thwacking against the ground.

A quick once-over revealed that the dog was fine, physically at least. The poor thing must be missing Meredith. "You're okay, boy," she murmured. "You'll be back with your owner soon." He licked her hand in response.

As she turned to go to the house, he whined again, adding a whimper for good measure. It was no good. She couldn't leave him out here alone all night.

"Come on, Huntley," she said. "You can bunk with Maxwell in the kitchen."

He rose to his feet with some difficulty, in contrast to his vigorous digging earlier in the day. "Wore yourself out, huh?" she asked. Many older dogs suffered from arthritic joints. If the stiffness continued, she'd suggest some helpful supplements to his owner.

"You're a good old boy," Harriet told him as they made their way to the house. She moved very slowly to accommodate his halting progress.

Maxwell greeted his sleepover friend with much excitement, prancing around the older dog until Harriet commanded him to calm down. She relieved Maxwell of his wheeled apparatus, and soon the pair was snuggled near the Aga, both snoring on their blankets.

Harriet took a final glance at the dogs, satisfied she'd made the right decision.

Charlie had been watching the proceedings from the safety of a kitchen chair, and she jumped down with a thump to follow Harriet up to bed.

Leaving a window slightly open for fresh air, Harriet climbed into the large, high bed that had once belonged to her grandparents. The primary bedroom was spacious, with polished antique furniture and a richly patterned needlepoint rug on the wide board floor. As in many of the rooms, there was a fireplace with a cast-iron insert, all in working order, according to Aunt Jinny. Harriet looked forward to cozy winter nights tucked up in bed with a fire on the hearth and a book in her hands.

Tonight, though, she left the soft duvet at the foot of the bed and used only a sheet. She thought about reading the novel on her bedside table, but it held no appeal. Instead, Harriet picked up her phone and opened a browser.

Ravenglen Manor burglary, she typed.

Her reward was a flood of articles about the incident. Besides those contemporaneous to the event, there had been occasional follow-up coverage over the years. The combination of an unsolved mystery, a fabulous jewelry collection, and Julian's colorful personality continued to intrigue the public.

Harriet had met him once, and she could already see what a powerful effect he exerted on the people around him. He would have bowled over a less strong-willed officer than DI McCormick. Harriet was glad the inspector hadn't allowed anything of the sort.

She chose to read in chronological order, wanting to learn facts as they were revealed. Julian Montcliff had discovered the theft when he returned home after a business trip to London. The first sign was disarray in the drawing room, where several valuable items were missing—two Royal Dux figurines, an enamel snuffbox, and a carved ivory statue.

Alarmed, Julian checked his safe and found it open and empty. Harriet gathered that besides freely displaying the valuable collection, Julian had been careless regarding the safe combination. He'd left it taped inside a desk drawer.

Immediate suspicion had fallen upon his household staff as well as the trade professionals who did repairs at the manor. Later articles mentioned that several were questioned—housekeeper Meredith Perkins, groundskeeper Walt Bennett, and plumber Terry Leaper.

Harriet's eyes widened when she saw the name Terry Leaper. Meredith Perkins as well. Was she now Meredith Bennett? In Harriet's experience, Meredith wasn't a particularly common name.

Julian's local friends had also been questioned, although the paper was discreet enough to leave out names. Was Aunt Jinny among them? Harriet guessed as much. That must have been troubling, judging by her own experience today with DI McCormick. It wasn't pleasant to be in the crosshairs of suspicion, even if one was innocent.

On that note, Harriet set her phone on the nightstand. If she kept this up, she'd be useless in the morning. At the foot of the bed, Charlie purred, which lulled Harriet to sleep.

Excited yips and barks woke Harriet early on Wednesday morning. Outside her window, a pink pearly dawn was brightening, promising another beautiful summer day. Charlie, who clearly hadn't left her spot all night, stalked up the bed and touched her nose to Harriet's.

Harriet laughed. "Good morning to you too." As she gently moved the cat aside and sat up, she remembered that Huntley had spent the night in the kitchen with Maxwell.

She fished for slippers under the bed as the dogs' ruckus continued. She was pretty sure they were fine. They wanted her attention—and their breakfast.

While Charlie darted ahead, Harriet tied on a robe and went downstairs. As she expected, the two dogs were playing, with Huntley running around Maxwell, who playfully nipped at him every time he went by. The night's rest seemed to have relaxed Huntley, who was moving much more freely.

Harriet greeted them with thorough pats and belly rubs. "Ready for some food?" she asked as she put Maxwell's harness on. The answer was the skittering of nails on the flagstone floor.

Soon, the crunch of kibble was the only sound in the kitchen. Harriet thumbed through the box and chose a French roast pod for the coffee maker. What a relief it had been to learn that coffee was almost as ubiquitous in England as it was in the States. She really appreciated sipping coffee every morning while she read her daily devotional.

Since the weather was nice, Harriet took her coffee mug, Bible, and devotional book out to the patio. The pets followed, Huntley collapsing to bathe in the sun and Charlie slinking off to explore the mysterious, dewy reaches of the garden. Maxwell sat under the table, close enough that Harriet felt his warmth on her ankles.

The day's passage was one of Harriet's favorites, Proverbs 3:5-6: *Trust in the Lord with all your heart and lean not on your own understanding; in all your ways submit to him, and he will make your paths straight.* Harriet sat back and pondered these wise words. Her decision to move to England and take over her grandfather's practice had been reached after much prayer and soul-searching. Although it was a wonderful opportunity, a once-in-a-lifetime offer, and a no-brainer, as some friends had put it, Harriet wanted to be sure she was following God's will for her life.

Only in that surrender, trust, and willingness to obey did Harriet find true peace. She'd tried the other route before, running ahead with her own ideas. That hadn't worked out quite so well, she reflected ruefully.

Namely the situation with Dr. Dustin Stewart, her former fiancé. One of Harriet's deeply cherished dreams was to get married and have a family, to enjoy a happy marriage like the one her parents had. Arthur and Charlotte Bailey were soulmates and true friends, both devoted and devout.

When she'd fallen for Dustin's good looks and charm, as well as his competence and compassion as a vet, she'd basically closed her eyes and jumped, assuming she would land on solid ground.

All too soon it had become apparent that he wasn't the right man for her. After months of hoping things would improve, she was devastated when Dustin broke their engagement. The memory still stung, and Harriet certainly didn't want to make another mistake. Hence, the prayer and seeking God before she accepted the inheritance. Before she packed up her apartment and moved thousands of miles to a new country.

Harriet looked up from the Bible, taking in the sunlit garden. Coming to Yorkshire had been the right decision. Hadn't it? She'd been so sure.

As if in confirmation, everything had been going so well. Busy and hectic, admittedly, even somewhat overwhelming at times, but that was to be expected. She'd stepped into a thriving practice without the guiding hand of her grandfather as senior partner. If asked, she would have said things were perfectly imperfect.

Until yesterday.

Harriet took a hasty swallow of coffee, trying to drown the knot of doubt forming in her midsection.

What if, despite her best efforts, she'd made a terrible mistake?

CHAPTER SIX

Harriet knew better than to continue down that road. Nothing good would come of it beyond more doubts, followed by fear, worry, and possibly a bad decision or two.

So she prayed instead, asking God to confirm His will in her life.

Then she drank the rest of her coffee and ate a quick breakfast of cold cereal. While rinsing her dishes, she remembered the hot water was out.

"And we're off to a great start with confirming that this was the right move," she muttered, grabbing her phone. Terry's number was in the clinic computer, so she popped in there to find it then decided to use the office phone.

He answered right away. "Are we still all set with Jolly's surgery?"

"Yes, we are. That's not why I'm calling. This is actually for personal reasons. I don't have any hot water in the house."

Terry chuckled. "I told Doc Bailey he was going to need a new water heater pretty soon. Sounds like that time has come."

"Really?" Harriet's heart sank. "How much will that cost?"

"Don't worry about it yet," Terry said, reassurance in his voice. "I'll see if I can keep the old one limping along a while longer. I can be there in an hour if that works for you."

"Wonderful." Harriet was relieved to get an appointment so quickly. She didn't have anything official until the afternoon, when she was supposed to go to Ravenglen Manor to meet the horses.

She was in her robe, so she hurried upstairs to dress, choosing jeans, a T-shirt, and sneakers.

Julian had said he still wanted her to be his vet as long as she was qualified. But that was before he'd all but accused her and Aunt Jinny of keeping some of the jewels for themselves. She'd check in with him later, once she geared herself up to make the call.

Polly arrived around eight, as usual. Harriet was in the kitchen, waiting for the coffee maker to finish brewing. She'd need more than one cup today.

"Good morning. Can I have one of those?" Polly wore a knee-length cotton skirt and crisp short-sleeved blouse. A messenger bag was slung over her shoulder.

"Of course," Harriet said, smiling. Being around Polly always raised her spirits. Although she was Harriet's employee, any formality between the pair had quickly dissolved.

Charlie, Maxwell, and Huntley charged toward Polly, eager for their share of attention. Allowing her bag to slip to the floor, Polly began dispensing pats. "You had some excitement here yesterday, I understand."

Harriet immediately felt remiss. "I'm sorry I didn't call or text you." She grimaced. "It was totally crazy."

Polly shook her head. "Don't worry about it. I heard the police were here until after dark." Pets duly greeted, she picked up her bag and continued to the table, where she chose a seat.

"Wow, word does travel fast around here," Harriet said. "Julian Montcliff showed up right after Van, before the DI arrived." She wondered again how he'd found out about the chest so quickly. He hadn't answered when she'd asked, and she hadn't dared press him.

"I think news spreads by osmosis in this town." Polly laughed, waving a hand in the air. "It's impossible to identify the source most of the time."

"Same where I come from," Harriet said. Seeing that the machine was finished, she removed the mug and handed it to Polly then made another for herself. "I'll tell you everything."

Polly sat with her coffee, totally absorbed as Harriet relayed the tale, beginning with her discovery of the chest. Harriet described the find, her surprise when Julian arrived, and the most troubling aspect of all—that suspicion had fallen on the residents of Cobble Hill.

"The police questioned Aunt Jinny and me at length," Harriet said. "Julian thinks the jewelry was here the whole time, ever since it was stolen. Anyone could have buried it here, but he seems determined to point the finger at Grandad."

Polly's eyes widened. "That's cheeky of him. As if Doc Bailey would ever do anything criminal."

"Exactly," Harriet said, feeling vindicated. "I can't even imagine such a thing."

"Neither can anyone who knew him," Polly said stoutly. "It's nonsense." Her expression became musing. "Though it is a mystery how the chest ended up here."

"Especially in a dog yard," Harriet said. "Everyone knows dogs like to dig. Although Aunt Jinny did say the yard wasn't always that large. I'm going to do some research and see what used to be in that spot."

"Research?" Polly asked, interested. "How?"

"By going through Grandad's journals and photographs," Harriet explained. "Maybe I'll find a clue as to what was happening back then. Including why someone might have chosen this property to hide the spoils. Perhaps I'll even find a tie to one of the initial suspects."

Harriet brought up one of the newspaper articles she'd found and showed her phone to Polly. "These are the people they initially interviewed. By the way, was Meredith Bennett's maiden name Perkins?"

Eyes on the article, Polly nodded. "Walt Bennett was her husband. Sadly, he passed away about twenty years ago." She handed the phone back. "Which might answer a question I have. Why didn't the thief ever come get the chest?" Excitement rose in her voice. "Maybe it was *Walt*."

"It's possible." Could the solution be that simple? Maybe the chest was still in the pen because the man who'd buried it had died.

Polly frowned. "Why didn't he sell any of the jewelry though? That doesn't make sense—to take it and then simply bury it forever."

Harriet had an answer to this. "According to Julian, some of it is missing. He thinks that the thief disassembled the jewelry and sold the stones. Maybe that's what Walt did with a few pieces at a time over the years."

"Could very well be," Polly said. "You should mention that theory to the police."

"I might have to." Outrage warmed Harriet's cheeks when she recalled Julian's attitude. "You should have seen the way he all but sneered at Aunt Jinny and me when he realized some things were missing. He practically accused us of dipping into the chest before calling the police."

Polly sucked in a breath. "The nerve of him. I don't think much of Mr. Julian Montcliff, even if he is related to the royals."

Harriet shared her assistant's opinion. "The thing is, I'm supposed to meet with him at two this afternoon at Ravenglen Manor, to be introduced to his horses." She picked up her mug and took a sip. "I'm not terribly enthusiastic now."

Polly put her hand on Harriet's arm. "I get that, but you should still go. Maybe you can pick up some information."

Harriet's brows went up. "Such as?"

"About Walt, who used to work there, and the other suspects," Polly said. "Julian seems quite free with his thoughts. Perhaps you can steer him into answering some questions or spilling what he knows."

"It's an idea," Harriet said reluctantly. The only mysteries she'd ever solved had to do with animal ailments. She had a disconcerting thought. "What if he tries to get information from me? About the missing jewelry, I mean."

"Then you can set him straight," Polly said.

Harriet doubted it. She had the impression that Julian was strong-willed and used to bowling people over rather than listening to other points of view.

"And another thing," Polly said. "We'd better be on guard against treasure hunters for the next few weeks. Once word gets out that you found the jewels here and that some of them are still missing, they'll be swarming all over this place."

Harriet pictured an army descending upon the farm, shovels over their shoulders. "I sure hope not."

Maxwell gave a yip, drawing Harriet's attention to the open French door, where Terry Leaper stood. How long had he been there? Terry cleared his throat. "Doc Bailey? I'm here about the hot water."

Terry Leaper was one of the robbery suspects. How much had he overheard?

Hoping she didn't appear flustered, Harriet rose from her chair. "Terry. Please come in. Thanks for getting here so quickly."

Polly threw Harriet a significant look before standing, mug in hand, and gathering her messenger bag. "There's my cue. I'll be in the clinic."

Terry set to work and soon had the hot water operational despite the heater being "on its last leg." Grateful for the reprieve, Harriet asked him to go ahead and quote a new heater. She couldn't conduct business at the clinic without a reliable source of hot water.

Meanwhile, Polly called Ravenglen Manor on her behalf and then relayed the message back to Harriet that Julian was "greatly looking forward to Dr. Bailey's visit." With that settled, Harriet decided to pop down to the village for provisions. She'd promised her aunt dinner and, in order to make good on that offer, she needed to buy some food.

The village of White Church Bay was less than a mile away, with access either by a footpath along the cliffs or by car. Since Harriet was buying groceries, she took the Land Rover and parked in the upper village, in a lot near the protestant church. Vehicle traffic in the lower village was discouraged due to steep, narrow streets and lack of parking.

After grabbing a cloth bag and locking the car, Harriet strolled toward the shops, studying every detail of the beautiful stone buildings, colorful flower gardens, and ocean views. The church was Gothic in style with tall stained glass windows adorning the front end, and set next to a graveyard. Grandad was buried there, along with his wife, Helen, Aunt Jinny's husband, Dominick, and Bailey ancestors dating back to the 1700s. Harriet was awed by her family's long history and deep roots in White Church Bay.

Moving on, Harriet passed by the White Hart, a classic inn fronted with white stucco and set with many multipaned windows. According to Polly, the Hart was one of the best restaurants in town, its dining patio in great demand on summer evenings. Harriet should treat Aunt Jinny to dinner there one night. That would be a very small thank-you for all her aunt had done to help her settle in.

A little farther on was another popular eatery, Cliffside Chippy, a fish-and-chips shop. Harriet's mouth watered thinking about the classic English meal of a battered fish filet and thick salty fries, or chips, as they were called here. Eating fish and chips while watching boats go by had been one of her favorite pastimes with her grandfather. He'd grab his cap and say, "Ready to go to the harbor, Harriet? There's a piece of fish with my name on it."

She always laughed so hard, taking him literally as children did. Now, as she began the descent into the lower bay, she imagined a line of fish filets labeled *Harriet, Polly,* and *Aunt Jinny.* She promised herself fish and chips one night soon.

The lane led down a steep decline, requiring Harriet to watch her step. Houses and small businesses lined the street, cheek by jowl, as the old saying went. Each building offered tiny, charming details—window boxes overflowing with petunias, lime-green shutters, a cat washing itself on a balcony. Some business names and motifs reflected White Church Bay's past as a smuggling village, a history shared with other Yorkshire coastal towns.

An enchanting corner shop with two bow windows displaying books and toys was one example. Tales & Treasures, its sign showing an open chest spilling gold, would be a perfect place to poke around on a rainy day. The sign reminded her of the chest Huntley had dug up. She had happily forgotten the cloud of suspicion hanging over Cobble Hill and her family.

Forcing the unpleasant thoughts away, Harriet continued on. Her goal, Galloway's General Store, sat down the hill, identified by bright blue awnings. She'd been glad to learn that the local market offered a decent range of groceries, produce, and other necessities. More extensive shopping required traveling to a supermarket on the outskirts of nearby Whitby. With Galloway's, she could get by for weeks between trips.

As Harriet approached, a menu idea began to take shape. She'd bake a chicken and serve it with mashed potatoes and fresh local peas or asparagus.

An older woman was coming out of the store, so Harriet waited, exchanging nods of greeting before she slipped inside, bells chiming as the door shut behind her. Harriet paused to get her bearings. As with rural general stores in the States, Galloway's took advantage of every square inch of space to display merchandise. Racks of canned goods. Baskets of produce and freshly baked bread. Meat and dairy coolers. Displays of personal care and cleaning products. Since they were on the coast, beach chairs and sand buckets.

On past visits, Agnes Galloway, the gregarious owner, had greeted Harriet warmly from her station behind the counter. Today Agnes merely glanced up briefly before returning her attention to the customer checking out.

That's odd. Harriet picked up a basket and made her way to the meat department. She chose a small whole chicken before moving on to the vegetables. Another woman stood in front of the peas, taking her time as she selected pods from a bushel basket.

"I love fresh peas," Harriet said, to make conversation. "I don't even mind shelling them. It's relaxing."

The woman gave her a once-over then turned away with a sniff of disdain. Heat flamed in Harriet's cheeks as she moved on to the asparagus. She'd been roundly snubbed.

Perhaps that woman was having a bad day. Harriet tried again in the fresh-baked bread area. "The whole-wheat bread makes wonderful sandwiches," she said to another customer. "It's nice that it comes presliced." She laughed. "Otherwise, I'd probably make a mess of it."

Her attempt at levity was met with a stare from icy blue eyes. Without responding, the woman placed a loaf of white bread in her basket and stalked away.

Harriet shivered. *Is it cold in here, or it is me?* She hastily did the rest of her shopping, anxious to get home.

"Find everything you need?" Agnes asked as Harriet unloaded at the counter.

"Yes, thank you." Harriet emptied her basket. "I'm making dinner for my aunt Jinny tonight."

"Oh, yes. Dr. Garrett." Agnes moved Harriet's items quickly. Instead of asking about Aunt Jinny as she usually did, the shopkeeper focused on her task while Harriet loaded the groceries into her cloth bag. There were no inquiries as to Harriet's health or matters at the clinic. Not even a comment about the weather.

The lady with the peas got in line behind Harriet, keeping her distance but sniffing every few seconds. That made Harriet feel like she had to hurry, so naturally she became clumsy. First, she dropped her wallet. Then she had trouble finding the right card and extracting it from the slot. Finally, receipt in one hand and shopping bag in the other, Harriet fumbled her way out of the store. But she caught the babble of voices rising before the door closed. Glancing over her shoulder, she saw customers clustered at the counter, talking to Agnes.

It all clicked in her mind. She realized what they were chatting about and why everyone in the store had been standoffish.

It had only taken a few hours for the town's gossip mill to do its work.

CHAPTER SEVEN

Harriet put her head down and charged up the lane, not even glancing at any of the intriguing places she passed. Her focus was reaching the safety of her vehicle and then rushing home, where she could vent to Polly. At least *she* was still on Harriet's side.

At the top of the hill, Harriet stopped to catch her breath. Was this the way it was going to be from now on? Were the villagers going to eye her with distrust and reject her friendly overtures? If so, how would the practice survive? The legacy entrusted to her would wither and die, Harold Bailey's once sterling reputation soiled forever.

Maybe her move here wasn't in God's will after all, and this was the sign she'd asked for.

Tears stung Harriet's eyes, and she blinked furiously. This was *not* the place to break down—in public, on the village's main road.

When she was able to breathe freely again, Harriet continued on, switching the heavy grocery bag from arm to arm. She avoided eye contact with the few people she encountered. She didn't know any of them, and with any luck, they didn't recognize her either.

Then she spotted someone familiar. In the graveyard next to the church, Pastor Will sat reading on a stone bench under a rowan tree. Harriet walked faster while watching him out of the corner of her eye. She couldn't stand the idea of being snubbed by her pastor, and she was too upset to attempt small talk at the moment. Only a little farther to the parking lot—

Too late. Pastor Will raised his head and waved, a friendly grin on his face. "Good morning, Dr. Bailey."

"Hello, Pastor Will. Lovely day, isn't it?" That much was true. As far as the weather was concerned, anyway.

He closed the book and approached the sidewalk, his long legs eating up the distance. "It certainly is. James Russell Lowell put it perfectly. 'What is so rare as a day in June?'" He ducked his head. "Sorry. Bit lame, I know." He gestured with the pocket-size New Testament in his hand. "During my breaks, I like to sit outside in the fresh air."

"So do I." Harriet inhaled. *Hold it together. A couple more pleasantries, and I can be on my way.* "I'll let you get back to your reading."

He gently caught her elbow. "Harriet, are you all right?"

She had every intention of insisting that she was fine and escaping to the safety of Cobble Hill. Then she made the mistake of meeting his kind gaze and found herself blurting, "Oh, Pastor Will, everything is going wrong."

Within minutes, Harriet found herself in the parsonage office, a cup of tea in hand. Pastor Will set a box of tissues on the table beside her and took his chair behind the desk. He picked up his own mug, and they sat in comfortable silence for a few moments.

Calmed by his gentle, accepting presence, Harriet soon felt able to voice her worries. First, though, she asked a question. "How is Meredith Bennett doing? Have you heard anything?"

"I have. She is much better," Pastor Will said. "She'll be getting out of the hospital tomorrow or the next day. Her granddaughter is going to stay with her, which is excellent."

"That's wonderful," Harriet murmured. "I'll have to contact her about Huntley." She cleared her throat. "Speaking of Huntley, did you hear what he dug up?"

The pastor's brows rose. "The Ravenglen Manor jewelry? Yes. That must have been quite a shock for you."

Harriet tried to swallow a sudden lump in her throat. "It was. I had no idea it was there, and neither did Aunt Jinny." She took a breath then poured out her heart. "Everyone seems to think my family had something to do with it. Julian Montcliff, the police, even Agnes Galloway and her customers. They wouldn't talk to me in the store this morning." She clenched her fist. "There's no way my grandfather stole that jewelry. He would never do such a thing. And that goes for everyone else in my family."

Pastor Will's gaze remained steady. "I agree with you. I knew your grandfather quite well, and he was a moral, upright man. A real pillar of the community."

Relief flowed over Harriet. Surely the village pastor was a good judge of character. He had to be. It was practically a job requirement.

"Thank you for saying that," Harriet said. "Polly shares your opinion, and so does Aunt Jinny." She made a disgusted sound. "The finger is also pointing at her. Apparently, she and my uncle used to be friends with Julian, so technically they would have had access."

"It's a troubling situation," Pastor Will said. "A theft of that magnitude… Relationships have been destroyed by far less." He swiveled in his chair. "Regarding Agnes, I'll have a discreet word with her this afternoon. Enlist her help squashing the gossip. She's a good sort, a lovely woman."

"Would you?" Harriet was relieved. "I understand why they're talking about it. Who wouldn't? It's just painful being the target. I'm really worried it will affect the practice." Tears threatened to form. "That would kill me. Letting Grandad down, I mean."

"Dr. Bailey—"

"Please, call me Harriet."

"Harriet. And call me Will. None of this is your fault. You truly fell into the situation."

She laughed. "Well, the hole wasn't *that* deep. Sorry. Go on."

"Harold Bailey meant a lot to this village." Will sipped from his cup, a contemplative expression on his face. "His door was always open to an animal in need. As for payment—well, a lot of people owed him money. He was flexible about how and when he got paid. The patients came first." He put his mug down and leaned forward. "Most people in town remember that. You have more support than you know."

"I sure hope so," Harriet said. Feeling she could confide in him, she said, "Proverbs three, verses five and six are my stronghold right now." He nodded in acknowledgment. "I'm doing my best to trust God, to believe that this is the right path, but—"

His smile was rueful. "I get it. Sometimes God's path isn't as smooth and easy as we might like. Believe me, I've been there."

"I guess I'll keep going then," Harriet said. "Hopefully the truth about why the chest was buried at Cobble Hill will come to light." Maybe she could nudge the reveal along with her research.

"Would you like me to pray?" Will offered. "I'd be more than happy to. And I'll continue to do so until this situation is resolved."

"Would you?" Harriet put down her tea. "I'd really appreciate it." She had a new friend, she realized with joy. How could she lose with Will in her corner?

Harriet found herself singing as she drove home. Running into Will was exactly what she needed after her experience at the general store.

A burst of awe lit her heart. Had the encounter been divinely guided? God knew what Harriet needed, even more than she did. Especially since she was still in the midst of a thorny situation. Will's support was encouragement for the journey.

Sometimes you can't get over or around, so you have to go through. With God's help and that of her friends, she would make it to the other side.

After she put away the groceries—which Will had insisted she put in the parsonage fridge during their chat—she popped into the clinic. "I'm back," she told Polly, who was working at the desk. "Want lunch in a few? I'll make sandwiches."

"That'd be nice," Polly said. "Thank you."

"How's it going?" Harriet asked. Paperwork was scattered over Polly's desk—patient files, supply catalogs, telephone message slips. Her stomach clenched as she asked the question foremost in her mind. "Do we still have a full book for tomorrow?"

Biting her lower lip, Polly brought up the screen. "We do, yes." She hesitated before adding quietly, "Now."

"Did we have some cancellations? I was afraid of that after my trip to the store."

Polly gave her a confused frown. "What happened?"

"A couple of customers wouldn't even speak to me. Agnes acted strange too."

Polly set her jaw. "Never mind them." She jabbed a finger at the screen. "For every cancellation, I had a call for an appointment." She picked up a file. "This client hasn't been here in two years. Now she wants her cat to have a checkup."

Harriet couldn't help but laugh at the irony. "Don't look a gift horse in the mouth, right?" Maybe there was no such thing as bad publicity after all.

Her assistant's eyes sparkled with humor. "Curiosity might bring them in, but our charm and skill will keep them here." Polly's expression sobered. "Don't worry, Harriet. It will all come right in the end. You'll see."

Harriet was warmed by Polly's unwavering faith. "Thank you. Pastor Will believes that too. It'd be a lot more difficult right now without your support, that's for sure. And his."

Polly's expressive eyes widened. "Our lovely pastor? When did you talk to him?" Then she put up a hand. "Hold on. Save the details for lunch." She began to type busily. "I'm almost at a good stopping point."

After a relaxing lunch with Polly, over which she relayed every detail of her trip to the store and her encouraging talk with Will, Harriet prepared for her tour at Ravenglen Manor. Polly pulled the files on the four horses for review, and Harriet decided to sit in the study to do so. Its bookshelves held a good selection of reference books Grandad had collected, so if she wanted to refresh herself on something she could easily do so.

None of the horses had any major problems, so Harriet quickly buzzed through the files. A glance at the camelback clock on the mantel revealed that she still had an hour before she'd need to leave. Maybe she should try to find her grandfather's journals.

Harriet studied the bookshelves for something that could pass for a journal. Everything within close view was a published book. To be thorough, she got up and scanned the rest of the shelves from top to bottom. She noticed many interesting books she'd like to read—an intriguing local history, a couple of novels, and an illustrated book of English animal art.

She found no sign of the journals, so she moved to the double-door cupboards below each set of shelves. The first one she opened revealed stacks of ledgers and old-fashioned checkbooks. Now here was a trove—records dating back to her great-grandfather, who had founded the practice. She would enjoy leafing through them when she had time.

The next cabinet held stacks of photograph albums, many of them very old, with board covers and black pages. Tiny triangles were used to secure the photographs. Harriet almost got lost in one with photographs from the 1920s. The images were of cars, farm wagons and horse plows, and views of Cobble Hill when the trees were much smaller. One even showed her great-grandfather as a child, posing with her great-great-grandparents in front of the house.

Harriet reluctantly put the album back for another time. A quick glance through the cupboard revealed much newer albums. Those she would return to later in the hope she would find photographs of the dog yard area.

The journals were in the third cupboard, two rows of brown leather books about eight inches tall. Harriet slid the first one out and carefully opened the cover. *1971* was written in blue ink on the first blank page. Grandad would have been just starting his professional practice, she guessed. A veterinary degree in England was a five-year program.

After confirming that the next journal was 1972, she counted the spines to 1983, the year of the heist. Harriet's heart beat a little faster as she gently extracted the book and opened it. It was the right one.

If only she had time to read it now. She put it on the desk, resolving to return to it later in the evening. Another glance at the clock told her she had better get ready to go.

A pretty figurine almost hidden behind a bookend caught her eye. She went over to the mantel and pulled it forward, seeing that it was a depiction of a milkmaid in eighteenth-century garb standing beside a cow, pail in hand.

Harriet picked up the piece, appreciating its smooth surface and detail, and flipped it over. A pink triangle was attached, reading ROYAL DUX BOHEMIA. There was also a number embossed on the bottom.

Royal Dux. A distinctive name, and she had recently heard it somewhere.

After a few seconds, she remembered. Two Royal Dux figurines had been stolen in the Ravenglen Manor heist.

Harriet picked up her phone and hastily scrolled through her history for the right article. After a couple false starts, she found it. A Royal Dux milkmaid figurine was among the stolen items listed.

Harriet stared at the milkmaid in horror. Was this the statue from Ravenglen Manor? What was it doing in her grandfather's study?

CHAPTER EIGHT

The clock chimed the half hour, and Harriet realized with a jolt that she had to get moving. She grabbed her purse and rushed out the study door, only to remember the files. She dashed back and grabbed them then stopped by the clinic's front desk.

"I'm off to Ravenglen Manor," she said. "You can leave anything important in my tray. I'll check it when I return."

"Of course." Since Polly had set up the tray, she knew the procedure well. She squinted at Harriet. "Are you all right? You seem a bit flustered." Then she nodded in understanding. "Is it about visiting Julian? Bearding the lion in his den, so to speak? Just play it by ear. That's what I do when—"

"No, it's about something else." Harriet shifted her weight, wanting to share but knowing time was short. "I found something I want to discuss with you, but it'll have to wait for now. I don't want to be late."

Polly glanced at the clock. "Yes, you'd better be getting on. By the way, if you see the mistletoe tree, you've missed the turn."

"Mistletoe tree?" Harriet echoed in confusion. "I have my GPS," she added, meaning her phone.

"Not that reliable in the depths of the countryside, I'm afraid." Polly opened a drawer and pulled out a map, which she then folded into a neat square.

Harriet peered over her shoulder.

"We're here." Polly marked Cobble Hill with a penciled X. She traced a route slowly, glancing up now and then to be sure Harriet was following. "Ravenglen Manor is here." Another X, and then she handed Harriet the map.

"Thank you," Harriet said, hoping she wouldn't need it. At some point, she should study the area and get the lay of the land. Many of her farming clients were located in far-flung corners. It wouldn't do to get lost if she had to make an emergency house call. Harriet strode toward the door. "I'm leaving now. Have a great afternoon."

"You as well," Polly called. "We'll catch up later."

Harriet started the Land Rover and entered the address of Ravenglen Manor into her phone. She was still in a daze from discovering the figurine. It had to be a coincidence. The company had probably made dozens, if not hundreds, of that design.

She put the vehicle into gear and pressed the gas. It was a very unsettling coincidence in light of the discovery in the dog yard. Should she tell the police? What if it was one of the stolen figurines? That would add to the case for her grandfather's involvement in the heist.

Which was ridiculous to even consider. Maybe he had bought it without knowing the provenance.

Realizing she was arguing with herself and wrestling with her conscience at the same time, Harriet forced herself to concentrate. She didn't need to get lost today, and it was too easy to drive on autopilot and miss a turn.

The route to Ravenglen Manor led along narrow lanes lined with hedges or rock walls. They bordered fields and woods, passed through farmland, and sometimes provided glimpses of the sea. Meeting another vehicle head-on required edging to the side, sometimes such a close encounter that Harriet winced. Not so much for the battered old Land Rover. It was the other cars she was worried about.

Somehow, despite keeping watch, she missed the turn, as she realized when she saw the mistletoe tree Polly had warned her about. A gnarled old apple tree stood alone on a rise, festooned with balls of greenery, the parasitic mistletoe plant.

Harriet gritted her teeth. There wasn't a place to turn around here due to the stone walls on both sides of the road. All too aware she was almost late, she continued until she found a wide enough spot.

On the way back past the mistletoe tree, she kept a close watch on the opposite side. At last, a break in the hedges revealed a tiny lane marked by a battered wooden signpost that read Ravenglen.

Relieved by this clue that she was literally on the right track, Harriet couldn't help musing. Was this really her life, visiting patients at historic manor houses in the English countryside? She'd visited large farms in Connecticut where the well-to-do kept horses, but there was something much more romantic and storybook about this setting. If only she could be sure of the reception she'd receive.

After half a mile or so, Harriet came across a tall set of stone pillars and an ironwork gate standing open in welcome. A bronze plaque informed her that this was Ravenglen Manor, built in 1620.

Four hundred years old. Harriet inched through the open gate onto a winding drive with woods on both sides. Birdsong echoed, and she glimpsed the leap of a doe. Around a final curve, she arrived at the house, a sprawling stone structure with peaked gables, red tile roof, and many chimneys.

The drive branched, the left fork forming a circle in front of the house while the other went straight, through an archway. Harriet drove through the arch. She'd been instructed to meet Julian at the stables in the rear.

Harriet pictured her grandfather at the wheel of this same Land Rover, driving through the arch. She wondered what he had thought of Julian Montcliff. If she was lucky, his journal would shed light on the events of forty years ago.

The cobbled yard was large enough to handle the carriages and wagons that used to travel here. To the left was the kitchen wing, and on the right stood the stables, a long, two-story building with several arched doors. One stood open.

As Harriet parked beside a small, white car, a young woman emerged through the open door. Dressed in jeans, a T-shirt, and muck boots, her brown hair in a braid, the woman watched Harriet's approach with her hands on her hips and a wary expression on her face.

Not exactly a warm welcome. Harriet arranged her features in a smile as she climbed out of the Rover. "Hello. I'm Dr. Bailey. Harriet. I have an appointment with Julian Montcliff to take over care of his horses from my grandfather."

The woman appraised every inch of Harriet and her vehicle. "He's around here somewhere," she finally said in a flat voice. She shook herself, as if remembering her manners. "I'm Stacey Bennett. Stable pro."

The name sounded familiar to Harriet. "Are you Meredith's granddaughter?" The woman nodded. "It's so nice to meet you. Her dog, Huntley, is boarding with me at Cobble Hill Farm."

Stacey warmed slightly. "Good to know. I'll be picking him up when she gets home."

"How is your grandmother?" Harriet asked. "I hope she's on the mend."

Stacey's expression softened. "She's getting there. They said she can go home either this afternoon or tomorrow. I'll be staying with her for a while."

"It's wonderful she has you," Harriet said. "Huntley will be glad to see his owner. He misses her."

"I'm sure." Stacey finally cracked a smile. "They're inseparable. The minute she's settled, I'll come get him."

"No rush whatsoever." Harriet hesitated before asking another question. "Does your grandmother remember anything about the attack? Such a scary thing to happen."

"No details at all," Stacey said, shaking her head. "Which, I suppose, is a relief. She won't have to relive it over and over."

Harriet didn't know if that was a good thing or not. The idea of someone accosting people in their homes was unsettling, and the police didn't have any solid leads. "I hope they catch him soon."

"So do I," Stacey said fervently. "I hope they throw the book at him."

A work van with a whining transmission lurched through the arch into the stable yard. *Leaper Plumbing.* This time, a young man drove, with Terry in the passenger seat.

"Terry works here?" Harriet asked then wished she hadn't.

Folding her arms, Stacey raised an eyebrow at her. "Why wouldn't he? He's got a sterling reputation."

"I realize that. He fixed my water heater this morning." The real issue was that Terry had been a suspect in the burglary. Harriet was surprised that hadn't made him avoid Ravenglen Manor. She supposed forty years was a long time, plus the manor probably offered a lot of lucrative work with all its bathrooms and likely ancient plumbing. Harriet was glad for the relatively modest size of her home and clinic. It must cost a fortune to maintain the manor.

Terry nodded a greeting as he climbed out of the van. Jolly pushed past him to run over to Harriet. Terry whistled. "Jolly. Come."

"He's no bother," Harriet assured Terry with a laugh, patting the eager dog. "We're quite good friends, aren't we, Jolly?"

"Until you put him under the knife." The younger man swaggered over and stood watching the scene, his posture mirroring Stacey's.

Terry blanched. "Carl Evans, how can you say that? You know how worried I am about the whole thing."

Carl's thoughtlessness annoyed Harriet. She was doing her best to reassure Terry, and his assistant wasn't helping. "It's a safe and simple procedure. I've done it more times than I can count, and it's always improved the animal's quality of life."

The young man grunted. "I guess we'll take your word for it, Doc. Seeing as how you're from over the pond."

Harriet bristled, a defensive reply crowding her lips. But such a reaction would be fruitless, either antagonizing Carl or rewarding him by rising to the bait. She was a newcomer, and the best thing she could do was let her skill speak for itself.

Whistling, Carl went around to the back of the van, opened the door, and began to rummage with a clank of tools. Jolly darted over and sat to watch.

"Don't mind my nephew," Terry said, his voice low. "He's a bit tactless."

Harriet managed to give him a small smile. "It's all right, Terry. People don't know me yet. I need to build their trust." And judging by the gossiping shoppers and cancellations, some might never give her a chance.

Something beeped, and Stacey's hand went to her pocket. "It's his nibs. He'll be a few more minutes. Wants me to show you around."

Assuming Stacey meant Julian, Harriet said to Terry, "Talk to you later. By the way, my water is nice and hot. Thanks again."

Terry beamed. "You're welcome, Doc. I'll have a quote for you on the new heater by Friday." He trudged over to the van and began conferring with Carl.

"Ready?" Stacey stood by the open door, her body language screaming impatience. As Harriet followed her inside, Stacey said, "Julian acts like these are my sole charges. I've got another stable this afternoon."

"You travel from stable to stable?" Harriet looked around, noticing two rows of neat stalls separated by a wide aisle. She counted eight, with four of them occupied.

"I do. I own a company called Stable Hand for Hire." She shrugged. "It's accurate if not splashy."

Considering how expensive a full-time stable hand would be, Harriet thought the arrangement was smart.

"I'll let Julian introduce you to the horses. They're his babies." Stacey strolled down the aisle to doors on the other end.

At the back of the stable was a corral with pastures beyond. Plenty of room for the horses to roam and graze, Harriet saw with satisfaction.

"He used to show horses years ago," Stacey said. "Now he rides for pleasure." She gestured for Harriet to follow. At one side of the stable was the tack room, with well-maintained saddles, bridles, and reins stowed neatly. Trophies and ribbons lined a high shelf, evidence of Julian's success in the ring.

"The supply room is this way." Stacey stepped through the tack room to another door. She cleared her throat when Harriet stopped to study a trophy. "I don't have much time."

"Sorry." Harriet scurried to join her, discovering a closet lined with cabinets and shelves of medicines and other supplies. "Quite an inventory."

"He likes to keep things on hand. Make sure that the vet has everything he or she needs."

"That makes sense, being so far out in the country." Harriet's respect for Julian went up a few notches. Whatever his faults, he took excellent care of his horses.

Stacey lifted a clipboard off a hook and handed it to Harriet. "This is the inventory. Part of my job is to keep it updated and order supplies."

Harriet flipped through the pages on the clipboard, scanning the list before handing it back. "Very thorough. I'm impressed."

The stable hand wore a pleased expression as she returned the clipboard to its spot. "I think I hear Julian now. Let's go meet him."

Stacey ushered her through the tack room and out into the main stable, where Julian was making a fuss over one of the horses.

"Welcome to Ravenglen Stables," he called as they approached. He wiped his hand on his trousers before extending it to shake, his grin wide and toothy.

"Nice to be here," Harriet said, returning the hearty handshake. She knew how to use a firm grip. "Lovely facility." Julian's demeanor was pleasant, even warm, a stark contrast to his suspicion yesterday. Harriet warned herself to be on guard.

"Stacey showed you around, right?" Julian asked as the stable hand slipped away with a murmur. "Let me introduce my babies." He put a hand on the chestnut mare's nose. "This is Lady. I've had her the longest, over twenty years."

With that, Julian was off, introducing Harriet to each horse with individual history, anecdotes, and a health overview. In addition to Lady, he owned a young mare and two geldings, all fine riding mounts. After the introductions, Julian let the horses out to graze and invited her in for tea.

"I saw your trophies and ribbons," Harriet said as they strolled toward the house. "Very impressive."

Julian ran a hand through his hair. "Ancient history now. I got tired of the circuit. And the constant training, especially the jumping."

"I can imagine," Harriet said. Some of her patients in Connecticut had been show horses. As with any sport, equestrian events required dedication and tons of time.

Instead of entering the rear wing, Julian took Harriet through the gardens along a gravel path. Flower beds were set strategically in an immaculate lawn, and roses adorned arbors or sprawled in hedges. Blooming wisteria climbed one wall of the house, a striking contrast with the stone. Water glinted beyond a row of weeping willows in the distance.

"What gorgeous grounds," Harriet said. "Everywhere you look, there's something beautiful to take in." So far, her visit to a historic manor was living up to expectations, although she still had reservations about her host. Resisting his charm took concentrated effort.

"That was my aim," Julian said as they crossed a flagstone terrace. He opened a French door for Harriet to enter. "During my tenure, I've made a point of restoring the gardens to their Stuart glory. While adding modern touches, of course."

The Stuarts' reign had come after the Tudors', if Harriet recalled correctly. If she was going to live in England, she had better brush up on the country's history. The past was still evident in structures, towns, and traditions.

"Welcome to my humble abode," Julian said as they entered a drawing room featuring coffered ceilings and gold flocked-velvet wallpaper hung with landscapes. Brocade-upholstered furniture, crystal chandeliers, and a gold French mantel clock added to the elegant ambiance.

"Not bad," Harriet said in a teasing voice. Then she smiled. "Really. It's magnificent."

Julian grinned. "I thought we'd have tea and chat in my study."

His study, with its big desk, bookshelves, and paneled walls, was adjacent to the drawing room. Another set of French doors gave access to the garden.

Julian indicated that Harriet take a seat on a sofa. He picked up the phone and spoke to someone then hung up again. "Tea will be right in." He sat in a nearby wingback chair. "So what do you think? Are you willing to add my little herd to your roster?"

"Are *you* sure?" she asked, deciding to lay her cards on the table. "After yesterday, I thought you might have doubts about moving forward with me as your vet." She steeled herself, expecting an angry response or even a repeat of his accusations.

Julian's eyes widened briefly—whether in surprise or something else, Harriet couldn't tell. Fiddling with his watch, he muttered, "I'm sorry about that. I might, er, have jumped to conclusions. In the heat of the moment, I mean."

Harriet remained silent, waiting. If she spoke, she would simply confirm what he'd said, which might shut down his apparent willingness to talk.

Lifting his gaze to hers, he said, voice brimming with sincerity, "I do apologize for my attitude yesterday, and should you be willing, I hope we can start over. I'm sorry we got off on the wrong foot."

"Thank you for saying that." Julian's continued patronage might help dispel the rumors about her grandfather, which was a point in his favor. "I'll be happy to provide care to your horses."

Julian squared his shoulders. "I'm glad that's settled. Now, as I said earlier, I'd like the horses to have semiannual checkups. Lady needs that anyway, at her age, so I figure they can all use the attention. I don't anticipate any issues, but if they arise, that schedule should improve our odds of catching them early."

"I completely agree."

A middle-aged woman wearing an apron over slacks and a blouse bustled in with a tray. She set it on the coffee table, checked it over, and said, "Do you need anything else, Mr. Montcliff?"

Julian eyed the tray, which held a tiered stand of baked goods and finger sandwiches along with a teapot, cups, milk, and sugar. "Unless you'd like lemon, Dr. Bailey?"

"No, thank you. Milk is fine." Harriet smiled at the woman, who maintained her formal demeanor.

"That will be all then, Sandra," Julian said. "Thank you." He opened the teapot lid to inspect the brew before filling two cups. "It's a real pleasure having you here, Dr. Bailey. Your grandfather and I spent many happy hours chatting in this library."

"Is that so?" As always, the mention of her grandfather made Harriet's heart leap. Hearing stories about him kept her own memories alive and deepened her knowledge and understanding of him. Each one was like a precious artifact that she'd unearthed.

"Indeed." Julian splashed milk into his cup, stirred, and then took a sip. "We were friends. We hashed over the horses, naturally, but we also talked about everything else. He was a very wise man. Talented artist as well." He grinned at her. "Do you see a Harold Bailey painting anywhere in here, by chance?"

Harriet glanced around the room, her gaze skipping over the artwork. "The small one over there. With the cow and milkmaid." She easily recognized her grandfather's style, which was a realistic yet romanticized view of English life.

Julian set his cup down and walked over to the painting. Harriet followed, feeling the wariness she'd set aside once more. Why was Julian pointing out this painting? Was he trying to imply something about her grandfather? The memory of the Royal Dux figurine sat heavy on her conscience. Even though Grandad's milkmaid wore modern garb, there was a similar composition to the work.

Her host bent close to the painting. "I think Harold's work stands up to any of the greats. John Frederick Herring. Sir Edwin Henry Landseer. John Emms."

Harriet had seen those names while glancing through the book on animal art. "I totally agree. That's one more thing on my list—getting the gallery up and running again."

"All in good time." Julian straightened the gilded frame slightly. "Anyway, you can see the influence of the past here. The old ways are much more picturesque, aren't they?"

"Sometimes." Harriet knew the labor that went into animal care and didn't begrudge farmers the convenience of modern equipment and methods.

Julian laughed. "In theory, anyway." He stepped away from the painting. "Oh, before I forget. Let me pay you for today." He detoured over to the desk and pulled out a checkbook.

"That's not necessary," Harriet said. Julian's account was set up for billing at the clinic, and he was up to date on his payments. Plus, she hadn't examined the horses yet.

"I insist." Julian uncapped a pen with a flourish. "You deserve the call fee. I was already confident in our arrangement before today, but I feel even better after talking with you about my animals."

Harriet returned to her seat, not bothering to argue further. "Thank you." While he wrote the check, she drank her tea and tried to gather her thoughts. Polly's suggestion to question Julian about the burglary nagged at the back of her mind. She had no idea how to bring up the subject. Especially since Julian was being so hospitable, although she wondered about his pointing out the painting.

Had it been completely innocent? He couldn't possibly know that Grandad owned a similar figurine—perhaps one stolen from here.

One thing she was certain about. She wasn't about to mention the statue to Julian.

Sandra appeared in the doorway. "Sorry to bother you, Mr. Montcliff," she said, smoothing the front of her apron with both hands.

Julian ripped the check from the book with a flourish. "What is it, Sandra?" He sounded slightly annoyed.

"It's the police." Biting her lip, she stepped aside to reveal DI McCormick and Sergeant Oduba. "You said to let them in."

"So I did." Julian hopped up from his seat and came over to Harriet, holding out the check. "Here you are. I'm afraid our visit has been cut short."

"Totally understandable." Harriet slid the check into her wallet. "I'll have Polly call to schedule the examinations." Her heart pounded so hard she could barely breathe. Had the police found the rest of the jewelry? Had they identified the thief? If only she could stay and find out.

"Dr. Bailey," DI McCormick said, and Harriet all but jumped out of her skin. "What brings you here?"

Harriet stood, slinging her purse strap over her shoulder. "Julian was introducing me to his horses. I'm the veterinarian of record for the stables."

"I see," the inspector replied, her tone implying that she understood far more than Harriet had said. "We'll be circling around to talk to you again soon, Dr. Bailey. I trust you're staying close to home?"

CHAPTER NINE

I'll be around," Harriet managed to stutter, her face flaming. "Not planning any trips." Although right now she'd love to get away. It wasn't much fun being so involved with a police case. Gathering her dignity, she turned to Julian. "Thank you for the tour, Mr. Montcliff. Our office will be in touch. I'll show myself out."

She forced herself to leave the room at her normal pace, painfully aware that all three watched her. In the drawing room, she slipped through the French door to the terrace instead of trying to find the way out through the kitchen wing.

When it came to solving the mystery, this visit had been a total bust. Polly would be disappointed. On the other hand, Harriet had gotten to spend time with four very delightful horses. That was where her real expertise and interests lay, not in solving forty-year-old crimes.

Harriet felt a wry smile creep along her face. At least she'd confirmed that she was in the right career. She'd be glad when this mess was over and she could focus all her attention on being the new Doc Bailey.

The delicious aroma of roasting chicken was drifting around the kitchen when someone knocked on the back door. "Come on in," Harriet called. She turned with a smile, potato and peeler in hand.

Instead of Aunt Jinny, the person she was expecting, Stacey Bennett stood awkwardly in the doorway. "Sorry to bother you. I'm here for Huntley."

At his name, the spaniel rose to his feet with a woof and scramble of paws. He and Maxwell had been hanging out together under the kitchen table.

"He's in here?" Stacey asked. "That's not what I expected when you said you were boarding him."

Harriet put down the potato and peeler and wiped her hands on a dish towel. "It's not the usual arrangement, but he and Maxwell are buddies. To be honest, he slept inside last night. He was lonely being away from his owner."

"Aw." Stacey patted Huntley's head. "Ready to go home?" His tail waved like a metronome. She glanced at Harriet. "What do we owe you?"

Harriet wasn't sure off the top of her head. "Don't worry about that now. I'll have Polly bill you."

Stacey shrugged. "If that's all right. Did he have a lead?"

"Right here," Harriet said, selecting Huntley's leash from a row of pegs. "He also had his blanket and dishes." She gathered his belongings from the kitchen. "I'll walk you out."

Harriet let Stacey and a leashed Huntley lead the way to the parking lot, Maxwell wheeling along behind them. "Maxwell will miss his friend."

"That's so sweet." Stacey opened the rear door of her sedan, and Huntley jumped inside. Then she went around and opened the other door so Harriet could deposit the dog's things on the seat. "Thanks again."

"Anytime," Harriet said. "Say hello to your grandmother for me and tell her I'm glad she's home."

"I will," Stacey promised, already moving to the driver's side door. "Sorry, I need to get going."

"Of course." Harriet would be anxious to get back to an injured grandparent as well. "Have a good night."

Harriet and Maxwell stood watching as Stacey started the car and set off. As she reached the bottom of the drive, a noisy little sedan came along the road. The new car stopped, and Terry's nephew, Carl, got out and came over to Stacey's window. When their voices rose, Harriet decided not to linger any longer. Their discussion was none of her business.

"Time to go in, Maxwell," Harriet said. As they made their way across the lot, a car door slammed, and the sedan took off. At least one mystery solved. Carl Leaper was the driver who annoyed Aunt Jinny when he raced by.

A dejected Maxwell returned to his spot under the kitchen table, and Harriet went back to peeling potatoes. She planned to mash the potatoes and sauté the asparagus in butter. It was a simple yet tasty meal, and there would be plenty of leftover chicken for sandwiches. Harriet enjoyed the relaxing chore of preparing a meal. It was a nice contrast to the mental energy it took to care for patients—and to ponder mysteries.

"Knock, knock." Aunt Jinny walked in, baking dish in her hands. "I took the liberty of making strawberry rhubarb crisp. I hope you don't mind."

"Mind? It's one of my favorites." Harriet kissed her aunt on the cheek. "Please make yourself at home."

"Is there anything I can do to help?" Aunt Jinny asked as she placed the dessert dish on the counter.

"Nope," Harriet answered firmly. "I have it all under control." She placed the pot of potatoes on the stove and switched on the flame. Then she pulled the bag of asparagus out of the fridge and carried it to the sink.

"Before I forget," Aunt Jinny said, "I wanted to invite you to Sunday lunch. Anthony and Olivia are coming with the twins." Jinny's son and Harriet's cousin, Anthony, was the father of six-year-old twins Sophie and Sebastian.

"I'd love to," Harriet said. "I've been hoping to spend more time with them." Anthony was only a year younger than she was, and they'd been great pals when she'd visited as a child.

"They'll be delighted to see you," Aunt Jinny said.

As Harriet washed the asparagus spears, she was uncomfortably reminded of her experience at the general store and what she'd found in the study. Rather than bring up a painful subject now—namely everything to do with the stolen jewels—she said instead, "I found out who drives the noisy little car that's been bothering you."

Aunt Jinny was seated at the table, Charlie on her lap. "Really? Who?"

Harriet snapped off the woody bottom of the stalks. "Terry Leaper's nephew, Carl. He stopped to talk to Stacey Bennett, and I recognized the car. Well, the sound of its engine anyway."

"Stacey is Meredith's granddaughter, right?"

"Yes. She came to pick up Huntley." Harriet selected a skillet and placed it on the stove. The asparagus wouldn't take very long, so she would wait until the potatoes were done. She opened the oven door and pulled the chicken out to check it. "She's going to stay with Meredith for a while."

"I'm glad," Aunt Jinny said. "Head injuries aren't something to take lightly."

Harriet inserted a thermometer into the chicken. "No, they're not. Stacey told me the police haven't identified the assailant yet, which is alarming." The temperature was perfect, so she left the chicken to rest before slicing.

Aunt Jinny glanced toward the open door to the terrace. "I hope he's found soon. Make sure you lock up at night."

"I always do. Plus, I have my early warning alarm." Harriet gestured to Maxwell from the stove as she poked the potatoes. They were soft, so she drained them. She added a chunk of butter to the drained pot, another to the skillet, and started the heat for the asparagus.

"Are you sure you don't want help?" Aunt Jinny asked.

"I certainly am," Harriet said. "You've cooked your fair share of meals over the years, so I insist you sit back and relax."

Aunt Jinny took her advice while Harriet completed the meal preparation. Soon they were sitting down at the table together, enjoying roasted chicken, fluffy potatoes topped with gravy, and tender fresh asparagus. Aunt Jinny's strawberry rhubarb crisp was the perfect dish to finish the meal.

"Scrumptious," Aunt Jinny said. "You're a wonderful cook, my dear."

Harriet beamed. "As long as I keep it simple."

Once the dessert bowls were scraped clean, Aunt Jinny asked, "Anything new happen today?" She didn't have to specify what she meant.

"Where should I start?" Harriet mused.

Concern creased her aunt's brow. "At the beginning would be good."

Over an after-dinner cup of tea, Harriet took Aunt Jinny through her day, including the trip to the store, the chat with Pastor Will, now "Will" to Harriet, and her appointment at Ravenglen Manor. "I don't understand Julian," she concluded. "One minute he's accusing us of theft, and the next, he's Mr. Hospitality."

"That's Julian," Aunt Jinny said. "It's how he's gotten away with so much all his life. He charms his way out of trouble to the point where people hesitate to hold him accountable because they like him so much."

Harriet had met that type before. "Thanks for the heads-up. I'll be careful around him." She paused before sharing what was really bothering her. "DI McCormick said that she wants to talk to me again. She even asked me if I was staying in the area."

"I'm sure that's strictly routine. She simply wanted to make sure you'd be around to talk to." Despite her reassuring words, worry shadowed her aunt's gaze.

Harriet knew she couldn't put it off any longer. It was time to mention the discovery she'd been holding back. "I found something interesting today."

Aunt Jinny set her mug on the table. "Show me."

Harriet led her to the study and pointed out the statue.

"What a nice figurine." Aunt Jinny picked up the milkmaid and rotated it. "Royal Dux. They did beautiful work."

"Do you remember where it came from?" Harriet asked anxiously. "Or when Grandad got it?" Perhaps he'd owned it before the Ravenglen Manor burglary.

Aunt Jinny shook her head. "I'm sorry, I don't." A crease appeared between her brows. "Why do you ask?"

Harriet inhaled. "Because a similar piece was stolen during the heist."

"What?" Aunt Jinny hastily returned the figurine to its shelf.

"I know. I was shocked too." Harriet took out her phone and brought up the article. "See? A Royal Dux milkmaid with cow was among the stolen items."

Aunt Jinny stared at the article. "I must have read this back then, but I never made the connection."

"It's easy to overlook," Harriet said. "What's a piece of porcelain next to emeralds and diamonds? I don't like the coincidence though." She picked up the statue. "See that number? What if it matches the number on the missing figurine?"

Aunt Jinny began to pace the study. "We need to tell the police about this."

Harriet's heart sank. "I was afraid you'd say that. I'm worried though. What are people going to say? It's more evidence pointing to Grandad, which isn't fair." She shuddered at the idea of new fodder for the gossip mill.

"But if we intentionally hide possible evidence, that's even worse." Aunt Jinny came to a stop in front of Harriet and put a hand on her shoulder. "Buck up, my dear. The only way out is through."

Harriet sighed. "I know. We have to do the right thing and trust God to take care of the rest."

"Besides, it might not be the same one," Aunt Jinny said. "They made hundreds. So think of the relief when we find out."

Or the shock when our fears are confirmed. Something deep inside Harriet told her the statue was related to the case. She gritted her teeth. *The only way out is through.*

She couldn't control the outcome, but she thought of something she could do to help. "I'm going to start reading Grandad's 1983 journal tonight." She showed the book to Aunt Jinny. "I also found a lot of photo albums, so I'll be working my way through those as well."

"If you have any questions or want someone to do it with you, please ask," Aunt Jinny said. She gave Harriet a quick hug. "Let's go clean up the kitchen. I've got an early morning."

Harriet smiled. "There's plenty of hot water, thanks to Terry."

After Aunt Jinny left, Harriet carried a fresh cup of tea, her grandfather's journal, and a stack of photograph albums to the reading nook. This was her name for a cozy area of the living room that included an alcove with a bow window, a tall wingback chair and ottoman, and a standing lamp. An end table provided space for books and her tea, which she set on a coaster.

Charlie and Maxwell tagged along. The cat curled up on the ottoman, and Maxwell chose the hearthrug in front of the empty fireplace. Harriet could picture Grandad there in the winter months, lounging by a crackling fire.

Harriet was caught by sorrow when she opened the journal. Her grandfather's neat yet spiky handwriting marched along the page, bringing back memories of cards and letters over the years. How she'd treasured those, reading them over and over as if that could bring them closer together. She could have picked out his handwriting from a lineup with ease.

Harriet read the first few entries to get a feel for her grandfather's style. He started each entry with the day's weather and then noted items of interest. These included patients, local news, and encounters with friends and acquaintances. Harriet found herself smiling frequently. The journal conveyed so much of his warmth, humor, and general good nature. A deep and abiding respect for people and animals was clear from his words.

Harriet leafed slowly through the journal. The heist had occurred in July, so she scanned the pages for any mention of Ravenglen Manor, Julian, or the theft.

Julian's name seemed to leap off the page on an entry dated June 10, 1983.

Follow-up with a lame mare, Bonnie, at Ravenglen Manor. She's responding well to treatment. Lovely creature. Julian was in something of a state, having received a huge estimate on plumbing and heating work that needs to be done. Once again, he's threatening to sell, saying he'll buy a bungalow somewhere warm. I told him I sympathize, especially when treating livestock during a deep winter freeze. I think I chiv-ied him into a better mood.

Harriet had been the recipient of Grandad's "chivying," or good-natured teasing, and could attest to how effective it was. She remembered more than one pout he'd eased her out of, how he had nipped self-pity in the bud. She felt for Julian and the manor's plumbing woes though. It was still being worked on, judging by Terry's visit that very day.

There wasn't any mention of Julian again until after the heist.

A very shocking event has the countryside in an uproar. Ravenglen Manor was robbed sometime over the weekend while Julian was out of town. Apparently, the entire Montcliff collection was stolen. Poor Julian. I do hope he had good insurance coverage.

Further on, Harriet found another mention.

Nothing new in the Ravenglen theft. The police have chased down any local leads, and opinion is now pointed toward a thieving ring targeting stately homes throughout England.

If it had been a gang, then they'd left quite a lot of loot behind. She made a note to research the other thefts and see if they had been solved.

After marking the relevant journal pages with slips of paper, Harriet moved on to the photo albums. She soon found herself entranced by the photographs of Cobble Hill in days gone by. Here were the great-grandparents she had never met. Grandad through the years as he grew into a handsome young man. His graduation from veterinary school, posing proudly with his father, and his wedding to Helen, her grandmother. Soon after, the appearance of Harriet's father and Aunt Jinny. There were many pictures of Aunt Jinny and Uncle Dominick's wedding and Harriet's parents' wedding. Then pictures of the grandchildren—Harriet and Anthony. Each year, there were a few Christmas pictures in front of the tree and the whole clan seated around a long table laden with food.

Harriet was swamped with nostalgia for those bygone days. Now that she was a resident here, she should try to create new traditions while honoring the old. Maybe she would host Christmas dinner at Cobble Hill and invite Aunt Jinny and Anthony's family. It was something to discuss, anyway. Maybe her parents would want to make the trip. That would be wonderful. She missed them.

Whenever she came across photographs showing the grounds, Harriet paid close attention. The stables hadn't been converted for dog boarding until the 1990s. She wasn't sure when the yard had been cleared.

A 1985 photograph of Grandad and his sheepdog, Sally, standing under the spreading branches of an oak, caught her eye. Harriet thought she recognized the shape of the lower branches. If she was right, a couple of feet to the right of Grandad was approximately where Huntley had dug up the chest.

Here was proof that the jewelry hadn't been buried in that spot since the heist in 1983. Several boulders would have been in the way.

So where had the jewelry been, and when had it been moved? More importantly, who had moved it?

CHAPTER TEN

T he next morning, Harriet took a deep breath before opening the door to the clinic. She'd faced her fair share of challenging days as a veterinarian. Overworked, understaffed, difficult cases, and outright heartbreaking ones. She'd dealt with it all.

But never before had her reputation—and that of her beloved grandfather—been in question. Rumors swirled, clients had canceled, and curiosity seekers filled the empty slots.

All eyes would be on Dr. Harriet Bailey today as the village of White Church Bay tried to decide for themselves whether her entire family was innocent or guilty.

Polly swiveled in her chair when Harriet entered the waiting area. "Good morning, Doctor." Her smile was wide and welcoming. "Isn't it a lovely morning?"

Every chair was full and every ear listening as Harriet said, "It certainly is." She gave the room a general wave and smile before picking up the top few files. Not that she was able to retain anything she read with this audience. Normally, the clients would be chatting or busy on their phones, not sitting rapt and attentive. It was unnerving.

Polly rose from her chair. "Mr. Gunderson is first," she said. "Martha, his French bulldog, is here for a regular checkup."

Harriet kept that file and set the others down. Stepping forward, she said, "Mr. Gunderson? Martha?"

"That's me." A slight, elderly man sprang to his feet, tugging on a leash attached to a white French bulldog with fetching black patches. As he made his way across the room, urging Martha along, he said, "Nice to see you, Doc. No tiara today?"

A hush fell over the waiting room. Rising to the occasion, Harriet touched her hair. "It's in for repairs, I'm afraid. Next time."

Everyone burst out laughing, and the wave of merriment carried Harriet and Mr. Gunderson into the exam room.

"Sorry to rib you like that, Doc," Mr. Gunderson said, wincing. "It sort of slipped out."

"Not a problem," Harriet said briskly, closing the door. "It was a nice icebreaker, in fact." She shook her head ruefully. "I know what everyone's thinking and really can't blame them."

"It's rubbish, and they know it," Mr. Gunderson said, lifting his chin. "Everyone loved Doc Bailey. The man wouldn't steal a sixpence, let alone a sack of jewels. Chin up, Doc. It'll all come right."

"I hope so," Harriet said, sighing. Getting down to business, she indicated the ramp. "Come on up, Martha."

Halfway through a standard exam that showed Martha was in perfect health, Mr. Gunderson said, "Something's been nagging at me."

"What's that?" Harriet asked, expecting him to comment on his pet.

"There were a few months when this place wasn't open."

"Sorry about that," Harriet said. "It took some time to settle the estate and for me to relocate."

He waved a hand. "No criticism of that. I meant, no one was here, on this property. Well, Dr. Garrett lives next door, but she doesn't go out to the dog yard, am I right?"

Harriet glanced at her client. "What are you getting at?"

Mr. Gunderson shrugged. "Someone could have taken advantage, that's all."

Understanding dawned. Mr. Gunderson thought the buried chest had been put there recently. He could be right. There would have been no reason for Aunt Jinny to investigate the dog yard, so someone could have easily buried the chest, and no one would have noticed the disturbed earth. This theory also fit with hers, that the chest had been buried well after the heist. After the boulders were moved.

"I'll mention your theory to the police," Harriet said. "If you don't mind. I don't have to mention your name."

"That would be best," Mr. Gunderson said. "I don't know anything for sure." He tapped his temple. "Just using my noggin."

"And a good one it is too." Harriet smiled at her client. "I'm happy to say that Martha is in excellent condition. I see she's due for a rabies shot. Do you want her to get that today?"

"Phew." Polly groaned as she sank into a chair at the patio table. "Talk about being run off our feet."

"I'm relieved we didn't have an empty clinic," Harriet said. She kicked her shoes off under the table and wiggled her toes. Behaving this casually at lunchtime was one benefit of working at home. "You booked some appointments this afternoon?"

Polly, who had taken a mouthful of sandwich, nodded and swallowed. "From one to three. Make hay while the sun shines and all that."

"Totally." Harriet finished a bite herself then asked, "Oh, guess what?"

At the same time, Polly blurted, "Guess what?"

They both laughed. "Great minds," Harriet said. "You first."

Polly gestured. "No, you go ahead."

Harriet pushed back her chair. The conversation would go better with props. "Just a minute."

The photo album and journal were upstairs in her bedroom. When she'd gone to bed last night, she'd felt uneasy about leaving them in the living room. She knew her fear was absurd—that someone would break in and steal those items over the actual valuables in the house. Nevertheless, she'd put them in a dresser drawer.

Back on the patio, she placed the journal and album next to her plate. "This is Grandad's journal from the year of the heist." She opened the book to the first slip of paper and handed it to Polly.

Polly read the entry. "Julian wanted to sell? That's interesting."

"What do you mean?" Harriet had a good idea but didn't want to put words in her friend's mouth.

Polly pursed her lips. "Don't mind me. I have a suspicious mind." She flipped to the next marked place. "Your grandfather wondered about Julian's insurance coverage."

Harriet lowered her voice to a whisper even though they were alone. "Do you think Julian faked the theft to collect the insurance?"

"It happens." Polly put a finger to her lips. "I never said that, all right? It's not something to bandy about lightly."

Harriet agreed. Unfounded accusations of criminal behavior could ruin a life. That was why gossip was so dangerous. "What we talk about stays between us." She opened the photo album to the right page and set it in front of Polly without an explanation.

"What am I—" Light dawned in Polly's eyes. "Those boulders. They're not there anymore."

"This photo was taken a couple of years *after* the heist. Far as I can figure, that's the spot where the chest was buried." Harriet realized Polly hadn't been out there. "Want to go see?"

"Absolutely." Polly jumped up from the table. "Lead on."

Harriet brought the photograph for reference to double-check her theory. They entered the yard through the outside gate and approached the hole Huntley had dug.

Polly glanced between the cavity in the soil and the oak tree then held up the photograph. "I think you're right." She waved the photo. "You need to show this to the police."

"I'll give DI McCormick a call." Harriet was happy to have something that might shift suspicion away from her grandfather. "I'll also show her a picture of when they changed this area into the dog yard in the early 1990s."

"At minimum, it proves the chest couldn't have been there since the heist."

As they headed back to the clinic, Harriet asked, "What did you want to tell me?"

Polly ducked her head. "I accepted Van's invitation to the tractor fest."

It took Harriet a moment to absorb what she'd said. Polly hadn't seemed the least bit enthusiastic when Harriet had relayed Van's message. Also, a tractor fest as a first date wasn't very romantic—unless both people loved antique machinery.

"Why?" burst from Harriet's mouth. "I'm sorry. That was rude."

"No, your reaction is perfectly understandable." After a beat, Polly added, "I couldn't refuse the opportunity to help investigate."

Harriet unlatched the gate. "I don't understand."

"I plan to talk to Van about the case." Polly's tone was placid. "I'm going to try to find out what's going on, if they really do consider Harold a suspect. Which I can't believe."

Harriet stopped short. "Polly, you don't have to go that far."

Polly faced her, resting her hands on her hips. "As far as what? It's a tractor show, that's all."

"Going on a fake date. Pretending you're interested in Van."

"Don't worry," Polly said. "I'm not going to lead him on. That would be cruel." She shrugged. "I'll make it clear that we're friends and that I don't see it as a date."

Harriet still had reservations, but she couldn't think of any other arguments, and it was Polly's business who she went out with. "I doubt he'll tell you much, but good luck." Then she remembered Julian Montcliff's arrival at Cobble Hill right after the discovery of the chest. Had Van spilled the beans to him? Maybe the detective constable wasn't as trustworthy in his role as one might think.

Harriet hoped that wasn't true.

Aunt Jinny called while Harriet was making a sandwich for dinner. It had been a long, busy day, and Harriet was both weary and content. "Hello," she sang into the phone. "How was your day?"

"Productive," Aunt Jinny said with a sigh. "Back-to-back appointments."

Harriet finished spreading mayonnaise and began laying chicken from last night's meal on the bread. "Would you like a chicken sandwich? That's my fancy dinner tonight."

Aunt Jinny chuckled. "No thanks. I'm having a salad. Anyway, the reason I called is that I've got some old photographs I thought you'd like to see. Pictures of me and your uncle Dominick living it up at Ravenglen Manor."

Harriet's interest quickened. "I'd love to look at them." She remembered her own discoveries. "I have a couple of things to show you too. When should I come over?"

"In about an hour, so we both have time to eat. We can meet up at my table outside. It's a lovely evening."

"Sounds great."

Later, Harriet cut through a thicket of trees to her aunt's house, accompanied by Maxwell and Charlie, who slunk from bush to bush like spies on a mission. Aunt Jinny waited outside, seated at the table under an umbrella.

"I see you brought company," Aunt Jinny said, smiling at Maxwell and Charlie. Her gaze fell on the tote bag Harriet carried. "What do you have there?"

Harriet set the bag on a chair to unload it. "One of Grandad's journals and a photo album." As she placed them on the table, she noticed an album in front of Aunt Jinny. Those must be the Ravenglen Manor photographs.

"Lemonade?" Aunt Jinny motioned toward a frosty pitcher that contained a carbonated, lemon-flavored beverage. While Harriet wouldn't refuse what the English called lemonade, she preferred the American version.

"Yes, please." Harriet sat at the table. Maxwell scooted underneath by her feet, and Charlie continued to prowl around the garden.

While Aunt Jinny poured, Harriet opened the photo album she'd brought over. "I think I found proof."

"Of what?" Aunt Jinny set the glass on a coaster near Harriet.

"Of Grandad's innocence." She slid the album toward her aunt. "Grandad is standing right where the chest was buried. See those boulders?"

Her aunt studied the photo. "Right. I remember those now. He had them moved so the dogs would have more room to run. Good work."

"Thanks, but all I did was leaf through old photos."

"But you did it," her aunt replied firmly. "And you found something."

Harriet set the album aside and opened the journal to the first slip of paper. "I found a couple of entries that mention Julian and the heist."

Harriet sipped the tart drink while her aunt read the entries. As she gazed out over the yard, memories of playing games with her cousin here drifted through her mind. She looked forward to spending time with Anthony and his family.

"This comment about Julian wanting to sell reminds me of something," Aunt Jinny said. "He was always complaining about the manor and all the upkeep it needed. At the same time, he was extremely proud of the place and his family history. His identity is deeply rooted there. Who would he be without the manor? I don't think even Julian knows."

"You mean he didn't really plan on selling?" Harriet had wondered that herself. Here it was forty years later, and he was still at the manor.

"Of course not." Aunt Jinny closed the journal and handed it back to Harriet before opening her photo album. "It was what you might call an idle threat."

Harriet scooted her chair closer so she could see the pictures.

Here were Aunt Jinny and Uncle Dominick as a young married couple—attractive, happy, and surrounded by friends.

"Those were the days," Aunt Jinny said dreamily. "We were very much in love."

"I can tell. You were a beautiful couple." Wistfulness panged in Harriet's heart. How she longed to be part of a perfect duo. All it required was meeting the right man. She'd already known her share of wrong ones.

Aunt Jinny reminisced as she flipped through, making comments about this picture or that. She pointed at a page. "This is the last gathering before the robbery—an elegant dinner party on the terrace."

Initial photos of the event showed small groups mingling. Aunt Jinny was lovely in a silk knee-length dress, her hair curled in the eighties style, and Uncle Dominick was handsome in slacks and a dress shirt worn with a tie.

In many of the photos, Julian stood with a slender dark-haired woman. "Who is that?" Harriet asked.

"Yvonne Russell, now Ellerby. She was Julian's fiancée at the time."

"They never got married?" Judging by the body language in the photographs, they were a happy couple at that time.

"No, sorry to say. Yvonne broke the engagement, though I never heard why." Aunt Jinny shook her head as she flipped the page. "I want to show you something. Ah, here it is."

In the photograph she indicated, Julian, Yvonne, Aunt Jinny, and Uncle Dominick stood in front of a fireplace, all smiles.

"See the necklace she's wearing?" Aunt Jinny tapped on the image of Yvonne. "It was incredible, diamonds and emeralds set in platinum. Julian called it the centerpiece of the Amelia Montcliff collection."

"Wow." Harriet peered more closely. "I didn't see *that* in the chest. I would have remembered it. Was it stolen?"

"I think so," Aunt Jinny said. "I'm not sure."

Harriet took out her phone and brought up the news stories about the heist. A quick scan gave her the answer. "Yes, it's listed among the missing pieces. One of the most valuable items, according to this article."

"That's too bad," Aunt Jinny said. "I hope it's recovered intact. Julian gave Yvonne that necklace as a birthday present. In fact, come to think of it, the dinner party was in her honor that night."

"That's quite a gift." Harriet thought of something. "So, even though he gave it to her, she left it at the manor?"

"I guess so. Maybe they thought it would be safer there." Her aunt grimaced. "Famous last words." She shuffled through a few more pages. "That's it for Ravenglen Manor. We saw Julian now and then after the theft, but it wasn't the same."

"Is Yvonne still around?" Harriet asked. She wondered if Julian's ex-fiancée might have any insight into the burglary.

"She's married to a veterinarian named Nigel Ellerby. You'll probably run into him at some point. Dad used to get together with other vets from the area to talk shop now and then."

"I'll keep an eye out for him." Harriet had planned to network with other veterinarians once she was a little more settled. Maybe Yvonne's former involvement with Julian should bump up that task in priority.

"Back to Grandad's journal," Harriet said. "Do you think it was a crime ring? He said the police were leaning in that direction."

Aunt Jinny rested her chin on her hand, thinking. "I'd prefer to think that. It would mean that strangers were responsible rather than someone we know."

"I get that," Harriet asked. "But doesn't it seem convenient that they struck while Julian was away?"

"They could have been watching the manor," Aunt Jinny pointed out. "I'm sure they wouldn't barge in willy-nilly. Don't they always talk about professional crime rings 'casing the joint'?"

"True." Harriet had to admit that a theft of that magnitude had likely required weeks if not months of planning. "They caught some members of a major theft ring recently, I read. I wonder if any of them had a connection to White Church Bay."

"The police probably wonder that as well," Aunt Jinny said. "Are you taking up detective work as a sideline?" Her voice was teasing.

"Not on purpose," Harriet said. "It makes me feel better to do something to help, even if it's not much. Especially with our family's reputation on the line." She gestured toward her grandfather's album. "The picture I found of the boulders, for example. Would the police think to dig that deeply?"

"Maybe not," Aunt Jinny admitted. "I'm sure they're pursuing other avenues. They have methods to trace stolen goods."

Stolen goods like the milkmaid figurine? Harriet's stomach flipped over. She really should call DI McCormick and report it. She would do that as soon as she got home. She'd mention the photograph as well.

All she could do right now was take the next step and pray everything worked together for good.

CHAPTER ELEVEN

Saturday morning, folded map on the seat beside her, Harriet set off for the tractor fest. The event was being held at Kettlewell Farm about ten miles away. She hoped to network with potential clients such as George Kettlewell, the host of the fest, and others in attendance. To that end, she'd slid a stack of business cards into her small crossbody bag.

DI McCormick still hadn't returned the phone message Harriet had left on Thursday evening, nor had she scheduled an interview with Harriet.

It's like having a sword dangling above my head. Unresolved issues and questions sat uneasily in Harriet's midsection despite her attempts to leave them in God's hands. At least she was getting plenty of practice at that exercise.

North Yorkshire had been enjoying a stretch of warm, sunny weather, and today was no exception. According to the forecast, temperatures were scheduled to climb into the eighties. Harriet was prepared with a water bottle, sun hat, and sunscreen.

The sound of tractor engines vibrating in the air was Harriet's hint that she was approaching the event. At an open gate to a field, a man in an orange vest directed guest traffic. Harriet slowed, inching forward as the vehicles in front of her ambled through.

Once parked, Harriet checked her bag before settling it into place across her torso. This certainly wasn't the first time she'd gone to a public gathering alone not knowing many people. She'd attended many conferences and animal-related events over the years.

However, this was the first such occasion in Yorkshire. Although Polly and Van were here somewhere, so she knew two people at least. Not that she planned to tag along with them like a third wheel, no matter what Polly said about it not being a date.

Following others on foot, Harriet made her way to the main event. She strolled past antique tractors and farm equipment on display, food and vendor booths, and musicians playing folk music on a makeshift stage. Onlookers stood along a fence, beyond which a caller announced participants in a draft-horse pull contest. In another area, a line of rumbling tractors paraded to the cheers of spectators.

Harriet's smile became genuine as she blended into the throng. These were her people, in love with their agricultural heritage and lifestyle. She'd attended a tractor fest with her grandfather when she was much younger, and this experience was close enough to her memory to make her feel as if Grandad walked with her.

How wonderful it was to see farms thriving in Yorkshire and traditions still being honored and enjoyed. And now Harriet was an integral part of this story, the latest in a line of vets practicing at Cobble Hill.

Harriet joined the crowd at the pull, thinking she should introduce herself to the horse owners. What beautiful creatures the horses, muscles rippling as they set to work.

Everyone cheered. The horse in the ring had broken the record set by the previous contestant, Harriet gathered. She joined in the applause.

"Magnificent beast, isn't he?" commented the man next to Harriet. He was middle-aged, with a comfortable belly and sturdy build. A flat cap shielded his eyes, and he wore trousers, a vest, and a checked shirt with the sleeves rolled up.

"He really is." Harriet decided to plunge in. "I'm Dr. Harriet Bailey of Cobble Hill Farm."

His thick brows rose. "Doc Bailey's granddaughter? I heard you were taking over." He extended a rough hand. "Dr. Barry Tweedy. I'm in the business myself. Knew your grandfather very well." His other hand covered Harriet's. "An excellent chap. Best in his field."

Warmed by this enthusiastic introduction, Harriet said, "It's so nice to meet you, Dr. Tweedy. I've been hoping to connect with other vets in the area."

"Call me Barry," the vet said, releasing her hand. He half-turned and whistled, lifting his arm in the air. "I want you to meet a couple of other chaps."

Soon, two other men joined them, both vets and dressed similarly to Barry. Dr. Gavin Witty was tall and thin, with curly reddish hair. He appeared to be in his forties. The third man was the oldest of the group, with tidy gray hair, craggy features, and an air of weariness. His name was Dr. Nigel Ellerby.

Harriet gave a little squeak of surprise, but covered it by saying, "How nice to meet you." This man was married to Julian's former fiancée. She glanced behind him, wondering if his wife was with him. There was no sign of Yvonne, however.

"We three get together now and then," Barry said. "Shoot the breeze about life. Discuss any troubling cases. Share treatment notes."

"Would you like to join us?" Gavin asked. "Harold used to be part of our confab group."

"I'd love to," Harriet said. "I've been hoping to network with other vets. I didn't expect it to fall into my lap like this, but I appreciate it."

"Nice when things work out, isn't it?" Barry said. "I had it in mind to give you a ring once you were settled in anyway."

"I bet the discovery of that jewel chest threw quite a spanner in the works," Gavin put in. "Hardly what you expect to find in a dog yard."

"Although stumbling across a stray fortune wouldn't come amiss," Barry said dreamily. "The missus and I could finally retire."

Gavin elbowed his friend. "In this case, the loot belongs to someone. It wasn't exactly pirate treasure."

"True, that." Barry nudged Nigel, who hadn't said anything since his greeting to Harriet. "Do you know what's up with the case? I understand Julian was a good friend of yours."

"Operative word there is 'was,'" Nigel said, his expression scornful. "He and I haven't spoken for years. Not since Yvonne and I got together after they broke up. Put his nose right out of joint, it did."

Barry chuckled. "I'm not surprised. Yvonne is a real beauty. His loss is your gain, right?"

"I put it like this," Nigel said. "The best man won." As the other two laughed, Nigel turned his attention to the horses, effectively closing the topic.

Harriet unzipped her bag and took out three business cards. She handed one to each man. "Here's my number. Please let me know when the next meeting is. I'll try to make it."

Barry took the card and read it over before tucking it into his pocket. "Our next meeting is Monday evening at Nigel's. Think you can come?"

Harriet checked her schedule on her phone. "I'm free. What time?"

"Around seven," Nigel said. "Glad to hear you can make it, Harriet." He slid a glance toward Barry and Gavin. "We could use some new blood. And brains."

The other two burst into laughter. "You're not wrong there," Gavin said.

Nigel gave Harriet the address, which she noted in her phone. Everything was falling into place. With any luck, she would meet his wife on Monday evening. She debated bringing up Aunt Jinny and her friendship with Yvonne, but decided not to bother. That topic would inevitably be a reminder of Yvonne's engagement to Julian Montcliff. Despite Nigel's bravado about being the best man, it couldn't be comfortable for him to dwell on her former engagement.

Why had Yvonne and Julian's engagement failed? Harriet wondered if the break-in at Ravenglen Manor had something to do with it. She couldn't see how, exactly, except that the stress might have exposed any cracks in their relationship.

The three men lingered at the horse pull for a while longer before excusing themselves. Barry and Gavin exclaimed how happy they were to meet Harriet and how much they looked forward to her attending their meeting. Nigel merely regarded her with hooded eyelids and politely wished her a good day.

Harriet also went on her way, deciding to introduce herself to George Kettlewell, the property owner. She stopped at the information booth to see if they could tell her where he was.

"You'll find George at the tractor show," an older woman said. "He's displaying his pride and joy, a Field Marshall Series 3A."

Harriet thanked the woman and headed toward the show. She enjoyed old tractors but was far from an expert when it came to identifying them by sight. But if she was in the right area, she had to assume she'd find George sooner or later.

Helpful placards in front of each machine listed the make, model, year, and owner. Harriet noted a variety of manufacturers, including Nuffield, Massey Ferguson, Allis Chalmers, and International. The oldest tractor was an Austin Model R from 1920, and for all models, owner pride was evident in their glossy paint and shiny chrome trim.

She found George in front of the red Field Marshall with its upright smokestack. He was explaining some details to several interested onlookers, so she stood aside and waited. Burly and balding, George was dressed in work pants with suspenders and a white shirt.

When the others moved on, he greeted Harriet warmly. "Good morning. Enjoying the show?"

"I certainly am," Harriet said. "Lovely tractor you have there."

"Isn't it?" George beamed with pride. "Used to belong to my grandfather. I found it rusting away in one of the barns and decided to restore it. Got together with some other fellows who had antique tractors and next thing you know, I'm hosting a show. Everyone has a nice time, and all the proceeds go to charity."

"That's wonderful," Harriet said. She put out her hand. "I'm Dr. Harriet Bailey, Harold Bailey's granddaughter. I've taken over his veterinary practice."

"So you're the new Doc Bailey," George said, an interested glint in his eye. He shook Harriet's hand with friendly vigor. "I've been wanting to catch up with you. Doc Bailey and his father before him took care of our farm animals. I'd like you to do the same, if you have time for us."

"I certainly do." Harriet made a mental note to pull the Kettlewell Farm files and acquaint herself with the usual services, breeds, and number of animals on the farm.

George's expression sobered. "I was truly sorry to hear about Harold. It's a real loss for us all. My condolences."

"Thank you," Harriet said, touched by the farmer's simple yet heartfelt remarks. "He left big shoes for me to fill."

"He did indeed." George grinned. "But something tells me you're up to the task."

Seeing that other people were wandering up to admire the Field Marshall, Harriet took her leave. A glance at her phone told her it was almost noon, as did the aromas drifting from nearby booths. She'd find lunch and then continue her rounds, perhaps circle back to the horse-pull area to meet farmers. She still hadn't found Polly and Van, and she hoped to at least say hello to them.

A colorful booth called Gary's Growlers caught her eye. Curious, she moved closer and discovered that a "growler" was a small, round pork pie. The size and portability made them a perfect festival food.

"Are those good?" Harriet asked a woman in line.

The woman eyed Harriet with amazement. "Never had a growler? Then you must. They're salty, savory, and delicious. Gary's pastry is flaky and tender, the best around."

Harriet edged into line. "They sound great. I'll take your recommendation." Besides, what was life in a new place unless it came replete with adventures, including the culinary kind?

With two pork pies in a bag and a cup of lemonade in hand, Harriet searched for a place to sit. Tables had been set up under a canopy, so she went in that direction. Polly and Van were seated together, and Harriet hesitated, torn between joining them or giving them privacy. Then Polly spotted her and waved, which made the decision for her.

"Have a seat," Polly said, pulling out the folding chair beside her. "I hoped we'd run into you."

Was she grateful for the interruption, or simply being polite? Harriet couldn't tell, but she set her lunch on the table and sat. "Hello, Van."

"How are you liking the tractor fest?" Van asked.

"So far it's great," Harriet said, unpacking her pork pies. "I ran into three other vets who knew my grandfather. They invited me to their professional meetup."

"Doc Bailey's friends?" Polly asked, eyes bright. "That's wonderful, Harriet. You're in the network now."

"I hope so." Harriet took a tentative bite of pie. "This is amazing," she said around the mouthful.

"Gary's?" Polly guessed before taking a nibble of her own growler. "They are the best."

A companionable silence fell over the table as they ate. Around them, a tide of fairgoers came and went, chatter and laughter a constant. Music drifted from a nearby stage, and children tossed a ball for an exuberant boxer puppy.

"I also met George Kettlewell," Harriet said. "He's going to keep his animal care with Cobble Hill."

"That's excellent," Polly said. "He's got a herd of a hundred dairy cows, plus he raises beef cattle every year."

"Enough to keep me busy," Harriet said with a laugh. She wasn't surprised anymore that Polly had this information at her fingertips. Not for the first time, she reflected how fortunate she was to have the young woman on board.

"I told Van about the photo you found," Polly said, opening the topic on everyone's mind.

Seeing that Van's expression was receptive, Harriet said, "It shows the spot where the chest was buried. There used to be boulders there."

"So I understand," Van said. "You'll need to show it to the DI."

"I plan to," Harriet said. "She hasn't returned my call yet." It was on the tip of her tongue to mention the figurine she'd found in the study, but she refrained. She didn't want to test Van's loyalty to the force or make him feel like she was urging him to take sides.

"She'll get back to you soon, I'm sure. They're very busy with the investigation. It's mostly out of my hands." Van held out his palms as if to demonstrate.

Harriet exchanged a glance with Polly. So much for getting the inside track from Van.

"I told Van they should include him more," Polly said. "After all, he's much more familiar with White Church Bay and its residents than they are."

"Lived here my whole life," Van said. "But you know how it goes. Major crime investigations are above my pay grade. Literally."

"That must be frustrating," Harriet said.

"I'll prove myself yet." Van's face colored with passion. "I don't want to be a detective constable forever."

"You won't be. I'm certain of it." Judging by the sincerity in Polly's tone, she wasn't merely flattering Van as part of her self-assigned mission.

Interesting. Harriet thought of a detail that had been bothering her. Thinking she might not have another chance to talk to Van informally, she decided to mention it. "Van, remember the day we discovered the chest? It really surprised me when Julian Montcliff showed up before the DI did. Do you have any theories regarding how he found out about the chest so quickly?"

Van scowled. "I have no idea, but I'd sure like to know. The DI was steamed. She thought I'd blabbed." He crossed his arms with a snort. "As if I would ever be so unprofessional."

So who had told Julian? The dispatcher? Did Julian have people watching for signs of his stolen heirlooms? Here was another mystery to solve.

A shout rang out, cutting through the cheerful sounds of the festival. "Help! Someone please help our dog!"

CHAPTER TWELVE

Harriet leaped to her feet so quickly her folding chair toppled over. She tossed her keys to Polly. "Can you get my emergency bag? I'm parked in the field."

"Right away." Polly darted from the table.

Leaving her lunch, Harriet ran toward a knot of people gathered around the pet emergency, Van on her heels.

"Let us through," he ordered. "She's a vet."

The crowd parted to let Harriet in, and she saw the young boxer lying on the ground, his chest heaving as he panted.

A young woman wrung her hands. "He just collapsed all of a sudden. He was running and playing a minute ago."

Two small children hovered near her knees, shock on their faces.

"What's wrong with Milo, Mum?" the boy asked. "Is he gonna die?"

At those words, the girl began to wail.

Their mother bent over and put her arms around the children, shushing them. "This nice lady is going to help him. Say a prayer." She sent a hopeful, teary smile toward Harriet.

Harriet knelt beside the distressed dog, who was also drooling. She had a tentative diagnosis, but she asked, "Did he eat or drink anything recently?"

His owner shook her head. "Not since breakfast."

"It's likely the heat then," Harriet said. "Let's move him to a cooler spot."

Van and another man carried Milo to the shelter of a nearby tree.

Polly returned with the bag, and Harriet thanked her. "We need cool, not cold, water—lots of it," she said to the crowd still watching. "Can anyone fetch some for us?"

"On it." A man trotted off with a couple of others.

Harriet opened her bag and found a cloth then dowsed it in water from the dog owner's bottle. She used it to gently pat the boxer's muzzle. His big brown eyes stared up at her with gratitude. "You'll be all right, boy," she whispered. "Hang in there. We'll get you cooled off."

George Kettlewell appeared. "Is there anything I can do?"

"A box fan would be great," Harriet told him. "Would it be possible to hook it up in one of the booths?" Power lines snaked along the ground to support the vendors.

"Right away." George shouldered his way through the crowd.

The men who'd gone for water returned with a large carboy, and Harriet began to drizzle cool water on Milo, carefully wetting him down. George brought the fan and directed the air at the dog. Harriet checked Milo's temperature, glad to see it was in the safe zone, and then gave him a small amount of water.

"How is he doing?" the young mother asked, casting glances of concern at her unhappy children.

"He's recovering already," Harriet said, patting the boxer's head. "I do recommend he stays overnight at the clinic so I can keep an eye on him and make sure there are no lingering effects."

"Whatever you think is best." The owner's voice was filled with relief. "Where are you located?"

"Cobble Hill Clinic, in White Church Bay," Harriet explained. She took the dog's temperature again. It was back to normal, so the water therapy could be discontinued, but he still needed to be observed overnight to make certain he was okay.

"Should I fetch the Rover?" Polly asked, still holding the keys. "I can drive it around and get it closer to here."

"That would be great," Harriet said. "You can follow me to the clinic or come by later," she told the owner.

"We'll go now," the woman said. "I won't be able to relax until I see Milo settled."

"I completely understand."

Harriet's phone rang. *DI McCormick.* Could there be a worse time, surrounded by an audience while treating an animal? Harriet considered letting the call go to voice mail, but the officer might think she was avoiding the police.

Harriet picked up. "Hello?"

"Dr. Bailey?" DI McCormick's tone was brisk. "Are you at the clinic?"

Was something wrong? Harriet's heart rate leaped. "I'm at the tractor fest at Kettlewell Farm, but I'm heading back to the clinic now."

"When can you meet us there?"

"Half an hour or so. I'm bringing in a sick dog, and I'll need time to get him settled. But then I can meet you in the house. I have some things to show you in the study."

"See you then." The DI disconnected.

Harriet drew in a ragged breath. What did the inspector want? She'd mentioned another interview but hadn't followed up, not even after Harriet's message.

Her attention fell on Milo, who gazed at her with trusting eyes. *Focus. There's a patient to care for, and he comes first.*

Polly and Van returned in the Land Rover. "What's wrong?" Polly asked Harriet quietly, so as not to alarm Milo's owners.

"Is it that obvious?" Harriet ran both hands over her face. "DI McCormick is coming to the clinic. She didn't tell me why." Her stomach churned with nerves. She had to show the inspector the figurine today, and she was petrified. She couldn't think of a single good reason why her grandfather would have stolen goods in his home.

"We'll come over too," Polly said firmly. "Won't we, Van?"

Instead of showing disappointment over cutting their date short, Van nodded in ready agreement. "See you there."

After gently loading Milo into the Rover, Harriet drove back to the clinic, the owner and her children following. Milo's family watched anxiously while she settled him in a cage where she could keep a close eye on him.

"He's doing really well," Harriet reassured them. "We'll keep him overnight to be on the safe side and set a time for you to pick him up in the morning. How's that sound?"

"I appreciate it." The woman laid a hand on her chest with a sigh. "Thank goodness you were there."

"I'm glad I was too," Harriet said. "There were several vets in attendance, so Milo would have been fine either way. I was simply the closest." She had caught a glimpse of Barry and Gavin in the crowd watching her. Since she'd had everything under control, they hadn't bothered to intervene. She was glad for that. More vets in such a situation would have meant they were more likely to get in one another's way, which would have affected the dog's care.

On a chorus of goodbyes to Milo, the young mother ushered her children out as Harriet promised to check in that evening.

After she shut the door behind them, Harriet leaned against the wall for a moment. She was so relieved that the young boxer would recover. One challenge met. Now on to the next. She needed to prepare herself for the visit from the police.

Harriet checked Milo's vitals again. "I'm going to be in the house," she told him, rubbing his ears. "Get some rest." Maxwell had trotted in to check the proceedings, and he positioned himself beside Milo's enclosure. "Maxwell, you'll come get me if I'm needed, right?"

Maxwell gave a little yip, which Harriet took as agreement. As she left the room, both dogs settled down with sighs, which made her smile. She'd check on them again in a little while.

Harriet washed up and went into the study. She opened the photo album to the picture of her grandfather near the tree and placed the figurine beside it, ready for the officers to view.

"We're here." Polly entered the study, followed by Van. "The DI hasn't shown up yet, has she?"

"No, which is fine," Harriet said. "I was able to get Milo settled, and Maxwell is in there keeping him company."

Polly clasped her hands. "What a good boy he is. He seems to know when other animals are hurting."

"I think so too," Harriet said. "Remember Huntley? He was whining in the dog yard, so I brought him into the house for the night. Maxwell ended up hanging out with him. It was so cute."

Van had picked up the figurine and was studying every inch of it, concern on his face. He tipped it over and read the bottom.

Harriet guessed what he was thinking. "You're wondering where that came from. So am I."

Polly glanced back and forth between them. "What's going on?"

Van set the statue down with a wince. "I must be wrong. Doc Bailey would never—"

Harriet jumped in to explain. "A figurine similar to this one was stolen in the Ravenglen Manor heist. I read about it in an article. Was something similar on the list the police had, Van?"

He nodded miserably.

Polly gasped. "What? You've got to be kidding." She stared at the statue in horror.

The doorbell rang.

"And there's the inspector, right on time," Harriet said.

As she trudged toward the door, Van said, "Hold on, Harriet. This may be unprofessional, but I'm saying it anyway." He swallowed. "I would have trusted Doc Bailey with my life. If this statue *is* from Ravenglen Manor, then he had a good, aboveboard reason to be in possession of it."

"Thanks for that, Van. I appreciate it." Harriet continued with lighter steps. *Add one more member to the Cobble Hill team—DC Van Worthington.*

Once again, DI McCormick was accompanied by Sergeant Oduba.

"Please come in," Harriet said to the duo. "How can I help you today?" Before Harriet had left the message about the photograph and the statue, the DI had mentioned another interview at Ravenglen Manor. Harriet had no idea what else she could tell the police about the chest.

The DI regarded Harriet with a cool gaze. "We have a few more questions for you."

That was nice and vague. Harriet wanted to ask for clarification, but refrained. It would probably become clear over the course of the conversation, and pressing the inspector would likely irritate her. Harriet didn't intend to alienate the primary investigator.

Polly and Van emerged into the hall. "We're going to put the kettle on," Polly said. "If that's all right."

"Please do," Harriet said, relieved they weren't leaving.

"DC Worthington," the DI said in a clipped tone. "What brings you here today?"

Van took the implied reproof in stride. With a smile and gesture at his casual clothing, he said, "Polly and I attended the tractor fest earlier. I'm also aware of the information that Harriet wishes to share with you."

The DI sighed. "You *are* our local liaison, I suppose. Carry on."

"I'll be in the kitchen if you need me." Van pointed his thumb in that direction.

Once the pair disappeared through the door, DI McCormick asked Harriet, "Where can we talk?"

Harriet led them into the study, allowing the DI to take the seat at the desk. The inspector didn't even glance at the open photo album or the statue. That was fine. Harriet would wait until the officers were finished with their business to present them.

Frowning, the DI flipped through her phone. "All right, Dr. Bailey. Tell us again how you discovered the chest of jewelry."

As Sergeant Oduba took notes or verified her previous interview—Harriet couldn't tell which—she once again walked them through every detail. Huntley digging in the pen, his barking, and how she'd retrieved tools to open the chest. The arrival of Aunt Jinny for dinner, as scheduled.

"Your aunt," DI McCormick said. "Dr. Garrett. How did she react when she saw the jewelry?"

Aunt Jinny? Surely, they didn't suspect *her*. Why would they? Because of her friendship with Julian? With that criterion, any number of people would be implicated. Plus the fact she lived in Cobble Hill's dower cottage, of course. Aunt Jinny's standing in the community apparently didn't shield her from the DI's investigation. That was as it should be, Harriet supposed, although she didn't like it one iota.

All too aware that the officers were waiting, Harriet cast her thoughts back, recalling the scene. "She was surprised when she saw the chest. Excited, even, thinking we might have found something interesting. Then—"

"Go on," DI McCormick said when Harriet paused.

"She said we needed to notify the police." Harriet shifted in her seat, anxious to make her point. "She must have realized what we'd found, and her *first* thought was to call the local station."

"Dr. Garrett didn't place any other calls?" DI McCormick asked. "Or send any messages?"

"No. She and I waited in the pen for Van to arrive. If anything, she seemed worried—" Harriet could have bitten her tongue. Why had she said that?

The inspector pounced. "Worried? Do you know why?" She curved her lips into the semblance of a smile. "Not that I want you to speculate. I merely wondered if she shared her thoughts."

"She didn't say a word," Harriet replied, a touch frostily. If they wanted to incriminate her aunt, she wasn't about to help them. "She was probably thinking what an ordeal we would face once the police were called in. And it has been. Some people in town won't even talk to me now. The old where-there's-smoke-there's-fire thing, I guess. As if I had anything to do with the stolen jewelry. As if *any-one* at Cobble Hill was involved. We're too busy treating sick people and animals to be robbing manor houses around here." The Baileys were all upstanding and productive members of society, and Harriet would make sure the police knew it.

A ringing silence filled the room. Harriet's face felt hot as fire, but she kept her chin up. She was trying to cooperate, to help solve the crime. Watching suspicion fall on one family member after another when the truth lay in another direction altogether was infuriating.

DI McCormick cleared her throat. "Please bear with us, Dr. Bailey." Her tone was almost conciliatory. "We need to confirm every fact during an investigation. It's not personal."

"I get that," Harriet grumbled. "Aunt Jinny was as shocked as I was to discover that chest." She rose to her feet. "I think this is a good time to show you what I found."

Harriet plucked the photo of her grandfather under the oak out of the album and passed it to the DI. "See the boulders? They used to be exactly where we found the chest. That means it couldn't have been buried before this picture was taken in 1985, two years after the theft. In fact, it couldn't have been buried there at all until the nineties, when those boulders were removed."

"Show me, please." DI McCormick stood and handed the photo to Sergeant Oduba, who studied it with interest.

Harriet moved to the doorway, waiting for the officers to join her. She was more than happy to take them out to the yard to prove her point. There was still the milkmaid figurine to deal with. Preceding it with something in Cobble Hill's favor would help.

They trooped out to the dog yard, Van and Polly following along at the DI's request. "Do either of you remember rocks being here?" the inspector asked them, her hand sweeping the area.

Harriet suppressed a snort of disbelief at this question. She'd told the DI when the rocks were moved. Van and Polly hadn't even been born yet. But she had to double-check everything, Harriet supposed.

Van and Polly looked at each other. "That was before my time," Van said.

"Mine too," Polly said. "The yard has been here for decades, I know that much."

"She's right," Harriet said. "As I said, it was built in the early nineties, when my grandfather started boarding dogs in the stables."

DI McCormick held up the photo and walked around the area near the oak.

"I think Dr. Bailey is right about the location," Sergeant Oduba said. "Be careful of the hole." He quickly caught his superior's elbow when she moved sideways and almost tripped.

Time seemed to drag as the inspector considered the site. "I agree with you," she finally told Harriet. "The rocks would have prevented the chest from being buried right after the heist." The relief that swept over Harriet was short-lived when the DI continued, "However, it could have been hidden elsewhere and buried after the pen was put in."

"You're still considering my grandfather a suspect?" Harriet didn't see any point in dancing around the topic. "There is one point you're forgetting."

"What's that, Dr. Bailey?" DI McCormick asked.

Harriet pointed at the cavity. "Dogs dig. A fact my grandfather was very well acquainted with. He wouldn't have taken the risk. It's amazing that none of the clinic boarders dug the chest up before now."

"She's got a point," Oduba said. "A property this size offers much better hiding places." He gestured in a sweeping motion.

Thanks—sort of. Harriet was disappointed that the DI hadn't regarded the photo as clear evidence of Grandad's innocence. What she had to bring to the inspector's attention next would only cement the officer's thoughts in a negative direction.

Suddenly, Harriet was anxious to get the ordeal over with and let the chips fall where they may. That had to be better than the sense of impending doom she felt whenever she thought about the figurine.

"When you're finished here," she said, feeling as though she were stepping off a cliff, "I have something else to show you. Remember the Royal Dux figurine I mentioned?"

CHAPTER THIRTEEN

Polly slid the mug of hot tea closer. "Drink up, Harriet. It will help."

"Nothing will help," Harriet groaned, but she picked up the mug. "Thanks for this. Thanks for being such a good friend."

"Of course." Polly propped her chin on her hand. Her eyes regarded Harriet with sympathy. "You've had a rough go of it."

Self-pity called her. Harriet drowned it with a healthy swallow of very sweet tea. "How much sugar did you put in this?"

"Enough to counteract any shock," Polly said. "I thought you might faint when Sergeant Oduba gave you the bad news."

"Me too," Harriet admitted. Although she'd been pretty sure that the milkmaid had come from Ravenglen Manor, a wave of dizziness had hit her when the sergeant confirmed it. He had checked Julian's original list of missing items for the insurance company on his device and confirmed the match.

Now the milkmaid was in custody, destined for the evidence room and eventually a possible return to the manor. Harriet pictured it on one of Julian's many mantels, home at last.

Where did Grandad get it? This question haunted Harriet. She picked up her phone. "I wonder if Aunt Jinny is home. I want to fill her in."

Harriet unlocked her phone to find that she already had a text from her aunt. WHAT WERE THE POLICE DOING THERE?

ANOTHER INTERVIEW, Harriet texted back. CAN I COME TELL YOU ABOUT IT?

PLEASE DO. I MADE COOKIES.

BE THERE IN A FEW.

"Want to pop over to Aunt Jinny's with me?" Harriet asked.

"Sure," Polly said. "I'm not doing anything for the rest of the day."

Thinking of Van, who had been called into work by DI McCormick, Harriet said, "That's right, your date was cut short. Maybe not a bad thing though?"

Polly pretended great interest in her tea mug. "It wasn't terrible. Van is an awfully nice guy."

"He is." Harriet eyed her friend. Maybe… She shut off that line of speculation. Far be it from her to intrude upon anything new and fragile. If there even was anything developing.

After they finished their tea, they walked over to Aunt Jinny's house. She was outside in the back garden, weeding a flower bed. She rose to her feet with a stretch. "Perfect time for a break."

Stripping off gardening gloves, she led them to the outdoor table, which held a platter of homemade cookies and a pitcher of orange squash, a concentrated drink made from orange syrup.

"Chocolate chip cookies?" Harriet exclaimed, taking one. "Exactly what I need right now."

"Me too." Polly also selected a cookie.

Aunt Jinny smiled, clearly pleased by their enthusiasm. She filled two glasses with squash and refilled her own. "So. Catch me up."

"DI McCormick came by for another interview." Harriet broke off a piece of cookie. "We went through finding the chest step by step, and then she focused on you, Aunt Jinny."

"Me?" Her aunt looked startled. "What do you mean?"

Harriet's ire rose again. "She wanted to know how you reacted to finding the jewels and if you called anyone. Besides Van, I mean."

"Someone must have tipped off Julian for him to get here so soon," Polly added. "First she blamed Van, and now she thinks it was you."

"That's outrageous," Aunt Jinny said with a huff. "Van wouldn't do that, and neither would I."

"Exactly." Harriet polished off one cookie and took another. "I got a bit short with her, to be honest. Told her we Baileys were too busy taking care of the sick to rob manor houses."

Aunt Jinny's mouth dropped open. "You didn't. You really are a Bailey, Harriet. We're pretty even-keeled, but push us far enough, and watch out."

"Your grandfather was the same way," Polly said. "He didn't put up with nonsense."

Harriet liked the idea of not putting up with nonsense. She often erred on the side of being too conciliatory and accepting.

"I also showed them the photograph of Grandad under the oak," Harriet said. "The DI had to agree that the chest couldn't have been buried there right after the heist." She frowned. "She suggested that it was put there later by someone at Cobble Hill."

"It was not," Aunt Jinny said crisply. "One of the dogs would have dug it up."

"That's what I told her." Harriet gave a satisfied nod.

Polly tapped the table with her forefinger. "This is what I think. Whoever put it there wasn't thinking about dogs. And I bet it was buried there after Dr. Bailey passed. With no one operating the practice, it seemed like a safe spot."

"Then Huntley and I came along and spoiled it." Harriet considered Polly's theory. "That means it happened recently, which is even more of a puzzle. Where have the jewels been since 1983?"

"A very good question," Aunt Jinny said. "Perhaps we should mention your thoughts to the police, Polly."

"We should, to clear Grandad," Harriet said. "And what about the rest of us?" There was still the figurine to deal with. "Oh, they took the milkmaid statue into evidence, Aunt Jinny. They confirmed that it was the one from Ravenglen Manor."

"Really?" Aunt Jinny exclaimed. "Where did Dad get it?" Her expression relaxed into amusement. "Maybe Julian paid him in porcelain."

Now Harriet was taken aback. "Pastor Will said something about that, how Grandad would wait to be paid. Did people give him things other than cash?"

Polly nodded. "He was paid in farm produce sometimes. Not so much lately. His barter system was a custom from a while ago."

"How can we find out?" Harriet asked. "I don't dare ask Julian. If he used the figurine to pay Grandad, it was pretty bold of him to list it as stolen."

"Julian is nothing if not bold," Aunt Jinny said. "He probably figured the police and the insurance company wouldn't search Cobble Hill for stolen goods." She made a face. "Sorry. I guess I'm a bit jaded about Julian. His attitude the other day got under my skin."

Harriet thought that was understandable, since he'd been quick to accuse the Baileys of theft. "If it makes you feel better, he apologized to me when I visited his stables."

"It does. Thank you." Aunt Jinny smiled. "In that case, scratch what I said. As for finding out about the statue, we can check Dad's old ledgers. Before the clinic's system was computerized, he used to write down transactions in a book."

Polly raised her hand. "You have me to thank for bringing us into the twenty-first century. One of my first tasks was digitizing the entire operation."

"Thank goodness. I can't imagine keeping track of everything manually," Harriet said with a grateful smile.

"Dad had a mind like a steel trap," Aunt Jinny said. "He could recall every detail of a case or a client's situation at a moment's notice. He was amazing."

"He was," Harriet said sadly. "I miss him."

Aunt Jinny sighed. "So do I, my dear. So do I."

"I thought the world of him," Polly added.

Harriet recalled a funny story about her grandfather and shared it. Soon the three were trading anecdotes and memories, bonded by their love for Dr. Harold Bailey, a giant among men.

Sunday morning, Harriet rose early. She usually slept in and had a slow morning before church, barring any emergency calls. She had a patient in the clinic, and if he was doing well, he'd be on his way home before she left for services. So even before making coffee, she went into the clinic.

Milo and Maxwell greeted her with eager expressions and excited wiggles, tags jingling.

"Good morning, boys," Harriet said. "I bet you want to go out." After checking Milo's vitals, which were normal, and outfitting Maxwell with his wheels, she allowed Maxwell to lead the way to the back door.

The pair did their business then romped around the garden, paws tracking through the dew-laden grass. Birds sang, and a gentle breeze wafted through the treetops.

"You are definitely ready to go home," Harriet told Milo, who was sniffing around the flower border. Since they were safely enclosed, she left the dogs to play while she went to make coffee. While waiting for it to brew, she called Milo's owner, who promised to come over within the half hour.

Perfect. Harriet would have time for breakfast and a shower before heading to church with Aunt Jinny.

Harriet drank her first cup at the table outside, watching the dogs with a supreme sense of well-being. Milo's sprightly movements warmed her heart. There was nothing more satisfying than witnessing a patient's recovery from illness or trauma.

She stored up these moments to help herself stay grounded when other troubles crowded in. The practice was her priority, right after loving and serving God. Loving her family and friends was right up there as well, of course.

Tires crunched in the gravel parking lot, a signal that her client had arrived. "Ready to go home, Milo?" she called. "Your people are here."

Barking in joy, he bounded toward her across the grass. After he was formally discharged and the family had left, Harriet and Maxwell returned to the house, where she gave him breakfast and made herself eggs and toast. Charlie, who had been off somewhere, came meowing for her meal, and Harriet filled her bowl as well.

"Is everybody happy?" Harriet asked. "I need to shower and dress."

Her two pets stared up at her then went their separate ways. Charlie curled up in an armchair in the corner of the kitchen, and Maxwell lounged in a patch of sunlight.

Harriet ran upstairs, mentally going through her options for church attire. People didn't exactly dress up—in fact, some churchgoers wore jeans or khakis. However, Harriet liked to wear a skirt or slacks, a contrast to the scrubs or jeans she wore almost every day.

Her final decision was a floral skirt, a silky shell and light cardigan, and leather sandals. Aunt Jinny called as she slipped on the shoes.

"Should we walk to church?" her aunt asked. "It's such a lovely day."

Harriet eyed her footwear. It should be fine on the path, which was fairly level. "Sure. I'll meet you out front."

The public path led along the cliff top, providing sweeping views of the water and White Church Bay that invited one to linger. This route was slightly shorter than going by car, so they would arrive on time even if they moved at a relaxed pace.

A few walkers were out, some with dogs and others with walking sticks that signaled their intent to travel long distances. One young man in a black windbreaker couldn't get enough of the views, stopping frequently to snap photos as he came along behind them. Whenever Harriet glanced back, he busied himself with his phone.

Harriet found it charming that England had a network of footpaths between villages. Many travelers hiked from inn to inn, a vacation on foot through the countryside. The States didn't have anything similar beyond the Appalachian and Pacific Crest Trails, both of which were difficult, isolated, and over two thousand miles long.

The walk was wonderful, but the sandals were a mistake. The third time her strap slipped, Harriet said, "These shoes weren't made for walking, that's for sure."

The young man behind them had stopped to take more pictures, loitering to enjoy the view. Harriet had been expecting him to overtake them and go by, impatient with their slow pace.

"I wear trainers and carry my dress shoes," Aunt Jinny said. She opened her bag so Harriet could see the heels nestled inside. "I'm sorry. I should have suggested it."

"Not your fault." Harriet finished tightening the buckle, and they continued. "I should have thought of that."

On they went, Harriet's enjoyment dimmed somewhat by her shoe struggle. Every few steps, she glanced down to check. Everything was fine for a while. The village streets were in sight now, so they walked faster, eager to reach their destination.

Then Harriet's sandal flew right off her foot and landed in the bushes. "Score!" she cried, trying to make light of the ridiculous situation.

"I'll see if I can find us a ride back," Aunt Jinny said. Her phone rang, and she answered. "Yes, Anthony. We're coming. Harriet has a bit of a shoe problem."

Having found the sandal, Harriet limped out of the bushes, one foot bare—and ran right into the young man, who was moving fast.

They both recoiled. "Sorry," Harriet said. "Didn't see you." She felt foolish standing on one leg. She put her foot down, and grit and pebbles immediately dug into her bare skin.

"No problem," the young man growled. Hunching his shoulders, he stalked on, glaring over his shoulder at Harriet and Aunt Jinny, who had ended the call.

"Do you know him?" Harriet asked as she bent to brush her foot and put the sandal on. He hadn't even said he was sorry—not that it was his fault, since she'd burst out of the foliage. Most people would apologize anyway, to be polite.

"Never seen him before," Aunt Jinny said. "Which isn't surprising. White Church Bay gets a lot of tourists." She watched as Harriet fussed with her sandal. "Anthony will run us home after church."

"He has room in his car?" Harriet straightened her skirt. At last the church was visible, and she would certainly make it there without mishap. She hoped.

"No," Aunt Jinny said. "He'll run us home then return for Olivia and the twins. I need to get back and check dinner."

"What are we having?" Harriet asked. "I'll help you."

"I put a pot roast in the slow cooker this morning," Aunt Jinny said. "I'll be making mashed potatoes and roasted carrots and brussels sprouts to go with it. The twins love roasted sprouts, believe it or not."

"So do I," Harriet said. "They remind me of baby cabbages. Only tastier."

On the sidewalk, they joined other churchgoers making their way toward White Church, where a bell tolled, calling everyone to worship. Folks smiled and waved to one another, and Harriet was glad that her outcast experience from Galloway's didn't seem to extend to church.

They filed through the entrance doors, the combined aroma of wood polish, stone, and candle wax comforting and familiar. A bronze plaque memorializing those who had been shipwrecked hung on the vestibule wall, reminding Harriet how tightly this congregation was bound to the sea. Maiden's garlands made of paper hung on a row of nails on another wall, unusual relics that had fascinated her as a child. Centuries ago, garlands like these were placed on the coffins of young unmarried women or carried before them during the journey to the cemetery.

Here in White Church Bay, the past continued to coexist closely with the present, honored rather than forgotten. Harriet found this continuity and sense of history reassuring.

Painted box pews lined both sides of the sanctuary aisle, and Harriet followed Aunt Jinny to her usual spot. Anthony and his family were already there, and they slid down to make room.

"Good to see you, Harriet," Anthony whispered. His wife leaned forward, smiling past a pair of well-behaved six-year-olds.

"You too," Harriet replied, retrieving a service book from the rack and opening it to the correct page. The organist started playing "Be Thou My Vision," further setting a reverential tone for worship.

Soon Will took his place at the podium, and the service began. Harriet found herself immersed in the familiar routine, the music and readings refreshing her heart and spirit.

Psalm 139:1–3 especially spoke to her. *You have searched me, Lord, and you know me. You know when I sit and when I rise; you perceive my thoughts from afar. You discern my going out and my lying down; you are familiar with all my ways.*

Here it was again, a reference to her path. God had His eye on her, and nothing surprised Him. If her destiny was truly in White Church Bay, then she could trust Him to make her paths straight and to take care of the obstacles she faced.

Harriet decided to take Him at His word, and peace flooded her soul. As the people around her stirred in preparation to exit the church, she reflected on her much-needed attitude adjustment. She was reluctant to leave, to step back into ordinary life.

Outside the entrance door, Will greeted parishioners. "Harriet," he said as she emerged. "So nice to see you today." Was she imagining it, or was that curiosity on his face? Was he wondering how she was doing after their talk last week?

"What a beautiful service," Harriet said. "I got a lot out of it. The psalm really spoke to me."

Will nodded. "I'm glad to hear that."

Conscious of the people behind her, Harriet was about to excuse herself and move on when Will said, "Harriet, you remember Agnes Galloway." Agnes came forward to join them.

Harriet's pulse leaped. She hadn't seen or spoken to Agnes since her unhappy experience at the general store. Was Agnes going to bring that up here, within earshot of half the town? Harriet took a breath, trying to calm her racing heart, and said simply, "Hello, Agnes. How nice to see you."

"Lovely to see you as well." Today the shopkeeper's expression was warm, her demeanor at ease. "I wanted to share something our event committee is planning." As she spoke, she edged away from Will so he could get back to greeting his congregation.

Harriet followed. "What is it?"

"The summer church fete is held every year on the fourth Saturday of June. This year, we'd like to give you a proper welcome during the lunch. You'll be our guest of honor, if you're comfortable with that."

"Guest of honor?" Harriet's head spun. The village wanted to welcome her, even with all that was going on with the police investigation, and while some were thriving on gossip about her family? "That's wonderful," she managed to stammer. "Thank you so much. Will I have to speak?"

"If you'd be willing to say a few words, that would be lovely." Agnes glanced in both directions before leaning closer. "I do want to apologize for what happened in my store the other morning, Dr. Bailey." Distress creased her features. "I was wrong to be so aloof with you. I also made sure to have a word with my customers after you left. It won't happen again."

Mortification needled Harriet's skin. How terrible that this even needed to be said. After a mind-boggled moment, she managed to say, "I'm so glad. Where else would I find my favorite bread?"

Agnes laughed, relief on her pleasant face. "You are a good sport, Dr. Bailey. We'll see you again soon, I hope."

"Count on it."

As Agnes moved on and Harriet looked around for Aunt Jinny, she set her jaw in resolution. They had to solve the mystery of the hidden chest before the fete. They *had* to. She would prefer a welcome to the community with no clouds hanging over her head.

CHAPTER FOURTEEN

Anthony and Aunt Jinny waited by Anthony's SUV. "Sorry," Harriet said. "I got caught up."

"Not a problem." Her cousin swung into the driver's seat. "I have to drag Olivia away every week."

As they set off, Harriet spotted Anthony's wife chatting with a cluster of young women. The twins laughed and darted around with their friends.

"It's nice you have such a close-knit community," Harriet said, who was seated in back. She felt a pang, longing for the day when she would be fully accepted.

Anthony glanced in the rearview mirror. "For the most part, yes." His smile was identical to Aunt Jinny's. "It can be a pain sometimes. Everyone has an opinion."

"I hear you." Harriet checked her heel. Yes, that was a blister. "I'm going to run home first to change, Aunt Jinny."

"Come over when you're ready," her aunt said. They were already pulling into the driveway.

"Be right back," Anthony said as they climbed out of the SUV. "Once I pry my family away, that is."

Inside the house, Harriet changed into shorts and a T-shirt then slid her feet into more comfortable flip-flops that didn't rub the tender skin of her heel. After checking on Maxwell and Charlie, she headed next door.

Entering through the rear door, she arrived in Aunt Jinny's kitchen, which she adored. Like the rest of the house, the kitchen was charmingly old-fashioned with ceiling beams, casement windows, and a farmhouse sink.

"There you are." Wearing an apron over her dress, Aunt Jinny checked the pot roast simmering in the slow cooker. "Do you mind helping chop the vegetables?"

"Not at all." Harriet washed her hands at the sink and then took a position at the butcher block island. A cutting board had already been laid out along with a knife and heaps of brussels sprouts and carrots. Harriet started slicing the brussels sprouts in half.

Aunt Jinny replaced the lid on the cooker and returned to the island, where she resumed cutting potatoes. "What did Agnes want? She didn't give you a hard time, did she?"

"No, she told me there will be an official welcome for me at the church fete." Harriet placed a sliced sprout on a sheet pan.

"That's nice," Aunt Jinny said. "I'm sure the committee will go all out."

Harriet cut another sprout. "She also apologized for the way she and her customers acted the other day. I really appreciated it. Otherwise, I was going to avoid her store."

"Agnes is usually lovely," Aunt Jinny said. "I'm glad she had the grace to apologize." She rinsed the potatoes and set them to boil.

"Pastor Will told me he would talk to her. It must have helped." Harriet arranged the sprouts in the pan. "Today's service spoke to me. The verse about God comprehending my path." A wave of emotion surprised Harriet, and she blinked rapidly, not meeting her aunt's eye.

"Harriet." Aunt Jinny put down her knife, moved around the island, and gathered Harriet in a hug. "Don't take everything on your shoulders, love," she said softly. "You're absolutely supposed to be here. It was all Dad could talk about in his last years—how he hoped you would be the next Bailey at Cobble Hill. He was so proud of you."

"Really?" Harriet tasted a tear. Was she actually crying? "I wish I'd come sooner." She buried her face in her hands as the tears overwhelmed her. "Why didn't I? I missed so much time with him."

Aunt Jinny gently patted her back. "Because you were gaining experience. Plus, you were engaged to Dustin."

Harriet laughed through her tears. "I hardly ever think about him anymore." She accepted the tissue Aunt Jinny handed her.

"That means you made the right decision." Aunt Jinny squeezed her then moved away. "Everything lined up to bring you here, to your forever home. Don't let other people discourage you. Especially not the gossips." She made a face. "Those who can, do. Those who can't, criticize."

Harriet managed a smile. "I'd better get back to work."

She had finished the sprouts and started on the carrots when two small blond whirlwinds burst through the door. "Grandma, we're here!"

Feet clattering, the twins ran to Aunt Jinny's side, where they received hugs and kisses. "I'm so glad to see you, my dears. Say hello to Harriet," Aunt Jinny urged.

The twins regarded her. "Are you our aunt?" Sophie asked, screwing up her adorable features. "I can never remember."

"No, I'm your cousin," Harriet said, recalling how confusing she'd found family relationships as a child. "Your dad is my cousin, so you're my first cousin once removed. But that's silly to say every time, so why don't you call me Harriet?"

With that explanation, Sophie gave Harriet a brief hug, followed by Sebastian as their parents came through the door.

"Jinny, we brought a salad," Olivia said, setting a bowl on the counter before coming over to give Harriet a hug. "So good to see you."

"Good to see you." Harriet felt thoroughly welcomed as she returned the embrace.

Olivia rested her hands on her hips. "Should I lay the table?"

"That's my job," Anthony said. "With the twins."

"Hang out with us, Olivia," Aunt Jinny said. "We're getting the vegetables in the oven."

"Only a few more carrots," Harriet said, arranging the pieces on the tray with the potatoes.

Sebastian appeared at her side, little fingers reaching for a sprout on the tray. Sophie was right behind him.

"Don't eat them all before lunch," their mother scolded, even as she smiled. With a giggle, they headed off with their stolen treats.

Once Harriet was finished, Aunt Jinny added olive oil, salt, and pepper to the vegetables, and into the oven they went. After setting the timer, she said, "Let's go out to the garden to wait."

By an unspoken agreement—or maybe Aunt Jinny had privately arranged it—the Ravenglen Manor heist was not discussed before or during dinner.

Harriet enjoyed an idyllic afternoon with her family. Watching Sophie's and Sebastian's antics. Catching up with Anthony, who worked as a pharmacist in York, about a half-hour train ride from their home in Pickering. Getting to know Olivia, a nursery-school teacher, better. In return, Olivia and the children enjoyed hearing about Harriet and Anthony's adventures as children.

"Can we climb the old oak too?" Sebastian was asking his dad when someone hailed them from the nearby path.

"Hullo," Doreen Danby called. "Up for a visit?" Doreen Danby, the woman who often brought baked treats to Cobble Hill, was taking a walk with her family.

Aunt Jinny gestured. "Please join us."

The Danbys owned a nearby farm, where they raised sheep and chickens along with their kids—Thomas Junior, Ava, Randall, Ella, and Terrance—who ranged in age from sixteen down to five. Introductions were made, and soon the twins were happily racing around the property with the younger Danby children. Tom Senior and Anthony chatted about sports while keeping an eye on the rampaging herd. The teens lounged in the sun with their phones, and Doreen joined the women at the table.

"Whew." Doreen sat and fanned her face with her hand. "The children have run me off my legs." Aunt Jinny poured her a glass of lemonade. "Thank you."

"They do keep us hopping," Olivia agreed.

Doreen took a good long drink and set the glass down. Her plain, pleasant features were concerned. "How are you holding up, ladies? Quite a shocking turn of events to find that chest."

"Understatement of the year," Aunt Jinny said. "At first, we were excited. Then I realized where the jewelry must have come from." She shook her head. "Although it wasn't buried there until years after it was stolen."

"How do you know that?" Doreen asked.

"Harriet found a photograph of Dad standing in that very spot before the dog yard was built. There used to be several boulders there."

Doreen regarded Harriet closely. "You've got your grandad's brains, you do. He never missed a trick. Come to think of it, he certainly would have noticed someone digging a hole on his property."

"Of course he would," Aunt Jinny said. "I wish I had."

"Anthony filled me in a little, but can you tell me more about the burglary?" Olivia asked. "Ravenglen Manor is near here, right?"

Aunt Jinny gave her daughter-in-law an overview of the story from beginning to the present. "The worst part is that we're living under a cloud right now," she concluded. "The police think someone at Cobble Hill might be involved."

"Seriously?" Doreen slapped the table with her palm. "That's ridiculous. Maybe I should give young DC Worthington a piece of my mind."

"Oh, he doesn't think so," Harriet said hastily. "His superiors are doing their job, which means investigating every possibility. It's not personal. That's what I keep telling myself anyway."

Doreen stared into space, pursing her lips. "It's probably the same fellow who attacked Meredith Bennett. Doesn't it seem obvious?"

"What do you mean?" Harriet couldn't see a link between the two incidents.

Doreen leaned forward and said in a low voice, "He pulled a ring right off her finger. A gold band set with diamonds all around."

Harriet gaped at her, shocked by this new detail. "Was that his intent, to steal her ring? I hadn't heard what his motive was for attacking her."

"Maybe so." Doreen hissed through her teeth. "'Twas an evil thing to go after an elderly woman in her own home. It's a good thing for him that she's on the mend. Otherwise, he'd be facing even more time than he already is."

Doreen's blunt statement caused a brief silence to fall. A breeze rustled through the trees, sending a chill down Harriet's spine despite the warm sunshine. She was so relieved and thankful that Meredith was all right. *Was* the break-in related to the heist? If so, how?

"Could it be that Meredith knows something about the jewels we found?" Harriet ventured. "She was working at Ravenglen Manor when it happened."

"Or perhaps the assailant thought she did," Aunt Jinny amended. "If only they could track him down. That would answer a lot of questions."

"Rumor has it that a crime ring was involved back then," Doreen said. "Maybe he's one of them."

"Wouldn't they be rather elderly by now?" Olivia asked. "We're talking about something that happened forty years ago."

"The thieves in the ring were rounded up a few years ago," Harriet said. "They operated for decades before that." She wondered if the culprits had actually been convicted and gone to prison. Sometimes court cases took years.

Olivia raised her eyebrows. "You're in the know."

"I have to be," Harriet said. "In defense off the family's reputation and all." She felt a thrum of excitement. "Doreen, your theory makes sense. An associate might have been trying to track down the hidden jewelry." That thought led to another. "Maybe it hasn't always been in that chest."

"Good point," Aunt Jinny said. "Someone might have found it and taken it for themselves. Then buried it in the dog yard because the clinic was closed for a while."

"Hooray, Doreen," Olivia crowed, clapping her hands. "You might have cracked the case."

"I'll mention your thoughts to the police the next time they interview me." Harriet rolled her eyes.

Doreen beamed at her. "Glad to help. Your family has been good to me, Jinny, and I'll do anything I can in return."

"What a sweet thing to say." Aunt Jinny smiled.

"Speaking of sweet, we love your baked goods," Harriet said. "Such a treat."

"More will be coming your way soon, I promise." Turning in her chair, Doreen whistled and waved her arm. "Tom?" she called. "We really should get going." She turned back to the women. "My in-laws are stopping by this afternoon."

The children finally allowed themselves to be parted, and the Danbys continued on their way.

"It was nice to see Doreen," Harriet said. "Usually, I only know she's been here when Polly shows me what she dropped off."

"She's a busy lady." Aunt Jinny sighed. "I can't believe the police are seriously considering us suspects." She stared up at the roof. "If I'd stolen those jewels, would those old gutters still be up there?"

Harriet took up her point. "Exactly. I love Cobble Hill, but it's hardly up to date. I just had to have the water heater fixed, and Terry says it needs to be replaced. Not to mention that the Land Rover is as old as I am."

"Dad was certainly frugal," Aunt Jinny said. "Many of the larger repairs and extras were funded by the gallery, believe it or not."

"What are you doing with the gallery?" Olivia asked. "Is it closed for good?"

Harriet winced at the reminder. "I haven't done anything yet. I do hope to reopen it though. I've been focused on the practice thus far, learning the ropes and making sure it's running smoothly with me at the helm."

"All in good time," Aunt Jinny said.

Olivia returned to the previous topic. "Aren't cars the first thing people splurge on when they come into money? I wonder if the police kept an eye on big expenditures by anyone local. That's what I'd do."

Aunt Jinny's brow furrowed, and Harriet said, "Did you think of something?"

"Almost." Her aunt laughed. "It escapes me. I'll probably remember in the middle of the night."

"That always happens to me." Olivia's smile was rueful. "A brain stuffed with as many details as mine is bound to lose track of one now and then."

Harriet could certainly relate.

As dusk fell, Harriet crossed the garden to the gallery. Olivia's question had pushed the issue to the top of her mind. She hadn't even been inside the building beyond one quick peek when she first arrived. The roof hadn't leaked, and all had seemed well, so she'd locked the door again and gone away.

Despite everything else on her plate, Harriet really wanted to take the first steps to either reopen or dismantle her grandfather's studio. The problem was that she had absolutely no idea which course to take. On one hand, she had zero experience in the art realm. On the other, she couldn't bring herself to squelch her grandfather's legacy.

Although many of his original paintings had already been sold— and there wouldn't be any more—prints were popular, according to Aunt Jinny. Some artists were more famous for prints and posters than their original paintings. With prints, sales were theoretically unlimited. They also tended to be much more affordable for the average art lover.

The gallery was housed in a former outbuilding constructed of local stone and with a thatched roof. Flower beds and bushes gave it a charming cottage air, as did the twenty-pane windows set with hand-blown glass.

Harriet inserted the heavy key in the door and twisted it with some difficulty. Her first repair would be to oil the lock.

Once she had the door open, Harriet flipped the light on and stood in the doorway. The air was musty and close. She opened the window next to the door, hoping it would help air the place out. She also left the door open.

Then she slowly took in the gallery, struck by the color and richness that flooded her vision. Harold Bailey had loved animals, and never was that more evident than in the talent and care he put into each painting.

Kittens playing in a shaft of sunlight inside a barn. A wider view of cattle cooling off in a brook. A close-up portrait of a black-and-white Shetland sheepdog.

A deep certainty took root as she strolled through the gallery, flipping through racks of prints and stopping to study paintings on the wall.

She couldn't lock this all away. The world should see her grandfather's genius. She should also select a painting for herself. Something she could hang in the study and gaze upon when she needed inspiration. When she was tired and cranky and wondering why she had gone into this challenging profession. The obvious love in Grandad's work would remind her and reawaken her own.

The painting she chose was small but beautiful, depicting a little girl hugging a spaniel with floppy brown ears. Harriet wondered if Aunt Jinny had modeled for it. In any case, it was heartwarming, reminding Harriet of the boxer she had saved and his young owners.

A scraping sound outside the open window caught Harriet's ear. What was that?

She held her breath, listening. Beside her, Maxwell tensed with a growl, the hackles rising on the back of his neck. "Hush," she told him.

There it was again, this time followed by a muffled exclamation. Adrenaline flooded Harriet's veins as the truth of her quandary sank in. She was alone at night in an isolated building, no one within earshot and only a vulnerable, handicapped dog for defense.

The same situation Meredith Bennett had faced mere days ago.

CHAPTER FIFTEEN

With a volley of barks, Maxwell bolted toward the door, wheels spinning. Harriet somehow managed to get ahead of him and slammed the door shut. Leaning against the wood, she locked the door and engaged the dead bolt.

Next, she ran to the window, although the opening was too small for human entry. As she prepared to pull down the sash, a scuffling sound caught her ear, followed by a muffled shout and running footsteps.

What on earth was going on out there? Cupping her eyes, she peered through the glass, unable to discern a thing.

After closing the window and locking it, Harriet eased her phone out of her pocket, fingers shaking, and dialed 999 for emergency services.

"Emergency. Which service do you require? Fire, police, or ambulance?"

"Police." Harriet leaned against the wall, her knees trembling. "I have a prowler." At least she and Maxwell would be safe in the gallery while waiting for help to arrive. She hoped.

The dispatcher promised DC Worthington would arrive shortly. Harriet straightened and began to pace. Who had been lurking out there? Had he followed her from the house and watched her every movement?

Shivering, Harriet went over the sequence of events in her mind. She'd been so comfortable strolling out to the studio. Totally and happily unaware of any danger. Nausea rolled in her stomach, and she put a hand to her mouth.

Maxwell whined, his nose touching her bare ankle. Harriet sank to the floor to pat him. "You're such a good boy, Maxwell. Thank you for protecting me." He would have made a valiant effort.

Someone rapped on the door.

Was Van here already? Or had the prowler returned?

Harriet leaned against the door. "Who is it?"

"Terry Leaper."

For a moment, Harriet had trouble placing the name. "I beg your pardon?"

"My dog, Jolly, is a patient of yours. I worked on your water heater."

Jolly was having surgery in the morning. Thinking that something might be wrong with the dog, she hastily unlocked the door and pulled the bolt back.

The plumber stood there, a hulking figure half in the dark.

"Sorry. I was having trouble switching gears." Harriet gestured. "This is—was—my grandfather's art gallery."

Vehicle noise caught her attention. Thinking it might be Van, she glanced toward the road. But the car kept going, the engine sound fading into the distance.

"I'm the one who should be sorry." Terry shuffled his boots on the slate walk. "Saw the lights on and thought I'd stop in. Make sure we're still all set for Jolly's surgery tomorrow."

Maxwell emerged from the gallery and sniffed around Terry's feet with great interest. Harriet agreed with him. She also smelled something off about the situation.

"You could have called," she told him. "No need to drive over here." Thank goodness Van was on his way. Otherwise, she'd duck back into the gallery and lock the door again.

Terry took his cap off and scratched his head with a sheepish expression. "I happened to be passing by, that's all. Didn't mean to bother you."

Headlights flashed in the treetops, and tires crunched on the gravel. That must be Van.

"You must excuse me," Harriet said. "I'm expecting another visitor. Van Worthington."

The plumber rocked back on his heels. "DC Worthington? I guess I'd best be going." He settled the cap firmly on his head. "Get out of your way."

"See you at seven tomorrow morning," Harriet called as he strode away. "No food or water for Jolly after midnight tonight." She'd already given him the instructions, as she did for every prospective surgery patient, but a reminder never hurt.

Terry hurried along the path and vanished in the darkness as the police car pulled into the gallery's small parking lot.

Van climbed out and hurried toward her, duty belt jingling. "Harriet, are you all right?" Maxwell yipped in glee, and Van bent to give him a pat. "Hello, little fellow."

"I'm fine," Harriet said. "Just shaken up a bit."

"Understandably. Take me through it step by step."

Van's kind tone and steady demeanor were already making her feel better. "I was in the gallery when I heard a noise out here." Harriet pointed. "The door and window were both open. The second time it happened, I locked the door, shut the window, and called 999."

"What kind of noise?" Van asked.

"A scraping sound the first time," Harriet said. "The next time, scuffling and a shout. Then someone ran away."

"Sounds like a prowler for sure." Van switched on his flashlight and examined the ground in front of the building. When he went around the corner, Harriet and Maxwell followed.

"The strange thing is, Terry Leaper showed up right after that."

"Could it have been him?"

"I don't think so," Harriet said. "He knocked on the door. But he said he was here to check on his dog's surgery tomorrow morning, which struck me as odd."

Van made a scoffing sound. "A likely story. Why didn't he give you a ring or text? Or send an email?"

"Yeah, the whole thing is fishy." Harriet didn't like to think that Terry Leaper was acting suspiciously. However, he had done work at Ravenglen Manor during the heist.

"Aha." Van trained the light on a certain spot. "Footprints."

There were several imprints in the soil beneath a window. Harriet thought they were from a man's shoe. An old wooden crate lay on its side next to the prints, as if it had been kicked over.

The window was high enough that Harriet had to stand on her tiptoes to peer in. To her dismay, the window provided a full view of the gallery. She sucked in a breath. "He was watching me."

Was his plan to come inside and accost her? Or did he mean to wait until she was walking back through the dark property?

"Give me a minute." Van went to the police car and rummaged around. He returned with an investigation kit and had Harriet hold the light while he measured and photographed the footprints.

Watching him methodically recording evidence of the prowler soothed Harriet's nerves. Shoe size and proof of trespassing were facts, something to grasp, instead of the worries and wondering that consumed her thoughts at times.

"Really should take a cast," Van muttered. "I don't want to risk the footprints getting messed up. Can you fetch me some water?"

"Sure." Harriet went into the gallery and grabbed the kettle from the kitchenette area. She filled it and carried it out to Van.

By the light of the bright police flashlight, Van mixed the cast material and poured it into the footprint. When he was finished, he suggested they go into the gallery and work on the report while the cast hardened.

"Want tea?" Harriet asked, carrying the kettle inside. "No milk, I'm afraid." When he shook his head, she dried the kettle and put it away.

"At a glance, those don't seem to be Leaper's prints," Van said as they settled in the tiny kitchenette area. "Unless he's got really small feet for his height, those are from another man. Of course these things vary, but guessing from his shoe size, I'd say we're looking for someone around five foot ten." Van pulled out his tablet.

"That's impressive," Harriet said. "Too bad you can't get hair and eye color from a shoe print."

"Too bad indeed." Van began to type on his screen. "The print will be a help regardless."

The implications of "another man" struck Harriet. "There must have been two people here tonight." Who was the other man?

"My conclusion as well," Van said. "I'll chase down Leaper tomorrow and see what he has to say. Maybe he saw something."

"Van." Harriet's throat thickened. "What if one or both of them attacked Meredith?"

The detective constable's expression was grim. "It would be wise to avoid coming out here alone at night again. Or anywhere else, for that matter, until we're able to catch whoever attacked Mrs. Bennett." He continued typing.

Harriet chafed at the idea that she wasn't safe on her own property. Then she thought of another twist. "If someone is lurking around hoping to find the stolen jewelry they hid, that proves Aunt Jinny and I are innocent. Remember Julian said some of it is missing?"

"No argument here," Van said. "Unfortunately, there is another possibility. It might have been an unrelated treasure hunter trying his luck."

Harriet groaned. A solution to the mystery of the buried chest seemed further away than ever. And now danger stalked her at Cobble Hill.

Van walked Harriet home, offering to check the house before she entered. The idea that the prowler might be waiting inside hadn't occurred to Harriet, and she was grateful for the detective constable's forethought.

"All clear," Van said when he emerged. "Even the attic."

The attic was another item on Harriet's to-do list. She hadn't even ventured inside it yet. She'd only peeked in once. The sight of the huge room stuffed to the rafters with Bailey belongings and discards had overwhelmed her.

"I can't thank you enough," Harriet said. "You've been really helpful."

Even in the dim glow of the back door light, Harriet saw Van's face color. "Not a problem. It's my job." He cleared his throat. "I'll wait out here until you're inside and the door is locked."

"Maxwell, come," Harriet said. The little dog obediently trundled through the doorway into the kitchen. "Good night, Van."

"Good night, Harriet."

Harriet locked the door then walked through the house, checking the other doors and the windows, even upstairs. When she came back down the staircase, Maxwell was waiting for her.

"You are such a good boy," she told him. "How about an evening snack?" His answer was the skittering of his claws as he ran for the kitchen.

Harriet fed him a few treats then put the kettle on, hyperaware of the windows lining the kitchen. Was someone out in the garden, watching her? With the lights on inside, she couldn't see well enough to tell.

After making the tea, she decided to retreat to the living room nook, pull the curtains, and read until she was sleepy.

Her usual relaxation technique failed utterly. The novel didn't hold her attention at all. Every few pages, she put it down, barely absorbing anything.

Harriet remembered the ledgers. Since she was wide awake, why not make the most of the time by working on the case? Maybe she would find a mention of the figurine, accepted as payment by her grandfather. Other possibilities were that it had been a gift, or he'd bought it without knowing its provenance, which meant she might find a receipt for it.

Harriet closed the book and stood. *One thing at a time*. She would check the practice ledgers first.

She decided to start with the year of the heist. After selecting a couple of the tall, heavy record books, she brought them back into the living room. The wingback chair was wide and comfortable, and she could put her feet on a round hassock beside a dozing Charlie.

The ledger pages, which showed funds collected and spent each day, were an education in themselves. Rather than simply noting a name and payment, Grandad had jotted notes regarding the care provided. *Burns farm, delivered litter of twelve pigs from prize sow.*

One column showed cash or check, another "in lieu of." Harriet quickly realized that it was the column where he recorded bartered payments. He'd gone home from the delivery with a *fine cured ham*. Harriet laughed, picturing him heading home in the Rover with the ham on the passenger seat.

Expenditures were eye-opening too. Everything was so much less expensive in her grandfather's time. It was all relative, although those long-ago days held the luster of what seemed to be simpler times.

Harriet decided to stop for the night when her eyelids began to droop. She had Jolly's surgery in the morning, which meant getting up at five thirty or so. Early even for her, and she wanted to be as fresh as possible for the procedure.

"Ready for bed?" she asked the animals. Maxwell ran toward the kitchen while Charlie didn't move. She would probably join Harriet at some point during the night, landing on the bed with a thump.

She let Maxwell out to do his business, watching warily from the doorway. "You make it quick and come immediately when I call, you hear me?"

Maxwell lifted his long nose as if to agree and didn't venture beyond the glow of the back door light. What a good boy he was, and brave as well. Harriet was touched that this pint-size pup would rush to her defense.

Once safely locked inside, she got him settled and headed up to bed. Morning would come all too quickly.

The blare of the alarm clock woke Harriet. Prying her eyes open to glimpse the pale gray dawn, she fumbled to shut off the racket.

Then she collapsed back, her arm grazing Charlie, who was curled next to her side, and stared at the ceiling.

She'd actually gotten a good night's sleep. For once, worries and speculations and questions hadn't soured her rest. The last line of Psalm 4 came to mind. *In peace I will lie down and sleep, for you alone, Lord, make me dwell in safety.*

"Thank You, Lord," Harriet said, sitting up. Either her words or her movement startled Charlie, who mewed in protest. She gave her a gentle pat. "Go back to sleep. I'll fill your dish before I go in to surgery."

Wearing a fresh set of scrubs and eager for her first surgery at Cobble Hill, Harriet unlocked the front door at six. Polly came along right after, hopping off her bicycle and parking it next to the entrance.

"Good morning," Harriet said. "Want a cup of tea before we get started?"

"You read my mind," Polly said, lifting the strap of her messenger bag over her head. "I made sure everything was ready before I left Friday."

"You're the best," Harriet said. Before the procedure, they would ensure that all was sterile and clean, with the correct instruments and medications ready. She was meticulous when it came to surgery, even fairly simple ones like lipoma removal. Grandad had always insisted that if she continued to take even the minor things seriously, she would maintain a high quality of work. It had worked for him for decades, so Harriet figured it was a good policy.

Cobble Hill had a small-animal operating room equipped with a thorough array of monitoring equipment. Extensive, in-house surgeries on horses and other livestock were handled by a veterinary hospital in the region.

Harriet surveyed the room, making a last check to be sure that everything was close to hand and the equipment was working. Grandad had spared no expense in the room. While she'd certainly seen more elaborate setups, her grandfather's surgery included everything she could need and wasn't cluttered with unnecessary things that could become hazards. Any vet would be happy to perform operations here.

Polly opened a closet that held gowns, masks, and other garb. "Fresh gear in here, even booties. Dr. Bailey insisted."

"Wonderful." Harriet glanced at the wall clock. "Jolly should be here any minute. I told Terry to arrive at seven." The previous night's events, especially concerning Terry, clamored in her thoughts, and she wished she had time to update Polly. But that would have to wait. Right now the priority was their patient.

No matter what was going on in her life, Harriet never allowed it to interfere with caring for a patient. Unless the world was ending, everything else was put on hold.

Terry arrived on time, the van with its whining transmission bouncing down the drive. He parked in the closest space and brought a leashed Jolly inside. When he saw Harriet waiting by the front desk, he quickly dropped his gaze.

Guilt? Or was he embarrassed and uncomfortable? Both were possible. "Good morning, Mr. Leaper. Polly has a little paperwork for you, and then we'll be ready to go." Harriet patted the retriever, who pushed his nose into her hand. "And how are you, Jolly?"

Polly gestured. "Come right over here, Mr. Leaper. I need to go through a few things and have you sign the consent form."

Terry reluctantly stepped over to the desk, dread in every movement. "He *is* going to be okay, right?"

"He'll be fine, Mr. Leaper," Polly said briskly. "We do these procedures all the time. You're welcome to wait, although Jolly will be spending the night with us. We'll simply need to make sure he doesn't pull a stitch once he starts feeling better." They'd also watch for infection and pain, but there was no point in sharing that with an anxious owner.

"I'll wait here during the surgery," Terry said, relief evident in his voice. "I postponed all my appointments this morning. Once I know he's on the mend, I'll leave him in your capable hands." He hunkered down on the floor to ruffle his dog's neck and chest. "These nice ladies are going to take care of you, Jolly. See you when you wake up."

The procedure went well, with no complications. Harriet found Polly both intuitive and knowledgeable. "You're the best assistant I've ever had," Harriet told her once Jolly was in recovery.

"Really?" Polly's face shone with gratification. "Your grandfather taught me all I know. The hands-on stuff, I mean. I've taken plenty of classes. And you work very similarly to him, so it's easy to anticipate what you need."

"Well, this Bailey is glad to have you." Harriet stripped off her gloves. Seeing that Jolly was stirring, she asked, "Should we put Mr. Leaper out of his misery and let him see his dog?"

They let Terry spend time with Jolly while they cleaned up. "Want to have lunch in town later?" Harriet suggested to Polly. "We deserve a treat."

She didn't have any appointments the rest of the day, so she should be able to leave for a while. Any emergency calls would come to her cell phone. She had the get-together for local veterinarians at Nigel Ellerby's home later in the evening. According to the follow-up email Barry Tweedy had sent with directions, "a light dinner" would be served.

"I'd love to," Polly said. "After we're done here, I'll be digging into the books the rest of the day."

"I have a lot to tell you," Harriet murmured, not wanting Terry to overhear. She tilted her head toward the other room, where he was still with his pet.

Polly nodded. "Can't wait to hear." She gathered the gowns, gloves, scrub caps, and slippers. I'll take care of these."

"We'll discharge Jolly tomorrow morning," Harriet told Terry. "Then he'll come back in two weeks so we can take out the stitches."

Terry stood, cap in hand, a tremulous expression of gratitude on his face. "I can't thank you enough, Dr. Bailey. Jolly—well, he means the world to me."

"Of course he does," Harriet said. "Thank you for trusting me with his care." Despite her suspicions and misgivings about Terry, she found herself liking him. Could a man who loved his dog so much be a criminal?

Someone knocked on the door, which Harriet had locked again so they wouldn't be interrupted during the operation.

Instead of a client with an ill pet as Harriet expected, DI McCormick and Sergeant Oduba stood there, peering through the window. She hurried to answer, thinking they were following up on the prowler. That discussion would be a little awkward with Terry still present, although he should be leaving soon.

When she'd opened the door, the sergeant held up an official document. "Good morning, Dr. Bailey. We have a warrant to search the premises."

CHAPTER SIXTEEN

Shock stole Harriet's voice. *A search warrant*? The implications came crashing over her head like a rogue wave on the rocky Yorkshire shore.

The police thought other stolen goods were hidden at Cobble Hill. Rather than pursue any other leads, they had made the Bailey property the epicenter of the investigation.

"What's going on?" Polly appeared at Harriet's side.

Harriet forced out a few words. "They have a search warrant."

"Seriously?" Polly snatched the document and scanned it. "You won't find any of that here," she said, offering it back to the sergeant.

He put up his hands. "Keep it. It's Dr. Bailey's copy."

Polly's brows drew together. "You'll have to give us a few moments. We just came out of surgery, and the dog's owner is still here."

"He needs to leave," DI McCormick snapped. Terry ambled out, and she started in surprise. "He's the dog owner?"

So the inspector knew who Terry Leaper was. Was he still on the suspect list? Harriet wished she could ask.

"I'm ready to go." Terry hovered by the front desk, casting anxious glances toward the officers. "What's going on?"

Was he worried they were here to arrest him? Harriet went over to the desk and handed him printed instructions for Jolly's aftercare. "I'll give these to you now, so you can familiarize yourself with them. See you tomorrow morning at eight. If anything changes with Jolly, we'll give you a call."

"Thank you, Dr. Bailey," he said, glancing over his shoulder at the officers. "*Can* I leave?"

"You're free to go." Harriet bit her lip, realizing she'd used a law enforcement phrase. Obviously, she'd read too many crime novels. Out in the parking lot, two other police cars arrived. Reinforcements made sense. It would take at least a month for two people to search a property this large.

Terry clapped his hat onto his head and made a beeline for the door. The officers stepped aside to let him out, and he dashed past without looking in their direction. Once outside, he hurried toward his van.

DI McCormick and Sergeant Oduba watched as he jumped in, backed up, and roared out of the parking lot. Other officers emerged from their vehicles, some carrying kits. DC Worthington wasn't among them, Harriet noticed.

"Where's Van?" Polly asked, echoing Harriet's thoughts.

"He might be busy," Harriet said. Or maybe his superiors didn't trust him to be objective in this situation. Harriet hoped not. Something like that could impede his promotion.

Sergeant Oduba went to talk to the team while DI McCormick entered the clinic. "Dr. Bailey, you're free to go about your business. But please stay on the property until we're finished."

"When will that be?" Harriet asked.

The inspector shrugged. "Long as it takes. We're searching all the buildings and the grounds."

"You'll want the key to the gallery, then. I'll get it for you." Harriet cringed at the idea of people handling her grandfather's artwork. The key was in the study, so she hurried there and back. "Please be careful," she said as she handed it over. "The paintings are irreplaceable."

"My officers are professionals," the DI said. "We might make a mess, but nothing will be damaged."

Harriet hoped that the DI's faith in her people was justified. "I'll be around, either here or in the house."

"We appreciate your cooperation," the inspector said. For an instant, something like compassion shone in her eyes. Then Sergeant Oduba returned, dragging the DI's attention back to their task.

"I can't believe this," Harriet said once the officers had left the room. "Do they really think the rest of the jewelry is here somewhere?"

"Maybe it is," Polly said. "It could have been stashed somewhere here when the chest was buried."

Harriet paced around the room, tidying things that were already in order. "But why wouldn't the thief have left everything in the chest? There was plenty of room."

"That is odd," Polly acknowledged. "Perhaps they separated some items out so that if the chest was found, they'd still have the other pieces to fall back on."

"I need to call Aunt Jinny." Her aunt was holding office hours, and everyone there must be wondering what was going on. Harriet picked up the landline and dialed.

The receptionist caught her aunt between patients. "Harriet, what's happening? I see two—no, make that three—police cars in the lot."

Harriet filled her in. "Polly and I will be hanging around while they're here. Come over when you get a chance. I don't have anything until a meeting of local vets this evening."

"Oh yes, Dad used to go to that. I'll pop in when I can." She gave a chuckle. "Never a dull moment."

"You've got that right." Harriet realized she hadn't told Aunt Jinny about the prowler. She hadn't wanted to disturb her late in the evening, and then she'd had the early surgery. There was no time to get into it now.

Harriet hung up. "She'll come over when she can," she said to Polly. "I need to tell you about the prowler who was stalking me last night."

Resting her hands on her hips, Polly gave her a mock glare. "Explain yourself at once."

"I will." Harriet glanced at the clock. "Over a cup of coffee. I need the boost."

"Coming right up," Polly said. "The operating room is shipshape, and everything else can wait." She waved the warrant. "We also need to read this closely. They listed everything they're searching for."

Curious, Harriet reached for the document. "We'll go over it together. I'll check on Jolly while you put the kettle on."

Trying to stay out of the way of the search team, they settled with coffee and tea out on the patio. As promised, Doreen Danby had left a tin of fresh apricot scones on the outside table, and they dug into those.

While nibbling on a scone, Harriet took Polly through the events of the previous evening, starting with her foray out to the gallery.

"I thought Terry seemed skittish when the police showed up," Polly said. "No wonder."

A pair of officers crossed the grounds toward the barn. Harriet hoped they had brought powerful flashlights. The barn was like a dark cave.

"Terry probably won't be visiting me at night again," Harriet said. "Come to think of it, the whole thing is really sketchy. If we hadn't already had Jolly's surgery scheduled, I would have dropped him as a client. And then I'd find a new plumber."

"I wouldn't blame you. That was very strange behavior." Polly sipped her tea. "It wasn't his footprint outside the window, huh?"

"No, it was from a smaller foot." Harriet shuddered at the memory. "I think he was spying on me." She bit her lip, unsure whether to share the next bit of information, then plunged ahead. "Van agreed that it might have been the man who attacked Meredith."

Polly's face was a mask of horror and anger. "I don't even know what to say. And you know how rare that is."

Harriet laughed, appreciating her assistant's attempt to lighten the mood. "I must say Van impressed me last night. He's a very good officer."

A small smile curved Polly's lips. "I think so too. People underestimate him, which can work to his advantage, right? Before they know what hit them, they're under arrest."

"I hope that happens with our mystery prowler," Harriet said. She pictured Van snapping cuffs on the mystery man and carting him off to jail. How satisfying that would be.

Once they had thoroughly hashed over the prowler incident, they moved on to the search warrant and its list of jewelry. Now and then Harriet heard voices inside the house or spotted an officer trekking somewhere. Hopefully they would be finished soon.

"Pearl necklace and matching earrings," Polly muttered. "Pigeon blood ruby and diamond brooch. Rings and more rings."

"It's incredible that one family owns so much," Harriet said. "I can't imagine wearing any of those things." Her taste ran to simple and discreet pieces like small gold hoops and a slim bangle.

Now that she had the list, Harriet could keep an eye out for the pieces, although she doubted she'd come across them. One never knew though. Maybe her grandfather had been paid in diamonds. The thought made her snort.

"What?" Polly asked.

Harriet shared the joke. "Last night, I started looking through Grandad's ledger books. I'm hoping to find that the milkmaid figurine was given to him as payment, which would explain why he had it. He took all kinds of things in lieu of cash, I'm learning. Even a whole ham, once, for delivering piglets."

"I remember him mentioning that," Polly said. "Thankfully when I came on board, it was all cash, check, or card. How do you account for a ham on the books?"

They shared a chuckle at the idea. "If I find the figurine listed," Harriet went on, "the police can question the person who paid with it and take Grandad off the suspect list." She finished her scone, energized by the notion. Having a task, no matter how small, was so much better than feeling helpless. Figuring out who possessed the stolen statue before her grandfather would be an important step forward in the investigation.

"I'll help if you need me," Polly said.

Thinking of the many ledgers, Harriet said, "I would love your help. Someone might have given him the statue years after the heist. Which means a lot of ledgers to search." She pictured the task—day after day, page by page, covering decades.

Slow and meticulous, but if there was information there, they would find it.

"What a mess," Aunt Jinny said, surveying the kitchen. The police had removed almost everything from the cupboards and left it for Harriet to put away.

"Wait until you see the living room and the study." Harriet gestured glumly.

Every book had been removed from the shelves, and the drawers were empty, their contents either on the floor or the closest surface.

"All that effort, and they didn't find a thing," Polly said with satisfaction.

That was the good news. DI McCormick and her team had left empty-handed.

Harriet put a hand to her mouth, contemplating the hours of work ahead. "I guess I'd better forget about going to the vet meeting tonight."

Aunt Jinny looked at her in surprise. "Why? We'll help you get this sorted in no time."

"I can't ask you to do that," Harriet protested.

Her aunt's grin was mischievous. "They might search my house next. If they do, you can help me tidy up."

"It's a deal," Harriet said hastily, before Aunt Jinny could change her mind. "Who wants to work where?" Upstairs was in much the same condition.

"I'll do the kitchen," Polly said. "First, this." She went over to the sound system housed on one of the bookshelves. Below the record player was a long line of vinyl albums owned by Grandad and his parents. Polly selected half a dozen to stack. "We need music."

Soon they were hard at work while the lively strains of show tunes and classic music from the fifties and sixties blared through the house. Every half hour or so, Harriet popped over to the clinic to check on Jolly, who was doing well. He'd already hit most of the markers she watched for in an animal recovering from anesthesia, such as drinking water and eating a little food.

The jaunty music made the task much more pleasant. Harriet, who was upstairs under Charlie's careful supervision, sorted everything, creating save, donate, and discard piles of clothing, linen, and toiletries. She found an old teddy bear she remembered from visits decades before and ferried it to her bedroom. Several vintage clothing pieces were also set aside. Cashmere sweater sets, silky bathrobes, and tweed A-line skirts, so old they had come back in style, were among them.

Footsteps tapped on the stairs, and Aunt Jinny appeared. "How are you getting along?"

Harriet placed another heap of men's cotton shirts on the donate pile. "Fine, except I keep getting distracted."

Aunt Jinny picked up a tie Harriet had placed on the foot of the bed. "I remember Dad wearing this." The silk tie depicted barnyard animals on a blue background.

"He loved ties with animals." Harriet held up another, red silk covered with monkeys and camels.

"Anthony might want some of these," Aunt Jinny said. "Please don't throw them away."

"I won't," Harriet said. "They'll go in the donation pile if he doesn't want them."

Aunt Jinny took in the heaps of clothing. "I'm sorry I didn't get to this before you moved in."

"You have enough on your plate," Harriet assured her. "I do have to admit, the police search is forcing me to deal with it all. Otherwise, I was quite happy to close the closet doors and ignore everything."

"I don't blame you." Aunt Jinny sat on the bed. "It took me ages to deal with Dom's things. Everyone told me to do it right after the funeral, but I didn't listen. I liked seeing his things around."

"I feel the same way about Grandad's belongings." Harriet made a decision on the last shirt. "There's so much family history in this house, and I love that." She was glad her ancestors had kept everything so faithfully.

Another set of feet climbed the stairs. Polly entered the bedroom, phone in hand. "I'm ordering pizza to be delivered. What toppings would you like?"

Harriet was suddenly starving. She hadn't eaten anything since the scone, and it had been a long and stressful day. "Veggie supreme with pepperoni." Popular English and American pizza flavors were very similar, Harriet had discovered to her delight. Pepperoni pizza was one treat she hadn't had to give up with the move, and today she needed its familiar comfort.

Around six, Harriet set off for the Ellerby home, located in a nearby village. The house was in order again, thanks to Aunt Jinny and Polly, and she'd made progress with the sorting. Polly had also offered to check on Jolly while she was out, which Harriet appreciated. He was doing well after his surgery, but the sooner they caught any issues that might arise, the better.

It was a glorious evening, the air warm and silky, fields and trees and rock walls touched with golden sunlight. Cows lifted their heads, chewing, to stare as the Land Rover puttered by.

Out here, between home and her destination, Harriet gained a little perspective. The mystery of the chest was not solved yet, but the fruitless search must have tipped the balance in her favor. Hopefully DI McCormick would now turn her efforts to other suspects: the prowler, Terry Leaper, other employees of the manor, the crime ring, and Julian's friends. Except for Aunt Jinny and Uncle Dom, of course.

Harriet ran through the possible suspects in her mind. Meredith Bennett had worked for Julian at the time of the heist. She had also been attacked, a diamond ring taken from her finger.

Had that ring originally been stolen from Ravenglen Manor?

A deep knell of certainty told Harriet she was on the right track. Too many dots were connecting. If she could see them, why couldn't the police? She would talk to Van soon and share her insights. At least he would listen to her, and maybe the others would listen to him.

A crossroads appeared ahead, and Harriet slowed, checked her directions, and took a right. Only a couple of miles to the Ellerby home.

With that realization, a cold ball settled in Harriet's midsection. The other vets had been friendly enough at the tractor fest. However, this meeting would be a test of sorts, a vetting of the newest veterinarian, as it were. She'd been around this block before.

Just because her grandfather was the venerated Harold Bailey didn't mean that others in the profession would automatically accept her. They would question whether she had the chops to run a successful practice. Her youth, newness, and even her gender would all be strikes against her.

Harriet set her jaw. She didn't agree with those criteria, naturally, but it was reality. She would meet the situation head-on and not allow them to intimidate her. She could almost hear Grandad saying, "That's my girl. Show them what you're made of."

A hanging sign inscribed THE ELLERBYS marked the property entrance. Harriet slowly proceeded up a winding drive, between pastures where several horses gamboled and grazed.

A stone Georgian house, flat-fronted and smothered in ivy, sat adjacent to a cluster of stone outbuildings with a fenced corral beyond. Several other vehicles sat in the parking area, including a small sedan Harriet recognized as Stacey Bennett's. The stable hand must work for the Ellerbys as well.

As Harriet got out of the Land Rover, Stacey and a petite, attractive woman with sleek gray hair strolled out of the barn. Yvonne Ellerby. Harriet recognized her from Aunt Jinny's photographs.

"That's a shame about your grandmother's ring. Julian told me the necklace needed to be cleaned," Yvonne was saying. "If I'd taken it with me that night, it wouldn't have been stolen."

CHAPTER SEVENTEEN

Harriet guessed immediately what they were talking about—the fabulous heirloom necklace Julian had gifted his former fiancée on her birthday.

Stacey groaned. "That's awful. Do you think—" She broke off with a frown when she noticed Harriet. "Hello," she said warily, as if wondering what Harriet was doing there.

In turn, Harriet wondered what Stacey had been about to say. She walked over to greet the pair. "Hi, Stacey. Nice to see you again." She extended her hand to Yvonne. "I'm Dr. Harriet Bailey, here for the vet meeting."

"Ah, Dr. Bailey." Yvonne's hand was cool and slim. "Jinny Garrett's niece. I'm Yvonne Ellerby. Welcome."

"Aunt Jinny mentioned that she knew you. Small world." Harriet didn't mention that she'd seen a picture of the necklace Yvonne had been talking about. Aunt Jinny hadn't been sure why it had still been at the manor after Julian gave it to Yvonne. Now Harriet knew, and she couldn't wait to fill Aunt Jinny in.

"I'll walk you to the house," Yvonne said.

"And I'll get back to work." Stacey disappeared into the barn.

"She does a good job," Yvonne said as they crossed the gravel toward the rear of the house. "I used to muck the stalls out every day, believe it or not." She touched her shoulder with a wince. "Now my arthritis won't let me."

Harriet murmured a sympathetic response before saying, "What a lovely home you have," as they took a path through a fragrant herb garden. Beyond the garden was a grassy stretch of lawn edged with flower beds and shade trees.

Yvonne stooped to pick a sprig of basil and offered it to Harriet. "I love herbs, don't you? For cooking, teas, tinctures, and countless other things."

Inhaling the aroma from the fragrant leaves, Harriet immediately longed to grow herbs at Cobble Hill. "I should plant some. Probably in pots though. I don't have time for a full garden right now." A hired service took care of the grass and the existing flower beds and shrubs.

"You must be busy, taking over your grandfather's practice." Yvonne opened the French door for Harriet, and they entered a stunning kitchen fitted with ivory cabinets and black appliances and countertops.

"It was rather like stepping in midstream," Harriet confirmed. "Even if the practice was closed for a few months." *Long enough for someone to bury a chest of stolen jewelry on the property.* Harriet was convinced that Polly was right about that detail. Who had done it was still a mystery.

"I'll escort you to the meeting," Yvonne said, leading her past an island holding a platter of sandwiches and a bowl of salad. On the stove, a pot of soup bubbled. "As you can see, I'll be serving dinner shortly."

"It all smells wonderful," Harriet said.

The veterinarians chatted in Nigel's study, the very picture of men at ease. The tall windows were open to the warm evening air.

Barry leaped to his feet, followed by the other two. "Dr. Bailey, you made it." He shook her hand, placing his other hand on top of hers. "So glad you could join us."

"It's nice to be here," Harriet said. She shook hands with Nigel and Gavin Witty.

As Harriet took her seat, the men continued their conversation. "The whole herd of hogs showed signs of strawberry foot rot," Barry said. "I've never seen it so bad. The wet spring, I suppose."

"It was extremely wet," Gavin said. "The pastures have barely dried out on some farms."

Hogs in pastures? In the United States, hogs were pigs. Ah! In Yorkshire, lambs born the previous year were called hoggs, she managed to dredge from her memory banks. Strawberry foot rot was a common name for a skin infection.

"Dermatophilosis?" Harriet inquired. "I rinse the lesions with enilconazole. I've found that it's not cost-effective to use systemic drugs in a large herd of animals."

Barry's eyes lit with approval. "You do know what you're about, don't you?"

"Wouldn't expect anything less from Harold's granddaughter," Gavin said with a smile.

Harriet took a breath. She had passed the first test.

During dinner, the conversation ranged over various conditions and treatments, intermingled with amusing anecdotes of encounters with "man and beast," as they called it. Although Yvonne checked in occasionally, she didn't join them.

"I could use your advice," Nigel said over dessert. "A pony with asthma. He's not responding to treatment. He's built a resistance to his bronchodilator." A bronchodilator was a medication that relaxed the lungs and widened the airways. "Inhaled steroids are too expensive, and oral medication is causing side effects."

Harriet cast her thoughts back to Connecticut, where she had treated a horse with asthma. "I have an idea," she said. "They did a study at an American university with promising results. We tried the treatment ourselves in my old practice and got some very good outcomes."

All three men regarded her with interest.

Harriet named the drug, which was a local anesthetic. "Inexpensive and well-tolerated, administered through an inhaler." She reached for her phone. "I'll share the study results with you."

Nigel gave her his contact information. "I'd like it as well," Barry said. Gavin chimed in with agreement.

"I'll check it out," Nigel said. "If it seems like something that'll work, I'll talk to my client. Would you be willing to attend if we give it a go, Harriet?"

"Be happy to," Harriet said as she sent the link, noting that they were on a first-name basis now. Her heart sang at the proof that she'd obtained membership in the good old boys' club.

Most importantly, she now had trusted colleagues to call upon and vice versa. Working by herself had been a stressful change. In Connecticut, she'd always worked with other vets. She was grateful that her days as a hermit in her career were over.

Around ten, Harriet set off for home. Full dark had fallen, so she drove slowly, watching for animals in the road. She hoped Nigel's client would agree to try the new treatment. She'd been impressed with the results of the simple, inexpensive medication back home. Discovering new and better ways of treating animal ailments was always exciting and so was sharing them with fellow veterinarians.

The clinic would be open for regular hours in the morning and, according to Polly, they had a full roster. That was a relief, especially since news of the search warrant might have leaked out, further damaging their reputation.

Barring any new problems with his stitches, Jolly would also be released tomorrow. Harriet shifted in her seat, uneasy when she thought about his owner. Something didn't add up with Terry, although there was nothing specific she could point to.

Perhaps most telling of all, Terry did the plumbing work for Ravenglen Manor and had for decades, even before the heist. He might have been involved in the original theft and could be trying to gain access to Cobble Hill for some reason. Was something else hidden there, something the police hadn't found? She hoped not. Van had promised to talk with Terry after the prowling incident, and Harriet made a mental note to follow up with him in the morning.

Harriet yawned as she made the final turn in her journey. The vet meeting had been mentally engaging and had also given her needed distance from the troubles weighing her down. Now she was ready for bed and a good night's sleep.

Headlights shone up ahead, illuminating the road and hedges. A vehicle sat on the shoulder of the road with its engine running, directly across from Cobble Hill. It took Harriet a moment to realize it faced the wrong way for that side of the road.

Harriet instinctively pressed the gas, eager to reach the driveway. As she passed the parked vehicle, she caught a glimpse of the white paint and lettering on the side. It looked like Terry's van, although she wasn't totally positive.

Did the plumber intend to prowl around the property again tonight?

The tires spit gravel as Harriet raced up the drive. She forced herself to slow down so as not to alarm Aunt Jinny.

She halted with a lurch, killed the engine, grabbed her bag, and scrambled out. As she locked the Land Rover door, engine noise on the road caught her ear. Headlights swung in the trees as the vehicle pulled onto the road. In the quiet, a distinct whining sound could be heard.

So it *was* Leaper's van. She remembered hearing it whine like that before. Not waiting to see what he was planning to do, she ran for the house and quickly locked the door behind her. Then she hurried to the front windows, Maxwell and Charlie at her heels, to watch the road.

The van moved very slowly past the property, the engine noise gradually fading in the distance. *He's gone.* Harriet took a few deep breaths, trying to slow her bounding pulse. She'd meant to check in with Van. Right now seemed like a good time.

Harriet took a moment to properly say hello to her pets and put the kettle on. Despite the late hour, Van returned her call as the kettle sang.

"Hello, Harriet. Is everything all right?"

"I think so." Harriet placed a tea bag in a mug. "Terry Leaper's van was parked across the road from Cobble Hill when I got home a few minutes ago. He drove off right after."

Van made a muffled exclamation. "I'll call him as soon as we're done here. Meanwhile, don't open your door to anyone. And call me immediately if anything else happens."

"I will," Harriet promised. "Thank you."

After a quick visit with Jolly, she set her tea down in the living room then pulled the drapes against any prying eyes. Her phone went on the end table beside her tea, within reach in case Van called back. It was wonderful to have her concerns taken seriously. It made her feel less alone in this situation, less like she was overreacting, even though she had Polly and Aunt Jinny. And Will. Not that she knew him well enough to keep him updated.

But she sent Polly and Aunt Jinny text messages to tell them the latest. She mentioned Yvonne's comment about the necklace, told them about the van stopped in front of the property, and shared that she had called Van.

Polly: ARE YOU ALL RIGHT? WANT ME TO COME OVER?

Aunt Jinny: I CAN BE THERE IN FIVE SECONDS.

Harriet: THANKS SO MUCH, BOTH OF YOU, BUT I'M OKAY. VAN IS ON THE CASE.

Aunt Jinny: HE REALLY IS AN EXCELLENT OFFICER. WE'RE LUCKY TO HAVE HIM.

Polly: WE ARE. WHY DO YOU SUPPOSE HE WASN'T PART OF THE SEARCH TEAM?

Harriet: I WONDERED THAT MYSELF. MAYBE I'LL ASK HIM. IF YOU THINK I SHOULD, THAT IS. I DON'T WANT TO MAKE HIM FEEL AWKWARD.

Polly: SAY YOU WERE SURPRISED NOT TO SEE HIM THERE. WHICH IS THE TRUTH, RIGHT?

Harriet: PERFECT, THANKS.

They chatted a little longer, touching on various topics. Then Van's number flashed on the screen.

Harriet: GOTTA GO. VAN IS CALLING.

Polly: GRAB IT.

Aunt Jinny: GOOD NIGHT XO.

Polly: GOOD NIGHT TO YOU BOTH XO.

"Harriet, it's Van," the detective constable said. "I spoke to Mr. Leaper."

"What did he say?" Harriet held her breath as she waited for his response.

"He said he's at home, watching telly. He hasn't been out tonight."

Harriet squawked. "What? I saw the van. I'm pretty sure it was his. It was making a whining sound, which his does."

"I took the liberty of driving past his house. He was there. Saw him through the window. No sign of the van."

Had he hidden it?

Van hesitated. "The thing is, where he lives—he couldn't have gotten home from your place by the time I called."

Harriet mulled that over. "Someone else must have been driving."

"That's what I think. If it was that vehicle," he added delicately.

"I admit I could have been wrong, but two whining white vans with lettering is quite a coincidence."

"I think so too. It probably was his van. Let me know if you see it again." He paused. "Or hear it."

"I will." Harriet thought about the question she had for Van. Did she dare ask it and perhaps damage their rapport? She decided to proceed with caution. "DI McCormick and her team searched Cobble Hill today. I was surprised not to see you with them."

Van sighed. "I was too busy with local matters, and the DI told me they had enough officers."

"I see. They didn't find anything, by the way." Harriet couldn't keep a note of satisfaction out of her voice. "I wish the lurkers would get the memo."

"The DI mentioned that to me as well," Van said. "Which means the investigation will continue in other avenues."

Harriet wished she could ask what those other avenues were. She wasn't quite sure of the boundaries of her friendship with Van though. She didn't want to put him on the spot or inadvertently press him to reveal inside information.

The mantel clock chimed.

"Oh my," Harriet said. "Is that the time?" She was rarely up this late.

"I'll let you go." Van sounded as if he suppressed a yawn. "Like I said, call me anytime, day or night. All right?"

"Yes," Harriet said. "I will. Thank you so much, Van. Good night."

One last task was sharing information from Van's call with Aunt Jinny and Polly. Neither answered her texts, which probably meant they were asleep. Harriet would take Maxwell outside for his last business and then toddle upstairs to join them in dreamland.

Mittens, the cat with hypothyroidism, was Harriet's first patient the next morning.

"What brings you in today, Miss Birtwhistle?" Harriet asked as she set the cat on the scale. He had gained a few ounces, which was a move in the right direction after the weight he'd lost despite his increased appetite. "Is he tolerating his medication okay?"

"He seems to be. He doesn't fight me when I rub it in his ears." Miss Birtwhistle watched anxiously as Harriet checked the black-and-white cat's vitals. "I wanted to be sure that he's on the mend. I do love him so."

"I understand. He's very lovable." Harriet used a stethoscope to check his heart and lungs. "His heart is sound, and his lungs are clear." She began to palpate his body, checking for any sensitivity.

Miss Birtwhistle sank into a chair with a sigh. "I slept so poorly last night."

Harriet threw her a glance. "Worried about Mittens?"

The older woman flapped a hand. "No, no. There's a young man on my lane who drives by at all hours. Startles me out of my sleep sometimes, his car is so noisy."

Carl Evans came to mind. Harriet had seen him driving a sedan of that description when he had stopped to talk to Stacey Bennett.

"Dr. Garrett, my aunt, said something about hearing him go by. Some men love their noisy cars."

"It's either that rattletrap or a van that makes the most awful whining sound." Miss Birtwhistle put a hand to her ear with a wince. "I have very sensitive hearing, you see. Certain noises bother me."

"The sound is distinctive," Harriet concurred.

Harriet ran her hands over the cat's soft fur, and he rewarded her with a contented purr. "I'm happy to report that Mittens is in very good shape. Continue the medication and bring him back in three months. Sooner if he starts overeating again or you notice something else. We can always adjust the dose."

Miss Birtwhistle beamed. Joining Harriet at the table, she picked up Mittens and kissed his nose. "Thank you, Dr. Bailey. You've made an old woman very happy."

"I'm glad. That's the best part of my job." She opened the exam room door. "Thank you for coming in. I hope you have a wonderful day."

"We will." Nose buried in her pet's fur, Miss Birtwhistle hurried away.

As Harriet started toward the front to greet her next patient, Polly said, "Mr. Leaper is here to pick up Jolly."

"Send him through, please," Harriet said. "Tell the next patient I'll be with them shortly."

She went to the back, where Jolly waited patiently in his cage. "You're going home, boy," she told him as she unlocked the door. He rose to his feet with a stretch, his plumed tail wagging.

"How is he?" Terry strode along the polished tile, boots squeaking. He held a leash in one hand.

Harriet gave the dog a quick once-over and adjusted the cone around his neck. "He's doing very well. I took him out earlier, and he's moving fine. There doesn't seem to be any pain." Jolly's movements hadn't loosened the stitches or made them bleed, which was important. "Keep the cone on until you come back, okay? We don't want him messing with his stitches."

"I will." Terry clipped the leash to Jolly's collar. "Appointment in two weeks, you said?"

"Yes, to take out the stitches." They began to stroll toward the reception area. "Do you have the aftercare instructions?"

"Not with me," Terry said. "I left them in the van, which I don't have today." He bent to pat Jolly's head. "I'm taking the day off to be with my dog. I missed him more than you can believe."

"No problem. Polly will print a fresh set." Harriet wanted to ask him where the van was, but he would certainly regard that as a strange question. Plus it was none of her business.

As they waited for the printer, Harriet glanced out the window. The noisy little sedan was parked in the patient pickup spot. So Terry and Carl sometimes swapped vehicles. She would pass that information along to Van when she had a chance. Maybe a conversation with Carl would prove fruitful.

After all, the truth had to be somewhere.

CHAPTER EIGHTEEN

"How about fish and chips tonight?" Harriet suggested to Polly. "We deserve a treat. Especially since we missed our lunch out yesterday."

After a full roster of appointments in the morning, Harriet had called at Kettlewell Farm to administer shots and perform checkups on several calves. Meanwhile, Polly had caught up on paperwork while holding down the fort.

"Sounds good." Polly tucked away the last file and closed the cabinet door. "I'm ready." She grabbed her handbag out of the drawer and slung the strap over her shoulder. "Are we walking?"

"I'd like to," Harriet said. "I need to stretch my legs." As they went out the back door, she thought of her aunt. "I'm going to see if Aunt Jinny wants to join us."

Polly waited while Harriet nipped next door.

"I'd love to go another time," Aunt Jinny told her. "I'm having company tonight. Yvonne Ellerby is stopping by. I don't even remember the last time we sat and chatted."

Maybe Harriet's visit to the Ellerby home had reignited Yvonne's interest in the friendship. Or, more cynically, the mysterious jewel chest might be the catalyst. But Harriet didn't say that, of course.

"Wonderful. I hope you have a nice visit." Harriet gestured to the path. "We're walking down and will be back later."

Harriet rejoined Polly, who stood near the path entrance, and they set off toward the village. As they walked, Harriet shared memories of her grandfather taking her to get fish and chips. "It was one of our traditions when I visited."

"He really was a grand chap," Polly said. "I'll never forget my job interview with him. He conducted it while delivering a litter of kittens at Cobble Hill. A stray cat had taken up residence there, and the kittens' arrival coincided with the interview time."

Harriet laughed. "Yes, that would be pretty hard to forget."

"'A trial by fire,' he told me after. 'That's the way it is in this work. You must be prepared to go into action at a moment's notice.'"

"That sounds like him," Harriet said. "What happened to the kittens?"

"All went to good homes," Polly said, smiling. "The mum too. People bring us stray cats and dogs at times, and after checking them over, we find them new owners."

"Our practice worked with several shelters in Connecticut," Harriet said. "We did spay and neuter and rabies services for them."

Polly asked a question about Harriet's former practice, and the conversation occupied them until they reached Cliffside Chippy.

The low-slung stone building offered seating inside and out. "Want to go down to the harbor to eat?" Polly asked. "We can watch the boats go by."

"That sounds fun." Harriet scanned the dozen or so outside tables on the patio, noticing a young man in a black jacket sitting hunched over his phone. A start of recognition surprised Harriet. Where had she seen him before? Perhaps sensing her gaze, he glanced up, his eyes hidden behind sunglasses, then settled his ball cap lower on his forehead.

"Let's hurry," Polly said from the open doorway. "A large group is coming, and I want to order ahead of them."

Indeed, a party of half a dozen adults and as many children made their way toward the restaurant. Harriet and Polly ducked inside.

"I recommend the haddock," Polly said as they studied the menu board above the serving area. The aroma of frying fish was mouth-watering. "The servings are huge, so I get the small."

"For here or to go?" the server asked.

"To go." Polly took some cash out of her jacket pocket. "Small haddock, chips, and a ginger ale, please."

"I'll have the same, and this will be on one check." Despite Polly's protest, Harriet pulled out her wallet and paid.

While waiting for their order, Harriet looked through the large window toward the picnic tables. The young man was gone.

She remembered now where she had seen him. Last Sunday, they had literally bumped into each other on the walking path. She had been stumbling out of the bushes, lost shoe in hand. Harriet smiled in chagrin at the memory. What a mistake wearing those sandals was.

Polly nudged her with an elbow. "Share the joke."

"It's nothing, really." Harriet told Polly the saga of the sandals. "We were almost to the village when one slipped off my foot and went flying. I was lucky we weren't near the cliff."

"I can just see it." Polly laughed. "What a hoot."

"Order for Harriet," the server called.

Carrying delicious-smelling sacks, the pair made their way down the steep lane to the harbor, chatting about the businesses and sights they passed. Harriet was glad they turned off toward the water before reaching the general store. She didn't want to talk or think about her humiliating experience there. Despite Agnes's reassurances, Harriet felt a little gun-shy about going back. She'd give it another week.

Benches stood on a grassy area above the seawall, and Harriet and Polly chose one. The aroma of brine and mudflats was strong so close to the water. A breeze ruffled Harriet's hair, and seagulls swooped and cried overhead.

"Hang on to your food," Polly warned. "They've been known to snatch chips right out of your fingers."

"Happened on the beach back home too." Harriet pulled a box out of her bag and opened it to reveal a slab of fried fish resting on thick, golden fries. "This is beautiful." She took a chip and bit into it, savory tastes flooding her mouth. She loved the English technique of applying vinegar and salt to fish and chips.

Polly handed Harriet a soda can and then popped the top on her own.

They ate in silence, listening to the squawk of gulls and the hiss of the incoming tide covering the flats. Brightly colored rowboats rested on the mud, waiting for the water to lift them. Children ran and shouted, and couples and groups strolled by.

Harriet had rarely had a meal in such a beautiful spot. And while it was a simple meal, it was incredibly tasty. "I think we should do this at least once a week."

"I totally agree."

The young man in the black windbreaker came along the path. Instead of continuing past their bench, he stopped and gazed out to sea. Then he lowered himself to sit on top of the wall. A covert glance confirmed that he was the person who had been at Cliffside Chippy. And, she was almost positive, on the path along the shore.

He hadn't done anything wrong, so why was she uneasy? Bumping into the same person multiple times in a small village like this wasn't exactly cause for suspicion. Forcing herself to focus on the view, she wished he would move along.

Polly closed the lid on her empty box. "That hit the spot." She wiped her hands with a napkin. "So what's next with our investigation? Going through the ledgers, maybe? We can do that when we get back, if you want. I have time."

Out of the corner of her eye, Harriet saw the young man watching them. She caught Polly's gaze, raised her eyebrows, and subtly tilted her head toward the listener.

Polly leaned forward and pretended to check her shoelace then sat back and changed the subject. "I'm debating whether or not I have room for ice cream."

Harriet polished off her last chip. "Not me. I'm stuffed." She wiped her fingers on a napkin. "What flavors do you like?"

"All of them." Polly rolled the sack top and set it next to her feet. She sat up a little straighter. "Here comes Van."

The detective constable strode along the seaside path, greeting the people he passed.

Polly waved when he got closer. "Van. Over here."

Van returned her wave and smiled then veered in their direction.

The young man in the black jacket scrambled to his feet and walked in the opposite direction.

Coincidence, or is he avoiding the police? Harriet was confident he had been eavesdropping.

"Van, do you know that man?" Harriet asked when he reached the bench.

The detective constable studied the young man as he hurried away. "Probably not. We get a lot of visitors here." His brow furrowed. "Was he bothering you?"

"No," Harriet admitted. "I've been seeing him around, that's all."

"He was listening to us talk about the investigation," Polly said.

Van's eyes widened in alarm. "What did you say?"

"Nothing," Harriet assured him. "We changed the subject to ice cream. Boring and innocuous."

"Not to me," Van replied, visibly relaxing. "I love ice cream." He took a seat on the end of the next bench, close enough to talk privately.

"I'm glad to see you," Harriet said. "I think I know who was driving the van last night. When Terry came to pick up his dog at the surgery this morning, I saw that he had swapped vehicles with his nephew, Carl Evans. So Carl has the van. I think he lives somewhere out past Cobble Hill."

Van rubbed his chin. "Interesting."

"I've seen Carl driving his car, and the whole neighborhood hears it go by. It's a noisy little thing."

Van nodded. "I know the car. He's got a bit of a lead foot too." He pulled out his phone and tapped on the screen. "Perhaps I'll have a chat with Carl. Let me know if you see him or his uncle anywhere near Cobble Hill, will you? There's no reason for them to hang around at night."

"It's very fishy for sure," Polly said, wrinkling her nose. "First Terry and now Carl. Did I tell you Carl asked me on a date?"

"No," Harriet and Van said at the same time.

"It was a few months ago," Polly said. "We were in school together, so I've known him for ages. His sister was one of my good friends—"

As she went on, Harriet noticed Van's deepening flush and the agonized expression in his blue eyes. Taking pity on him, she said, "What did you tell him, Polly?"

Polly grimaced. "I said no, of course. I don't like Carl. He's a bit of a chancer." The word referred to someone who wouldn't hesitate to resort to shady ways to get what he wanted.

"Not nearly good enough company for you," Van said, his features easing in relief. "I'm glad you realized that. Better safe than sorry."

Harriet had to agree.

"There's Pastor Will," Van said. "Now *he's* a good sort."

Polly studied the detective constable, her brow furrowed.

Harriet wondered what was troubling her assistant, but knew that if Polly wanted to talk about it in front of the others, she would. So she called out as the pastor walked over, "Fancy meeting you here."

"How is everyone?" Will asked. After they all exchanged greetings, he smiled at Harriet, who still held her dinner box. "I've been thinking about grabbing myself some fish and chips on the way back to the parsonage."

"They're great today. We went to Cliffside Chippy," Harriet said. "I used to go there with my grandfather."

"Best place in town." Van rose from the bench. "I'd better continue my rounds. Nice seeing you all."

The foursome ended up walking part of the way together, chatting about this and that, before Van resumed his route through the lower streets. Polly and Harriet waited while Will stepped into Cliffside Chippy to order his meal.

Conversation dwindled as the trio tackled the steep hill to the upper village. Every now and then, Harriet caught Will's eye, and he would smile. Last time they'd been alone, she had almost cried, which made the situation somewhat uncomfortable. She was glad Polly was there as a buffer.

At the top, they paused to catch their breath. "Never have to worry about staying fit around here," Harriet said. Seeing their amused faces, she clarified. "I meant staying in shape. Toned." She'd forgotten that *fit* meant attractive in England.

Will grinned. "We get it. It was good to see you both."

"Wait a second, if you can," Harriet said, surprising herself. Why was she reluctant to let him go? Rather than examine that, she went on. "I was wondering…" Her thoughts scrambled. What had she wondered? She remembered and clumsily asked, "When you welcome me at the fete, do I need to give a speech? Agnes said a few words would do, but I wanted to make sure you weren't thinking something different."

Will appeared to shift gears mentally. "No, that's fine. A short speech saying you're glad to be here. Which I hope is true." His brown eyes were warm.

Harriet found herself calmed and reassured by his kindness. He really was a good man. "I am. For the most part." She felt heat in her cheeks. "You know what I mean."

"You mean besides the prowlers, buried chests, and police searches?" Polly asked, rolling her eyes. "That'd be enough to drive anyone out of town."

"What's this about prowlers?" Will sounded worried. "Did they hurt you, Harriet?"

"No, not at all." This gentle man could be protective too, Harriet realized. "Scared me though."

He touched her arm lightly. "Let's sit down. I want to hear what happened. If you don't mind me asking."

"Of course not."

They found seats on benches near the parsonage. From there, Harriet had a view of the harbor and the headland curving beyond. After admiring it for a moment, she began with the prowler outside her grandfather's studio and gallery.

In the telling, Harriet could see what a complex and confusing situation she was facing. Judging by his questions and comments, Will seemed able to follow and cut through to the most salient points.

"Someone must believe there's more to be found on the property," he said. "The question is who. There were two men at the studio that night. One was Terry Leaper. Was Carl spying on you or someone else?"

"It might have been Carl," Harriet said. "Maybe his uncle came by, saw he was at Cobble Hill, and told him to leave. I did hear someone running away."

"That would fit," Polly agreed. "Terry then knocked on the door to cover for his nephew. He must not have known about the footprints under the window."

"I wonder how big Carl's feet are," Harriet said. "I can't imagine who else would be poking around."

"Unless it was the man who attacked Meredith," Will pointed out. "I haven't heard any indication that Carl is a suspect in that case. Meredith claims she doesn't recall many details of her attacker's appearance. She might be afraid that he'll come back if she identifies him."

"Poor Meredith," Harriet murmured. "Her granddaughter said the intruder stole a ring. I've been wondering if it was from the Ravenglen Manor collection."

"You mean *Meredith* might have masterminded the heist?" Will sounded shocked. "I can't imagine that. Not only is she entirely harmless, but she doesn't exactly live in the lap of luxury."

Harriet shrugged in apology. "I didn't mean to sound like I was accusing her. She worked there at the time, that's all. Maybe the ring was a gift from Julian, which wouldn't be unheard of. He gave his girlfriend at the time a fabulous necklace. The timing of the attack on Meredith, right before our discovery of the chest, seems odd to me."

"Or it was a coincidence," Will said. "The ring was probably the most valuable item she owned."

"You're right," Harriet admitted.

"Huntley digging up the chest right at that time does seem like a big coincidence," Will mused. "Unless he's part of the ring, sent to retrieve the loot." They all laughed.

"I'll suggest that to the DI," Harriet joked. "But that reminds me. Julian got wind of the chest really fast. He showed up at Cobble Hill even before the inspector. Van says he didn't tell him. So who did?"

"And who is sneaking around, scaring the daylights out of Harriet?" Polly asked. "The chest wasn't buried there for forty years, which Harriet proved with her picture of the site. So when was it buried there? And who buried it?"

"I'll pray about this," Will said. "The Lord promises to guide us into all truth, right? We definitely need His help untangling this situation."

Will offered a quick, discreet prayer right there, and Harriet and Polly gave an enthusiastic "Amen." Soon after, they parted ways. Will went into the parsonage while Harriet and Polly continued on to Cobble Hill.

Seeing lights on in Aunt Jinny's kitchen, Harriet said, "Do you want to stop by? Yvonne Ellerby is supposed be visiting. She was Julian's fiancée at the time of the heist."

"I'd love to," Polly said. "Being so close to the situation, she might know something. Even if it didn't seem like much at the time."

Harriet had the same idea. Maybe revisiting the incident in hindsight would reveal new clues.

As Harriet and Polly approached the house, voices drifted through windows, which were open wide to the evening air.

"I don't believe you." A woman's sharp tones rang out. "You knew the chest was there all along, Jinny. You can't fool me."

CHAPTER NINETEEN

Harriet trotted the rest of the way to the back door, not waiting to hear Aunt Jinny's response to these lies. Hearing a visitor in her aunt's home make ugly and unfounded accusations was reason enough to react.

Harriet barged into the kitchen with Polly right behind her. Aunt Jinny sat at the island, and Yvonne stood nearby, hands on hips and scowling. They both gaped at Harriet, startled expressions on their faces.

"I heard what you said," Harriet told Yvonne, matching her stance and the scowl that had returned to the other woman's face. "If you're going to talk like that, you'd better leave."

"Harriet—" Aunt Jinny protested.

Harriet put up a hand. "No, Aunt Jinny. This has gone too far. My aunt had no idea the chest was buried at Cobble Hill, Yvonne. It's really none of your business, but it wasn't sitting in that spot for forty years. We have proof the burial was much more recent. And that's all I'm going to say." She folded her arms over her chest and glared, silently daring Yvonne to argue.

In the back of her mind, Harriet was aware that she might have irrevocably damaged her relationship with Yvonne's husband, Nigel, and by extension Gavin and Barry. That was too bad. She'd have to deal with the fallout. No one got to waltz into her aunt's home and accuse her of grand larceny.

Yvonne returned Harriet's glare for a few seconds before tearing her gaze away. "I guess I'd best be going," she muttered with a dramatic sniff. "I know when I'm not wanted." She scooped up her bag and scurried out of the kitchen, heels clicking. A moment later, the front door slammed.

Aunt Jinny's face crumpled in distress. "Oh, Harriet. How could she? We used to be friends."

Harriet shook her head. The theft at Ravenglen Manor had done far more than financial damage. It had fractured relationships and gouged rifts that still weren't healed.

"When—not if—we learn the truth about why the chest was buried here, we'll shout it from the rooftops," Harriet said. "People will be apologizing, not accusing." She just wished she knew how much longer it would take.

Aunt Jinny's eyes were pensive. "I have to admit I didn't see that one coming." She made a face. "I thought we were going to pick up our friendship. I missed her."

Harriet wondered if the intention had been one-sided. Perhaps Yvonne had simply wanted to learn whatever Aunt Jinny knew about the heist. Or the whereabouts of her necklace.

"That's too bad." Polly carried three steaming mugs of tea to the island.

After a few sips, Aunt Jinny told them more about the visit. "At first, everything went well. We caught up on our lives and shared pictures." She smiled. "She thought my grandchildren were cute."

"They are," Harriet said. "No one can deny that."

"Thank you, dear. Anyway, she brought up the old days, how we first met, some of our antics back then. I got out the photo albums, and we had quite the trip down memory lane."

"Then she mentioned the necklace," Harriet guessed.

Aunt Jinny nodded. "I knew I should have skipped that page. She started going on about how the necklace belonged to her, even if they hadn't gotten married. That it was pure rotten luck that it was stolen. If only she'd insisted on taking it home...you get the idea."

The album still sat on the island, and Harriet flipped to the photo of Yvonne wearing the necklace. Polly came to peer over her shoulder.

"It was one of the finest pieces in the collection, right?" Harriet asked.

"I believe so," Aunt Jinny said. "That photograph doesn't do it justice. It was stunning in person."

"What a shame," Polly said. "I do have a question though. Why didn't Julian get it cleaned *before* he gave it to her? Wouldn't he have wanted to make the best possible first impression?"

This reasonable question fell like a stone into a pond, creating ripples in Harriet's mind.

"It does seem odd," Aunt Jinny said. "He was certainly aware of her birthday. The party was all she talked about for weeks."

"He might have wanted to keep the necklace at the manor until they were married," Harriet suggested.

"Why not make it a wedding gift, then?" Aunt Jinny countered. "He was one for a splashy gesture though. In this case, he seemed so generous, yet he really hadn't handed it over." She lifted her mug. "I wonder if the cleaning was an excuse to hold it back."

Another theory formed in Harriet's mind, but she wasn't ready to voice it, even to those closest to her. Instead, she skirted the issue by saying, "We can't forget that the police blamed a crime ring targeting stately homes."

"That was after local inquiries didn't go anywhere," Aunt Jinny said. "None of the pieces appeared in the usual channels, whatever those are."

Harriet thought of the chest. "A good amount of jewelry was still in the chest forty years later, don't forget."

"And still in White Church Bay," Aunt Jinny added. "If it had been thieves from out of town, they would have carried off the loot to wherever they were based. If the police are worth their salt, they're back to local suspects again."

"Local suspects like the Bennetts?" Polly asked. "They worked at the manor."

"Possibly," Harriet said. "And Terry. He was in and out of the manor working on the plumbing."

Polly picked up a spoon and stirred her tea. "Or it was a combination. Maybe the crime ring worked with the employees or tradesmen, since they had knowledge and access to the manor. The jewels in the chest could be the locals' share."

"That's possible, Polly," Aunt Jinny said. "Although Terry, Meredith, and Walt never struck me as criminal masterminds." She frowned. "It makes me uncomfortable to even think that about them."

"Pastor Will agrees with you," Harriet said. "We were talking about Meredith's stolen ring earlier, and he defended her. Not that I was actually accusing her of anything."

Aunt Jinny's brows rose. "Stolen ring?"

"Her granddaughter said that her attacker took it off her finger. Assuming it was valuable, I wonder if it came from Ravenglen Manor."

"It may have been a gift from Julian," Aunt Jinny said. "Maybe when Meredith and Walt got married."

Or he gave it to them for services rendered. Again, Harriet decided not to voice her speculations. "We could always ask her, I suppose. Although I'm hesitant to bring up difficult subjects after her injury."

"We can see if she's up for visitors before going over," Polly suggested. "If we do go, we'll be gentle in how we broach the topic."

"That makes me feel better about it." Harriet was glad to have a partner help her investigate. She glanced at the clock. "It's not too late. Maybe I'll continue going through the ledgers tonight." To Aunt Jinny, she said, "I'm seeing if Grandad recorded the milkmaid figurine as barter somewhere."

"Good idea," Aunt Jinny said. "If it was payment for services, he wouldn't have mentioned it to me. He was very discreet about such matters."

"I can help for a while, if you'd like," Polly offered.

"I would love that." Harriet thought of the late hour, the possibility of prowlers, and Polly alone on her bicycle. "I'll run you home after. No arguments."

Seated on the sofa in the living room, Harriet and Polly leafed through ledgers with Maxwell and Charlie snoozing nearby. Occasionally Maxwell snored lightly.

Polly chuckled at an entry. "I can hear Dr. Bailey saying this. Brings him right back to mind, it does."

"Computers have made the records more efficient, but they're often much less personal. Listen to this. 'Unexpected snow on the moors. Ewes caught in storm decided to deliver at the same time. Six fine lambs and frozen fingers are the result.'"

"That's him all over," Polly said, a reminiscent expression on her face. "Such a kind man. Funny too."

"To be honest, reading these felt like a chore at first," Harriet said. "Now I'm treasuring them. His journals as well. It feels like a way to hold on to his memory."

"We're lucky to have them. He had so much wisdom and experience."

Regret stabbed Harriet. If she had moved to England sooner, while her grandfather was still alive, she would have learned so much from him. She forced her thoughts back on track. She had loved Grandad, and he had loved her. She couldn't change the past, but she was following in his footsteps now, the way he had always hoped. Instead of lamenting old decisions, she needed to embrace the future.

They read on, occasionally sharing an entry or a laugh. Harriet was years past the heist in her ledger review when she finally found the milkmaid. She thought. Blinking, she read the entry again.

"Polly. Listen." Harriet sat upright, book gripped in both hands. "'Cow statuette, MB, as payment rendered.' Do you think that's the milkmaid figurine?"

"Cow statuette?" Polly's brows drew together. Then her face cleared. "I'll bet it is. He would be more focused on the cow, wouldn't he?"

"He did favor animal art," Harriet agreed. "All his other porcelain statues are of animals or people with animals."

"MB might be Meredith Bennett," Polly said. "Though I suppose we can check the client roster for other people with those initials. What year was it?"

Harriet checked the date. "Five years after the heist, in 1988." She considered the idea of Meredith using porcelain to pay her bill. "If Meredith stole the jewelry, wouldn't she have the money to pay Grandad?" Maybe this entry was proof that Meredith wasn't involved in the heist, even though the figurine had come from Ravenglen Manor.

"True." Polly smoothed a page. "Julian might have given it to her."

"But he listed it on the police report as stolen," Harriet burst out. "Why would he do that if he'd given it away as a gift?"

"He forgot?" Polly cringed. "That sounds far-fetched though. I'm starting to have doubts about Julian Montcliff."

"So am I." Harriet unfolded her legs and got up from the sofa to grab her phone. "I'm going to send Van and DI McCormick a picture of the entry. Maybe they can sort it out with Meredith and Julian." She couldn't hold back a smile as she aimed her phone camera at the page. "And scratch Grandad off the suspect list once and for all. If this entry and the Royal Dux figurine match, it's additional proof he wasn't involved in the heist."

Polly helped Harriet return the ledgers to the study bookcase. "There are a lot of them, aren't there?"

"For sure." Harriet slid the last one into place. "I'm glad we didn't have to cover the whole collection." She left the ledger with the figurine entry on the desk in case the police wanted to see it. Now that she knew what the books contained, she'd select one to read every so often. Same with the journals. It would be like getting to have another conversation with her grandfather.

They loaded Polly's bike into the back of the Land Rover, and Harriet took her home. Polly lived with her parents in the upper village, in a neat cottage with beautiful flower gardens. Harriet left the engine running while she helped Polly unload the bicycle.

"See you tomorrow," Harriet said. "Thanks for all your help."

"No problem." Polly began to walk the bike toward her home. "Thank you for the fish and chips."

"That seems like ages ago, doesn't it?" Harriet could use a bedtime snack. "We'll go again soon."

To Harriet's relief, the ride back to Cobble Hill was uneventful. No vehicles followed her or lurked in the lay-by. She pulled into the drive and parked close to the door. She trotted to the house without sparing a glance at the dark areas of the property.

While the water heated, Harriet selected one of Doreen's scones. Instead of tea, she made a cup of hot cocoa. Then, her contented pets sprawled at her feet, Harriet sat in the nook and enjoyed her snack while reviewing the day. A busy day in the surgery. Fish and chips on the shore. Van. Will.

Seizing on a light topic for a change, Harriet thought about Polly's reaction when Van complimented Will, right after they'd discussed Carl Leaper asking her out. Had she thought he was suggesting that she try dating Will? Harriet hadn't gotten that impression, but it was interesting that Polly might have—and had appeared to be upset by the idea.

Harriet smiled. She remembered all too well the confusing moments early in a relationship. How one tended to read too much into things that meant nothing. Were Polly and Van headed toward something significant?

The shrill ring of the surgery line broke into her musing. A call at this hour meant only one thing—an emergency.

CHAPTER TWENTY

Harriet hastily picked up the phone. "Cobble Hill Vet Clinic. Dr. Bailey speaking."

"Hi, Doc. It's Stacey Bennett. Lady, Julian Montcliff's mare, has a bad case of colic."

"I'll be right there." The causes and outcomes of colic could range from minor to life-threatening, especially in an older horse. It was fortunate, considering the late hour, that Stacey had been at the stables and noticed the mare's condition.

Harriet sprang into action, body and mind alert. She had no time to waste.

In the clinic, she added medical supplies and medications to her bag, mentally going through a checklist of what she might need. She also made sure she had the number of the closest equine hospital in case Lady needed surgery.

She prayed it didn't come to that.

Harriet jumped into the Land Rover, and the engine started with a roar. The Beast might not be beautiful, but it was reliable.

At midnight, the countryside lay in quiet slumber under twinkling stars and a waxing moon. Harriet was glad she'd already visited the manor. There was a very real possibility she would have gotten lost in the maze of lanes at night if it were her first visit.

Signposts were difficult to read and turnoffs almost invisible in the shadow of shrubbery.

Harriet sped up the drive to Ravenglen Manor and parked at the stables, where lights blazed.

Julian emerged to meet her, his face fraught with worry. "Thank you for coming so quickly, Dr. Bailey."

"Not a problem." Harriet collected her bag and shut the Land Rover door. "Lead on."

Stacey stood next to Lady, lead in hand. The mare shivered, stamping her feet and tossing her head. "I tried walking her, but it's not helping."

"You did the right thing by calling," Harriet said. "Let's get her inside."

The other horses watched, heads hanging over the stalls, as Harriet and the others helped the stricken mare into a box stall. The horse's huge eyes followed Harriet with a pleading expression.

"I'm here to help you, girl," Harriet murmured, stroking Lady's velvety nose. Her first task was to verify the diagnosis of colic and then determine the likely cause. Following that, she would administer the appropriate treatment.

Harriet quickly performed her exam. One of her worst fears was an intestinal obstruction. As she worked, she asked questions about Lady's medical history, recent diet, and for a description of the event.

"She's been known to be greedy," Stacey said. "I've had to cut back her grain at times and make sure there's nothing for her to get into."

"What would we do without you, Stacey?" Julian murmured. "You're my eyes and ears in the stable."

The mare's history of overeating was a clue that Lady was experiencing indigestion and a sluggish system, both more common with age.

"Her belly is fine," Harriet said with relief a few minutes later after she'd checked several things. She sent up a prayer of thanks. The signs were very encouraging. She explained the next steps to Julian and Stacey. "We should see improvement soon."

Julian heaved a huge sigh. "Thank you, Dr. Bailey." He patted the mare's neck. "You're going to be all right, old girl." To Harriet, he said, "I've had her since she was born, you know." Tears sparkled in his eyes.

Touched by the evidence of his attachment to the mare, Harriet said, "Our animal friends are precious, aren't they?" With Stacey's assistance, Harriet began to administer treatment. With any luck, it would bring the mare quick relief.

"I'll get out of your way," Julian said. "Come up to the house for a hot drink whenever you're ready."

"Will do," Harriet said.

Hours later, Harriet dragged herself to the house, utterly exhausted. The mare was on the mend. She'd provided instructions to eliminate grain until the horse's system was regular. Meanwhile, she could graze on fresh grass, and regular walks would also be helpful.

Julian answered when she knocked on the door. "How is she?"

"Much better," Harriet said. "With monitoring, she'll be fully back to normal within a day or two."

Harriet followed Julian to the kitchen, filled with the aroma of fresh coffee and something sizzling in a pan on the stove. "You can wash up in the sink then have a seat," Julian said, indicating the island. "Coffee?" He held up a mug. "I'm making a full English, if you'd like one." A full English breakfast included eggs, sausage, bacon, baked beans, tomato, and mushrooms, all fried. Even the bread was toasted in the fry pan.

Harriet usually didn't eat in the middle of the night, but she was famished. "Yes to both, please," she said as she washed her hands. "Thank you."

He brought her the full mug, indicating milk and sugar nearby. "Your grandfather and I enjoyed many a breakfast in this room. Emergencies always seem to happen at night, don't they?"

"They sure do." Harriet added milk to her mug and stirred. Thinking of her grandfather eating a meal in this very kitchen caused her to warm to Julian. Which might not be a good idea. Not until the mystery of the chest was solved, at least.

Harriet enjoyed the excellent coffee while watching her host tend the stove. He broke eggs with dexterous ease and flipped food with aplomb. Bread was sliced perfectly with quick passes of the knife.

"I've done this a few times," Julian said. "Comes with being a bachelor. After all, I can't drag my staff out of bed in the middle of the night simply because I'm peckish."

Although Harriet wondered why he and Yvonne hadn't gotten married, she didn't dare ask something so personal. Had the theft here at Ravenglen Manor created a wedge between them? Or had they drifted apart, with someone finally making the difficult decision to end things? That was the way it had gone with her and Dustin.

Julian put together a plate and set it in front of Harriet then nudged the salt and pepper shakers closer, along with marmalade and a bottle of brown sauce.

After serving himself, he sat at the island. "I'll spell Stacey soon so she can eat."

That was thoughtful, Harriet acknowledged as she attacked her meal. "This is delicious," she said after several bites.

Julian nodded his thanks and then asked some questions about the mare and her treatment.

Harriet gave him her analysis as well as recommendations to prevent future bouts of colic. Being an older horse, Lady was more susceptible to digestive upsets, and her routine would need to be adjusted accordingly.

"Like all of us." Julian patted his trim middle. "I can't eat like this every day. It's usually shredded wheat and hot milk for me." He slid off the stool and carried his empty plate to the sink to rinse it. "Would you like more coffee?"

"Yes, please." Harriet set her fork down. "Mind if I visit your washroom?"

Julian pointed. "Go through those doors into the main hall. You'll find it next to my study."

Like the other rooms in the manor, the bathroom was elegantly appointed. A marble sink was set in a mahogany cabinet, glossy white trim contrasted with flocked gold wallpaper, and the flooring was tiny hexagon tile.

Harriet would love to do something similar at Cobble Hill, when she could afford it. Not quite as fancy though. An array of scented individual soaps sat on the counter, and she picked one up and unwrapped it.

Seeking a place to rest the used soap, Harriet peeked into a porcelain dish. It already held a ring, so she perched the soap on the sink instead.

Then she went back for a closer look at the ring, teasing it out of the dish with forefinger and thumb.

A gold band set with diamonds all around. That was how Doreen had described Meredith's stolen ring.

Could it be? A wave of heat rushed over Harriet from head to toe. If this was the same ring, why did Julian have it? Had *he* attacked Meredith?

Harriet tried to imagine Julian wrestling a ring off an older woman's finger. The picture wouldn't come clear. The incident seemed totally out of character for him. He would be much more likely to charm the ring away from someone.

She placed the ring on the counter and patted her pockets for her phone. Then she took several pictures of the ring before putting it back in the bowl.

She hurried out of the bathroom. Julian would be wondering where she'd gone.

"Still want that coffee?" Julian asked from the sink.

Harriet wanted nothing more than to get out of there, away from Julian and Ravenglen Manor so she could think.

"Actually, I'd better not, thanks. I need to check on Lady before I head for home." Harriet pasted a smile on her face. "Thanks again for a great breakfast." Good thing she'd eaten before finding the ring. The discovery would have stolen her appetite.

"Understandable." Julian rinsed a plate. "Tell Stacey I'll be out soon, if you would."

"I'll do that." Harriet paused on her way to the door. "I'll be back this afternoon. If Lady gets worse or seems to be in pain before then, call me immediately."

Julian wrung out a sponge. "I certainly will. Thanks again for coming out, Dr. Bailey. Much appreciated."

"Anytime." Harriet lurched into movement again, hoping she was acting and sounding normal. She didn't feel normal.

"Oh, and Dr. Bailey? One more thing."

Cold flashed over Harriet's body, pinning her in place. Had he noticed her change in behavior and guessed the cause?

"Bring the bill when you come back. I'll write you a check."

Harriet started moving again. "I will. Thank you."

Outside, she took several deep breaths of cool air as she crossed the gravel to the stables. She needed to put Julian and the ring aside and focus on her patient.

Inside the stables, Stacey was still watching over Lady. She smiled when Harriet entered the stall. "She's doing so much better. I can tell."

Harriet checked the mare over, agreeing with Stacey's assessment. The look of distress was gone, and her belly sounds were normal.

"Definitely much better." Harriet began packing the instruments in her bag. "I'll be back in the afternoon to check on her." She remembered Julian's request. "Julian said to tell you he'll be out soon so you can go eat."

Stacey made a scoffing sound. "Big of him," she muttered under her breath. When Harriet raised an eyebrow, she arranged her features into a pleasant expression. "One of his fry-ups, is it? I sure could use something to eat."

"How is your grandmother?" Harriet asked. "And Huntley?"

Stacey checked the mare's water. "They're fine, thanks. We're planning a trip soon to see properties farther inland."

"Really?" Harriet's ear perked up. "You want to move?"

"Yeah." Stacey leaned against the stall wall. "We need a change. Nana especially. She's lived in White Church Bay all her life, but she doesn't feel safe here anymore. I'm hoping to get a place with some land. Maybe have my own stables with a horse or two. Something small."

Harriet could understand that someone who loved horses so much would want their own. "Pleasure riding?"

"Partly. I'll do lessons. Plus keep working at other stables." She pushed up her sweater sleeves. "I like to keep busy."

"So do I," Harriet said, glancing around to be sure she had everything. "Fortunately, that's not a problem in my line of work."

Stacey rolled her eyes. "Got to love these late-night emergencies, right?"

"I don't mind," Harriet said. "It's part of the job." She was grateful to have no morning appointments so she could sleep in. "Call me immediately if she's in distress again or has any problems, okay? Otherwise, I'll see you in a few hours."

"Will do." Stacey yawned.

Harriet hesitated, wanting to ask Stacey about the ring. She could show her the photo she'd taken to ask if it was the same one.

What if it was? She pictured Stacey confronting Julian and his furious denials. At the very least, he would fire her. He might even get violent if he had indeed plucked the ring off Meredith's finger.

The police wouldn't be happy either, if she interfered.

"Is there anything else, Dr. Bailey?" Stacey asked, her eyes curious.

Harriet forced a smile. "No, all set." She picked up her bag and gave Lady a pat before leaving the stall. "See you later."

Despite her questions and worries, Harriet slept soundly until late morning.

"Come on, Maxwell, there's a good boy." Polly's cheerful voice drifted through the open window.

Harriet's last task before collapsing into bed was to leave Polly a note asking her to care for Maxwell and Charlie when she arrived for work, due to the emergency call at Ravenglen Manor.

She stretched out fully, thinking about the day ahead. This afternoon, she'd return to Ravenglen Manor to check on Lady. Other than that, she would catch up on paperwork and go over the books. Working in her own practice meant staying on top of the bills, something she hadn't had to do in Connecticut.

As she slid out of bed, Harriet smiled, thinking of her grandfather's ledgers. Thank goodness she had a computerized system and Polly. Otherwise, everything would take three times as long.

Harriet took a quick shower and dressed before venturing down for coffee and a second breakfast. A scone would probably do after her feast at Ravenglen Manor.

"There you are." Polly came through the back door, Maxwell and Charlie in tow. "Did you get some rest?"

"I sure did, thank you." Harriet started the coffee. "You won't believe what happened."

"What?" Polly sounded alarmed. "Is Lady all right?"

"She's fine." Harriet grabbed her phone from the charger and brought up the photograph of the ring. "This was in a dish in the bathroom. I think it might be Meredith's."

Polly studied the photo. "It was right in plain sight? If it is hers, why would he leave it there?"

"I have no idea. It gave me a shock, I tell you. I didn't hang around long after that. What if he was the one who attacked Meredith?"

"You should send this to Van," Polly told her. "The police need to know about it."

"I suppose." Harriet squirmed at the idea. "What if I'm wrong? Julian would fire me as his vet." Even as she said it, her conscience began to nag. "You're right. I should send it and let them sort it out. Catching whoever did this is more important than my potentially losing one client."

Polly set the phone on the table. "Good decision. If he attacked Meredith, you don't want him anyway."

They were discussing the ins and outs of the mystery over scones when the clinic phone rang. Polly answered. "Yes, Dr. Tweedy. I'll see if she's available."

Barry Tweedy, from the vet group.

"Dr. Tweedy wants to know if you can demonstrate that new asthma treatment today on a pony named Rumpelstiltskin," Polly asked after putting the phone on hold.

Harriet reached for the phone. "Good morning, Barry. What time were you thinking?" Dr. Bailey was back in action.

CHAPTER TWENTY-ONE

Rumpelstiltskin and his owner lived near Ravenglen Manor, which worked well for Harriet. Her plan was to administer the treatment and then swing by the manor to check on Lady.

Her photos of the ring were now in Van's hands. As with the photo of the ledger entry regarding the milkmaid figurine, he'd thanked her. She hadn't heard a thing from DI McCormick.

Harriet's destination was a cottage on the edge of the moors. She parked on the road behind a shiny green Land Rover and a van almost as battered as her own vehicle and carried her bag around back, as directed.

Nigel Ellerby and Barry Tweedy were in the barn with Rumpelstiltskin and his owner, a young woman named Gwendolyn.

"This is Dr. Harriet Bailey," Barry said to Gwendolyn. "She's our newest associate, hailing from the States. Dr. Harold Bailey was her grandfather." He grinned. "This is the new Doc Bailey, and she deserves the title."

Gwendolyn shook Harriet's hand. "I remember Doc Bailey. So sorry for your loss."

"Thank you." Harriet inclined her head in acknowledgment. "Tell me about your pony."

Rumpelstiltskin was an adorable Shetland with a tan coat and shaggy blond mane and tail. Gwendolyn told her about his struggles with asthma, and Nigel relayed the treatments they'd already tried. Harriet checked the results of the lung function tests. That was the baseline they would use to gauge results.

Once Harriet had taken in all the information, she unpacked the equipment she'd brought, explaining how the treatment would work and the studies behind it. Then she demonstrated the procedure, talking through each step with her audience. The dose was carefully calibrated for the pony's weight.

Rumpelstiltskin didn't seem to mind the treatment. Afterward, his owner let him out into the pasture to graze.

"How will we know if it works?" Gwendolyn asked. "If he doesn't have another attack?"

"Lung function and exercise tolerance tests," Harriet said. "You should see a steady improvement in his numbers."

"I can handle those," Nigel said. "Dr. Bailey, will you help me assess the results?"

Harriet watched the pony trotting around the grass. "I'd be happy to."

"Thank you so much, Dr. Bailey," Gwendolyn said, hands clasped to her chest. "I've been so worried about the little guy."

"Glad I could help," Harriet said. She was also glad that a professional rapport had been established between her and the other local area vets. She would no doubt be calling on them as well when she was stumped or needed a second opinion.

Mission accomplished, Harriet drove to Ravenglen Manor, her nerves tightening with every mile. Did the diamond ring in the dish belong to Meredith? If so, why did Julian have it? She had the unsettling sense that deceit lurked behind a facade of wealth and propriety.

The police had the photo of the ring. The ball was in their court. Hopefully Van would show the picture to Meredith and find out if it was her ring.

As Harriet reached the manor gate, she saw a white van proceeding down the drive ahead of her. It was the Leaper Plumbing van. *Because I wasn't stressed enough.*

By the time she parked, the van's rear doors were open and the driver was nowhere in sight.

Before going into the stables, Harriet went to the back door to let Julian know she was on the property. After a moment, he answered, kitchen towel in hand. "Dr. Bailey. Here to see Lady?"

"I am. Do you want to come with me to the stables?"

Julian peered past her at the van. "Leaper Plumbing?" He finished wiping his hands and set the towel aside. "Which one is it? Terry or Carl?"

"I don't know," Harriet said, wondering why that mattered.

Without explanation, Julian stalked ahead of Harriet across the yard to the stable. Harriet paused to grab her bag before following.

Inside the stable, Julian, Carl, and Stacey stood near Lady's stall. As Harriet approached, Julian was saying, "Carl, I've spoken to you about this before. When you're here to work, please leave Stacey alone."

Scowling, Carl said, "I never start the clock until tools are in my hand. It's none of your business if I stop to talk to a friend."

Stacey's wide gaze darted back and forth between the men. "It's all right, Carl. We'll catch up later."

He swung around to stare at her. "Promise? I haven't been able to get ahold of you for days. Thought you were avoiding me."

Julian frowned. "Maybe she was. Learn to take a hint, Carl. Never pester a woman. Besides, she's also here to work."

Carl's mouth opened as though to retort, but then he clamped it shut and walked away. He marched past Harriet without even glancing her way, and a moment later, something clanged out in the yard.

Julian was affable again by the time Harriet reached the stall. He unlatched the door. "Shall we?"

Harriet glanced at Stacey, who stood with her head down and arms wrapped around her middle. Something—or someone—had upset her. Was it Carl, or Julian?

Harriet was glad to see that Lady was doing much better, almost back to her usual perky self. "It seems we caught the problem in time," she said with satisfaction as she packed away her instruments. "Keep an eye on her though."

"We will," Julian said, running a hand along the mare's nose. "Think she can join the others in the pasture?"

"I don't see why not," Harriet said. "She's ready to graze."

A cell phone rang, and Julian put his hand to his pocket. "Better take this. I'll leave Lady in your capable hands." He answered the phone, talking as he left the stall.

Harriet allowed Stacey to take the lead in ushering Lady through the stable and into the pasture beyond. Stacey had a nice touch with the horse, kind yet firm.

After closing the gate, they stood by the fence and watched Lady trot over to join the rest of the herd. Soon she was head down, eating grass, her tail swishing back and forth.

"It does my heart good to see her out there," Stacey said. "I was so worried."

Harriet had been as well, although she didn't voice it. As a vet, it was important to project confidence even when the situation felt dire. That didn't mean she couldn't empathize with her human clients. But she had learned that if she remained calm, it helped them do the same, which in turn helped their animals.

She also wanted to talk to Stacey while she had the chance, with no one else in earshot. Rather than ask questions bluntly, she decided to share something first. "I had a prowler at my house the other night."

Stacey's head whipped around. "You did? Did he attack you?" She searched Harriet over as if checking for injuries.

"It didn't get that far, thankfully," Harriet said. "I was out in my grandfather's studio when he was prowling around." *And peering through the window, apparently.* "Fortunately, I realized something was wrong and called the police."

Stacey's gaze was now on the horses as she chewed her lower lip. "I wish Nana had. I wish I'd been there. She's so easily taken in. I think she let him inside."

Harriet could see that happening, especially if Julian had come to call. "Did she ever say what the visitor wanted? What pretext he used?"

She shook her head. "It's as if the head injury erased her memory."

That could happen during trauma as a protective response from the body. Did she dare ask about the ring? Pressure built in Harriet's chest as she pondered. Finally, she took a breath and went for it. "Your grandmother's ring, the one that was stolen. Any leads on it?"

Stacey shook her head. "Not yet. DC Worthington said they checked the local pawn shops, but it hasn't shown up. I've been watching online in case someone tries to sell it."

"Good idea." Harriet shifted uneasily. The conversation had done nothing to alleviate her fear that Julian had the ring. "So awful. Was the ring a gift from her husband?"

"Sort of," Stacey said. "Julian gave it to them for her wedding band when they got married. A gift for their years of faithful service."

The dots connected with an almost audible ping in Harriet's mind. The ring had originally been part of the Ravenglen Manor collection. Had Julian reported the ring missing after the robbery? That would have been shady.

The answers seemed to dangle just out of reach. Wary of probing Stacey further or sharing her suspicions, Harriet took her leave. "Please call me if you need anything or have a question about Lady. Better safe than sorry."

"Thanks again, Doc," Stacey said, remaining at the fence. "Have a good day."

"You as well," Harriet called as she strode toward the stables. She needed to collect a check from Julian and then she would be on her way.

Once again, Julian answered the door when Harriet knocked. "What's the verdict?"

Harriet fumbled for words, her thoughts still on the stolen ring and Julian's possible role. *The mare. He's asking about Lady, not my verdict on his potential guilt.* "She's fine. I'd say she's nearly back to normal. I brought the invoice, as you requested." She handed it over.

Julian took the page and scanned it. "You undercharge for the peace of mind you've brought me. I'll write you a check. Follow me to the study."

Harriet studied her hands. "Mind if I wash up first?"

"Join me when you're ready."

He politely let her lead the way, with Harriet detouring to the washroom while he continued to the study.

As soon as she closed the door, she checked the dish.

The ring was gone.

CHAPTER TWENTY-TWO

Harriet stared at the empty dish that had held the ring. Did Julian suspect she'd noticed it? Had he hidden it somewhere, planning to deny everything?

Or had he merely put it away, as anyone would secure a valuable item instead of leaving it lying around?

These thoughts circled in an endless loop while Harriet washed her hands. She didn't dare ask Julian about the ring. Even under normal circumstances, that would be nosy. If he was a friend, she might mention loving the new ring, but never with a client. She didn't often visit homes, and when she did, boundaries were in place. Her purpose was to treat patients, not notice and remark on clients' personal lives or belongings.

"Everything all right?" Julian asked as Harriet entered the study. He was seated at his desk, bent over his checkbook.

What did he mean? Harriet wondered if something about her expression or body language was signaling her uneasy thoughts and suspicions. "Perfect," she said in a sprightly tone, perching on a chair. "Lady is so much better this morning. When I left her, she was grazing in the pasture with the other horses."

Julian ripped out the check and extended it, requiring Harriet to stand up and take it from him. "Any news from the police on the chest?"

This unexpected question caused Harriet to plop back down on her chair. "Not that I've heard." In light of his remarks about Cobble Hill, she wanted to share that she might have cleared her grand-father's name by finding the origin of the figurine. Meredith Bennett, or someone else with her initials, had given it to him. Plus, she'd proven that the chest hadn't been buried in the dog yard area since the heist, due to boulders in the way.

She didn't say any of this, of course. The police could fill him in if they chose.

Julian tapped his pen on the desk. "I was glad when they called in DI McCormick. This case was obviously over our little detective constable's head."

Defensive words about Van's capabilities rose in Harriet's throat. Swallowing hard, she managed to suppress them.

"But I'm starting to think she's not much better," Julian complained. "Every time I call for updates, I get her voice mail. And she never returns my calls."

"Maybe she's busy tracking down the thieves?" Harriet suggested.

Julian's brows shot up. "Thieves, you say. As in more than one. What's your theory about the heist? Everyone seems to have one."

So did Harriet—more than one, actually—but she didn't want to share them with Julian, since she couldn't fully trust him. He stared at her, waiting for an answer, so she finally said, "Well, if it was a crime ring like the papers said, maybe they divided the jewelry." That was safer than pointing to his former employees as suspects. She really didn't want to open that can of worms.

Then she heard the problem in her own statement. The chest hadn't been there since the heist. It couldn't have been, because of the boulders. And it would be crazy for an out-of-town crime ring to come back to White Church Bay years later to bury the jewels in the local vet's dog yard. The culprit had to be local.

The burning question was, where was the rest of the jewelry? Already sold or hidden somewhere else?

Harriet rose abruptly, sending her chair rocking. At Julian's surprised reaction, she hurriedly explained, "Just remembered I need to get back to the clinic."

He stood as well and extended his hand. "Thank you again, Dr. Bailey. I'm grateful to have you on board as our vet."

She forced herself to shake his hand and act as though all was normal. "Thank you for engaging our services. And please call right away if Lady has a setback."

Clutching the check, Harriet hurried out of the study. The pieces were starting to come together, and she wasn't sure she liked the shape they made.

"Here you go." Harriet placed Julian's check on the desk where Polly was putting together a deposit. "Julian's a prompt payer. I have to give him that much."

Polly glanced up sharply. "What's the matter? Come on, spill. I can tell something's wrong."

"Tell you in a minute." Harriet was already dialing Aunt Jinny. "Are you free right now?" she asked when her aunt answered. "Excellent. We're coming over."

They set the landline to forward calls to Harriet's cell phone so that clients wouldn't get voice mail during an emergency. After locking up and leaving a note, they went next door.

Aunt Jinny was in the kitchen, mixing up a pitcher of fresh lemonade. "What's up?" She filled three tall glasses. "I made this because you like it so much."

"I do." Harriet took a seat at the island. Where to begin? Her mind was so clogged with thoughts and emotions, she had trouble framing a sentence. Finally, she managed to simplify what she was thinking. "I think the heist was an inside job."

Aunt Jinny and Polly stared at her. "You mean *Julian* did it?" her aunt asked.

"Maybe," Harriet said. "And what if Meredith was involved somehow?" She took out her phone and brought up the picture of the ring to show them. "Stacey, her granddaughter, said it was a gift from Julian. Now it's back at the manor."

"It might not be the same ring," Aunt Jinny said.

"True." Harriet studied the picture. "It might not be. But what if Meredith is faking her loss of memory? If she was involved in the heist, she wouldn't tell the police that Julian had taken it."

"But why would he do that now?" Polly asked, ever practical.

"He might have seen it as evidence of a connection between them. Maybe Meredith threatened to go to the police. People's consciences can start to bother them over the years."

"Yes," Aunt Jinny said wryly. "The nearer to heaven, the heavier sin's burden. I've seen it before."

"I can't imagine Meredith as a thief," Polly said. "She's such a sweet person."

"She is," Aunt Jinny agreed. "However, all of us make mistakes." Her face twisted. "Though that would have been a big one, which makes me think Meredith must have gotten more out of it than a ring." Her expression cleared. "I have an idea."

"Do tell," Polly urged.

Aunt Jinny got up from the table and returned a moment later with a laptop. She opened a browser and typed something in. "I'm reviewing local property records. They're public." After a few minutes of tapping and searching, Aunt Jinny turned the laptop around. "Take a look. The timing of this transaction is very interesting."

The screen showed a property transfer to Walter and Meredith Bennett. "That's where she lives now," Polly said.

According to the record, the transfer had occurred in 1984, the year after the burglary at the manor. Most telling, there wasn't a mortgage recorded. The young couple had paid cash. Had Julian given them money along with the ring and the milkmaid figurine?

Or Julian might not have been involved at all. Maybe Meredith's husband was the mastermind and had sold some of the jewelry on the black market to get the cash for the property. How and when some of it had been buried at Cobble Hill was still a mystery.

Aunt Jinny picked up her lemonade and took a sip. "Don't get me wrong. I'm not saying they didn't save every pound for years before that. However, paying cash does seem odd to me, especially considering their jobs as staff at Ravenglen Manor. It's worthy of investigation, anyway."

Harriet had to agree. "Let's send this info over to Van. He can ask Meredith where she and Walt got the money to buy their home."

"See, Dr. Bailey?" Terry pointed. "The area is a little red."

Terry had called first thing Thursday morning, and Polly had fit him in between regular appointments.

Glad to see Jolly still wore his cone, Harriet examined his surgery site closely, trying to determine if the incision was infected or if any stitches had come loose. To her relief, the answer to both was negative. "The area is bruised from the surgery," she explained. "It should get better every day. By the time the stitches come out, he'll be good as new. You did the right thing by calling when you weren't sure if something was wrong."

The plumber's expression eased. "Well, he'll still be a wee bit bald in that area."

Harriet smiled as she smoothed the dog's long fur. "For a while, yes, but eventually it should grow back. Do you have any other concerns today?"

Terry hesitated. "Uh, yes." After a long pause, he said, "Remember the other night, when I came by the studio?"

How could Harriet forget? She'd been petrified by the disturbance outside followed by his unexpected knock on the door. "I sure do."

He took a step away from the table, shifting on his feet as if agitated. "I was there because of my nephew," he burst out. "I'm worried about him."

"Carl?" Harriet supplied.

Terry nodded. "He's supposed to take over my business. Been working with me since he got out of school. Don't get me wrong—he's a very talented plumber. He's got the Leaper knack."

Harriet was waiting to hear how Carl fit into the night at the studio. Had he been the watcher outside the window?

"I'm sure he does," Harriet said to keep him talking. Although riveted, she was also conscious of the other patients waiting to be seen. Footsteps, voices, and faint barking penetrated the closed door.

"I thought he was at your place that night," Terry said. "That's why I came by."

"Why would he be at Cobble Hill?" Harriet asked. She could guess, but she wanted to hear it from him.

Terry picked up his cap and worried it in his long, calloused fingers. "He's been acting shifty for a while. He forgets I've known him since he was this high." He demonstrated with one flat palm. "I could tell when he was up to no good then, and I still can."

"Up to no good?" Harriet's gears began to turn.

"It's something I sense. He sneaks off at all hours. Won't tell me anything."

So far, Harriet hadn't heard anything that wasn't normal behavior for a young person seeking more independence.

"He was excited about that chest buried here," Terry went on. "I figured he was prowling around looking for more treasure."

"So it was him at Cobble Hill that night?" If so, Harriet was going to call Van and pass the information along.

Terry shook his head. "No. It was someone else. The guy was looking through your window when I came up to him. We scuffled, and then he ran off."

Electricity bolted through Harriet. "Do you know who it was? Why didn't you stay and tell Van about him?" Terry had made a hasty retreat when the detective constable arrived.

"Never saw him before." The plumber ducked his head, a sheepish expression on his face. "I should have told the detective constable. I was worried Carl's name would come up, and I didn't want to make matters worse for him."

"How would you have made things worse?" Harriet asked.

"He's had some trouble," Terry admitted. "Years ago. That's one reason I took him on. My sister begged me to."

Harriet hoped Carl hadn't blown the second chance provided by his uncle. "I don't see how that would relate. The heist was forty years ago, well before your nephew was even born."

Terry shifted his stance again. "The police called him in for questioning. Someone gave them an anonymous tip that Carl knew something about the Ravenglen Manor jewels."

"What happened with the police?" If they'd arrested Carl, no one had told Harriet.

"They let him go. This time. You can see why I've been so worried."

Terry thinks Carl is involved somehow. But Harriet refused to voice that. "You want the best for your nephew. That's understandable." Not that Terry should sneak around her property—or anyone's—while keeping tabs on Carl.

"Thank you, Dr. Bailey. I knew you would understand." He patted Jolly, who readily walked down the ramp.

Harriet wasn't quite sure she did understand. She wished she had time to ponder Terry's revelations, but a full roster of patients awaited. "Let me know if the surgery area changes at all. Otherwise, we'll see you at the appointment to have the stitches out."

"Was that the last one?" Harriet asked Polly as the door closed behind a woman with two Pekingese dogs in tow.

"Until one thirty," Polly reported. "We have several afternoon appointments."

Harriet leaned over Polly's shoulder to scan the patients and their complaints on the monitor. "I suppose it will be a while before we get caught up." Some of the appointments were clients loyal to her grandfather. They'd waited for her to reopen rather than transfer to a new practice. Every client who said that made her more certain that Cobble Hill Farm would continue to prosper.

"Probably, but we'll get it done, and job security is never a bad thing." Polly swiveled in her seat, stretching with laced hands. "Lunch?"

"I'm ready." Harriet thought about the contents of her fridge. She didn't have much in the way of leftovers.

"I took the liberty of ordering for us." Polly gestured to the door with a grin. "And here it is."

To Harriet's surprise, DC Van Worthington stepped inside, a large sack in his hands. "Special delivery."

"Van," Harriet exclaimed. "How nice of you."

"There's a sandwich in there for me as well," Van said. "If you don't mind the company?" His brows rose in inquiry.

"Of course not," Polly said. "I was hoping you'd have time to eat with us."

"You are more than welcome," Harriet agreed. She had things to discuss with the detective constable.

After Polly locked the door and flipped the sign, they made their way to the garden table. Harriet brought out cans of soda and extra condiments as her contribution to the meal.

"What do we have here?" Harriet asked as she unwrapped the paper around her sandwich.

"Ploughman's lunch," Polly said. "Cheese, ham, pickle, mustard, and arugula."

Harriet took a bite of the thick sandwich, tangy mustard and peppery herb making her tongue tingle. "This is great."

"From the Happy Cup," Van said. "They do a nice sandwich."

Harriet hadn't been to the tearoom yet, and now a visit was definitely on the agenda. She waited until they'd finished their sandwiches before bringing up a difficult topic. "Van, remember the ring photo I sent you?"

He shrugged. "I passed it along to the DI. And there it sits."

"It's probably not a priority, but I figured that wasn't my place to decide. I was at Ravenglen Manor today, treating a horse. The ring's no longer in the washroom, which doesn't mean much, I suppose." Unless Julian was worried she'd seen it.

"What are you thinking?" Van asked. "I can see the wheels turning, Harriet."

She laughed. "You already know me too well. Let me take a step back." She arranged her thoughts before going on. "Stacey, Meredith's granddaughter, said the intruder had stolen a gold-and-diamond ring from her grandmother. She also told me that Julian gave Meredith the ring."

Both listeners nodded.

"I know it's speculation, but there are two points I want to make. One, a ring of similar description was on the Ravenglen Manor stolen list. Two, what if Julian took his gift back, and that's the ring I saw in his washroom?"

Polly gasped. "You think he attacked Meredith?"

"I don't want to believe it," Harriet said. "And I realize I'm jumping to conclusions here. The ring in the washroom might not be Meredith's."

Van's expression was contemplative. "I get where you're going, Harriet, and how you got there. But Julian has an alibi for the attack on Meredith."

Harriet was surprised. "You questioned him as a suspect?"

"Not exactly," Van replied. "Meredith lives near Ravenglen Manor, so I asked Mr. Montcliff if he'd seen any unfamiliar vehicles go by that morning. He told me he was in York most of the day at a meeting with his bank. I followed up with the bank, and they confirmed that he was there until noon."

Meredith had been attacked late that morning, so Julian was in the clear.

"Okay, that's solved then. He couldn't have done it." Harriet was relieved, mostly because the act was thoroughly deplorable. She didn't like to think a client of hers would stoop so low.

"How thorough of you," Polly said to Van in open admiration.

Van grinned at her. "That's what I aim for. There's a connection between the two—Mrs. Bennett retired a few years ago from her job at the manor. Her insistence that she didn't recognize the assailant required further investigation. You could see she was petrified, even in the hospital where she should have felt safe."

"She was probably telling the truth," Harriet said. "Unless she was protecting someone else." *Carl?* A thrill ran through her. Carl was Meredith's granddaughter's friend, and Meredith likely knew Terry, since both had worked at the manor around the same time. "I have more."

Harriet relayed what Terry had said about his nephew during his appointment earlier. "I know Carl is friends with Stacey, because I've seen them together a few times." She mentioned witnessing their argument at the foot of the Cobble Hill driveway and their discussion earlier at the barn. "I got the impression from Julian that Carl spends a lot of time 'bothering' Stacey at the manor. Not sure what she thinks about it."

Van typed something into his tablet. "I might try to follow up on that."

"Terry told me Carl was questioned about the Ravenglen Manor heist due to an anonymous tip," Harriet said.

An uncomfortable expression crossed Van's face. "I really can't get into that."

"No need," Harriet assured him. "I wouldn't want you to compromise your professional integrity. I'm just saying it all fits. Maybe Carl terrorized Meredith and took the ring." How it ended up in Julian's bathroom was still a mystery.

Van typed on his tablet again. "Thanks, Harriet. I don't believe we've asked Mr. Evans for an alibi."

Polly nudged her boss. "I'm impressed, Harriet. Good work."

Harriet squirmed under the praise. "I didn't do anything. I put bits and pieces together, that's all."

"That's a large part of police work," Van said. "Making connections where others don't see them. Backed up by evidence, of course."

Speaking of evidence… "If you talk to Carl, maybe you should check his shoe size. Terry said it wasn't Carl outside the studio the other night, but who's to say he's telling the truth? It would be natural for him to want to protect Carl."

Van made another note. "Will do." He tucked his tablet away and stood. "And on that note, I'd better get back to work."

Polly got to her feet as well. "Thanks again for bringing lunch. I really enjoyed it."

Van flushed. "Anytime, Polly. See you soon. You as well, Harriet."

"Keep us posted," Harriet called as Van strode away. "As much as you're comfortable with, that is."

Once he was out of earshot around the corner of the house, Harriet grinned at Polly. "He's not so bad, is he?"

Ducking her head, Polly began gathering up the wrappers and stuffing them into the paper sack. "Go on with you. He's a friend, that's all."

Harriet didn't bother to argue. Instead, she hid her smile and helped Polly clean up the remains of the meal.

The afternoon ended up busier than Harriet expected, with Polly squeezing in a few more patients with Harriet's approval. Harriet was very aware that she was building her own reputation as well as cementing her grandfather's legacy. Timely, appropriate, and compassionate care had been his hallmark—and was now her aim.

Even as she dashed from one exam and treatment to the next, questions about the Ravenglen Manor heist lingered in her mind. Was Meredith involved? Or was she another innocent bystander like the Baileys? Harriet included herself in this because she'd had to deal with the chest in the dog yard.

Greed and the opportunity for wealth blinded people sometimes. No doubt whoever had buried the chest hadn't considered the impact on Harriet's family's reputation, or simply hadn't cared.

Besides Meredith, Carl seemed to be smack-dab in the middle of it all. Working at Ravenglen Manor. Friends with Stacey. Lurking around Cobble Hill.

He'd been in trouble before. Had he seen an opportunity he couldn't resist?

Or was he the fall guy for his uncle, who was also a central character in the saga? He'd worked at Ravenglen Hall at the time of the heist. A plumber's van was the perfect cover to hide nefarious activity while the owner was away.

Maybe Terry had stolen the jewelry and Carl had stumbled upon his cache. The rest of the jewelry might be gone, sold intact or stone by stone.

Harriet leaned her head against the exam room wall with a groan. One patient had exited, and she was supposed to go up front to greet the next.

"Are you all right?" Polly poked her head around the half-open door. "It has been a whirlwind. Sorry about that."

Harriet straightened. "I'm fine. I just got bogged down thinking about the case."

Polly bit her lip. "It's worrying me as well. It feels like the more we learn, the further away we are." She took a step into the room. "We should go visit Meredith this evening," she said in a low voice. "I've been meaning to take her something after her ordeal to show her that we care."

"You're absolutely right. We should have done something a long time ago." Harriet hadn't even sent a get-well card.

"Let me call for flowers or maybe a potted plant. We'll swing by and pick it up on the way." Polly glanced at the wall clock. "Meanwhile, you've got a poodle who needs a checkup."

Harriet forced her legs into action. "I'm coming." She touched Polly's elbow. "Thank you. For everything."

Polly smiled. "My pleasure." She hurried back to the front desk.

After they closed for the evening, Polly called Meredith to see if she was up for a visit. "She's excited to see us," Polly told Harriet after hanging up. "And so is Huntley."

"I'm excited to see them too." Harriet went to her bedroom, changed into jeans, and grabbed the Land Rover keys. They'd swing by the florist on the way and pick up the cheerful red geranium Polly had ordered.

When Meredith's cottage came into view shortly after passing the Ravenglen Manor gates, Harriet said, "Now I understand why Van asked Julian if he'd seen anything when Meredith was attacked." Her first time traveling out there, she'd been more focused on navigating the large, awkward vehicle along the narrow lane than studying her surroundings.

"I thought your theory was worth exploring," Polly said. "Meredith would be afraid to report Julian to the police. His word has a lot of weight around here."

"Alas, he has an alibi," Harriet said. "Not that I like thinking he would or could do such a thing. It was despicable."

"It was." Polly stared out the window at the passing scenery. "It's a good thing Pastor Will came along when he did."

"It really was." Harriet shuddered to think how long the older woman would have lain injured and helpless. She also ignored how her heart lifted at the mention of Will. She had enough mysteries to contend with right now without adding another about herself.

As Harriet pulled into the drive, she saw Huntley running around outside, barking. "That's strange," she said. Huntley's distressed behavior made her uneasy.

"Something's up," Polly said. As soon as the Land Rover halted, she was out the door.

Harriet was right behind her, and as soon as her feet landed, Huntley ran up, whining. "What is it, boy? Is your mistress okay?"

Polly put a finger to her lips, tilting her head toward the cottage. She began to move stealthily in that direction. Harriet followed.

Huntley ran ahead, stopping to look back as if urging them to hurry.

The front windows were wide open to the fresh air, and as they drew closer, a man's angry voice drifted from inside. Harriet and Polly edged behind bushes lining the cottage. Keeping their heads low, they peeked inside.

Harriet immediately recognized the young man looming over Meredith, who shrank back in her chair. She'd seen him on the seaside path and at Cliffside Chippy, always wearing the same black windbreaker.

He leaned forward and rested both hands on the arms of the chair, speaking right into Meredith's face. "Where is the rest of the jewelry? Don't give me any guff this time."

CHAPTER TWENTY-THREE

I'm calling the police." Polly hunkered down and dialed while Harriet watched the scene in horror, praying help would arrive quickly.

"Did your granddaughter take it?" the young man demanded.

Meredith pressed back against the chair, her face filled with fear. "What do you mean? She wasn't even born yet."

He pushed his chin forward. "Don't waste my time with that nonsense. The boss said his stuff is missing, and he charged me with finding out where it is."

Who was his boss? And was this the man who had attacked Meredith previously? Had he returned for another intimidation attempt?

"It's not here, I can tell you that much." Meredith's voice quavered as she lifted her hands and held them in front of her chest, trying to ward him off. "I'm begging you to believe me."

"We need to do something," Polly whispered. "We can't afford to wait until the police get here. He could hurt Meredith."

Harriet nodded. The man's anger seemed to be escalating, and they couldn't stand there and watch while he took his rage out on Meredith's belongings—or Meredith herself.

Maybe if they announced their arrival somehow, he would leave. Then they could question Meredith and get some answers.

Harriet had seen the man enough times that she could verify his identity once the police collared him. Or maybe there would be mug shots available, if he somehow evaded immediate capture.

There had to be a reason why he was questioning Meredith. Had she been involved in the original heist, as Harriet had come to suspect? Or maybe it was Stacey who was involved somehow. Stacey and Carl, perhaps. They both spent time at the manor on a regular basis. Shock tingled Harriet's spine. Had they found the cache of jewels from the heist and buried them in the dog yard?

"Why would I believe you?" the man growled. "You had that ring." He moved back slightly and stood, glancing around. "I've half a mind to tear this place apart."

"No, please don't." Meredith began to cry. "My home is all I have. Does it look like I'm rolling in money?"

His lip curled with scorn as he kicked at the rug. "Not with this tat." Harriet recognized the word for an item of low quality.

Meredith took the opportunity to stand up. "That's an antique, you oaf. Everyone doesn't like shiny new junk."

He took a step toward her, fist clenched. "Who are you calling an oaf?"

"We have to get in there." Polly's tone was decisive. She whispered a plan in Harriet's ear.

Hunched over, they ran out of the bushes, past the front door, and around the corner of the house. Huntley, thinking it was a game, trotted along eagerly.

"Pray it's unlocked," Polly whispered when they reached the back entrance. She reached for the knob, twisted it, and pushed.

The door swung open freely. Harriet hunkered down in front of Huntley. "Go help your mistress. Get the bad man." She ruffled his neck fur and gave him a gentle push.

Polly moved away from the opening as Huntley charged inside, barking his head off. A yelp followed by shouts sounded from inside.

"That's our cue," Polly said.

They ran into the cottage. In the front room, Huntley stood on the young man's chest.

"Get this monster off me," he cried, arms and legs waving.

"Don't thrash around like that, or he'll bite," Meredith said.

As if understanding, Huntley lowered his muzzle and growled. Harriet hadn't known the old dog had it in him.

The young man froze and stared up at the dog. "Don't let him bite me."

Polly picked up a fireplace poker and pointed it at the man. "Don't move. The police are on their way. Huntley, stay."

Meredith leaned against a wall, visibly trembling. "He forced his way in here. I was napping, so I thought it was a bad dream or a memory of what happened before."

"So this isn't the first time he's been here?" Harriet asked.

"I'm pretty sure he's the one who attacked me." Meredith held out her left hand. "He stole my wedding band right off my finger."

"It wasn't yours," the young man howled. "I was doing my job."

"Your job is attacking helpless women?" Polly's scowl was fierce. "You're a coward, aren't you? Lily-livered and spineless."

The young man groaned. Huntley growled again, and his prisoner fell silent.

"What's your name?" Polly asked. "And who sent you?"

The young man didn't answer.

Polly pointed the poker at him. "Wallet, please."

He didn't move until Polly poked him with the poker. "Hold on. Hold on." The young man dug a wallet from his back pocket with some difficulty, since he was lying on it, and tossed it onto the floor.

Harriet picked it up, flipped it open, and read the license. "Who sent you, Damien Vitty?"

Damien scowled. "I'd rather not say."

"The police will get it out of him," Meredith said with satisfaction. "You're going to go away for a long time, young man. Especially if you refuse to cooperate."

In light of Damien's comment about the ring, Harriet had a good idea who had hired him. Julian Montcliff, in search of the missing jewelry.

"You've been following me around, haven't you?" she asked. "It wasn't a coincidence when I saw you on the cliff path, was it?" Once while walking to church with her aunt and the other while eating fish and chips with Polly. There had also been moments at Cobble Hill when she'd sensed something or someone watching her from the bushes. Not to mention the time someone had spied on her through the studio window.

"I'd rather not say," he repeated, grumbling.

Harriet eyed his feet, which were clad in sneakers. They were of average size for a man. "I bet that was you at the window that night. We found your footprints." Perhaps Terry hadn't been lying when he said he didn't recognize the man. Van could use the cast to see if Damien's shoes matched.

Meredith gasped. "What nerve. Spying on a young woman."

"I was in my grandfather's art gallery," Harriet hastened to explain. "Damien is more interested in the missing jewelry than in me personally, I'm sure."

"I wanted to see what you were doing in there. I wasn't going to hurt you."

Polly huffed. "The way you didn't hurt Meredith, you brute?"

"It was an accident," Damien said. "She fell." He tried to peer past Huntley, who was still on top of him. "I'm sorry, ma'am," he told Meredith.

She sniffed, crossing her arms. "A bit late for that, isn't it?"

Harriet wasn't sure if his remorse was genuine, but it was a start. Now that he'd confessed to spying on her at the gallery, which meant he'd been lurking around Cobble Hill, she had another question. "Did you tell Julian I found the chest?" She'd heard something in the bushes that day. Maybe it hadn't been small wildlife after all.

Damien closed his eyes and didn't respond.

A siren whooped, and tires rumbled on the drive. "That'll be the police," Polly said.

Harriet rushed to greet Van, who was with Sergeant Oduba. "Am I glad to see you," she cried as she ran out the front door. "We caught the man who attacked Meredith."

"He's still here?" Van hurried up the path.

"Yes. Huntley and Polly are guarding him." Harriet pointed the way. "He's also the one who spied on me at the gallery. His name is Damien Vitty. We made him show us his ID."

She stood back to allow the officers to enter first. Although they hadn't found the missing valuables yet, Damien Vitty would soon be off the streets. He wouldn't be terrorizing Meredith Bennett again. Or anyone else, for that matter.

An hour later, when the statements had been taken and Damien Vitty had been hauled off to be booked, Harriet and Polly drank tea with Meredith at her kitchen table. Huntley slept in the corner, content after gobbling more treats than Harriet normally would have recommended, but he'd earned them.

"I can't believe it's over." Meredith lifted her cup with a shaking hand. "I haven't slept well since it happened."

"Don't blame you there," Polly said. "It's frightening to be attacked in your own home."

Meredith lowered the cup. "I'll never be able to thank you two enough. You were both so brave."

Harriet smiled at the snoring dog. "It was easy with Huntley in the lead. He's so protective."

"Damien lured him away with treats," Meredith said. "The police found the bag outside last time. Huntley is generally docile unless he believes I'm in danger, which never happened until recently."

"We hope it never does again," Polly said. "The whole thing was awful. I hope they figure out why he targeted you."

Meredith's lips twisted. "I have my suspicions."

Harriet did as well. If only Damien had told them who had hired him. Was it Julian, desperate to recover his missing jewelry? Or someone else with the same goal? Hopefully Damien would tell the police.

"Where's Stacey?" she asked. "Still working?" She would feel better about leaving if Stacey was there.

Meredith glanced at the clock, frowning. "I suppose so. She said she'd be here an hour ago." She picked up a cell phone, peering at it through her glasses. "I'll give her a ring." A moment later, she shook her head. "Right to voice mail. That isn't like her. She always answers her old gran."

A trickle of unease slithered down Harriet's spine. "Where is she working today?"

"At the manor. She's been spending a lot of time there with those horses. Julian can be demanding." Meredith pressed her lips together. "Cares more for his horses than people."

Apparently so, if he *had* hired Damien Vitty.

Now Harriet was really concerned. What if Damien had questioned Stacey before coming back to the cottage? Maybe even attacked her?

Polly picked up on Harriet's concern. "We can go over to the manor and check on her, if you'd like," she told Meredith.

"Would you, dear? I'll be fine here, now that the police have taken away my attacker."

"If you're sure," Polly said. "We can call someone else to stay with you."

The older woman shook her head. "I'll be fine." She patted Polly's hand. "Please go. I'm worried about my granddaughter. She's been acting strange lately."

"What do you mean?" Harriet asked. Terry had said the same thing about his nephew.

Meredith pursed her lips, frowning. "It's hard to describe, but I can tell she's keeping secrets from me. Going outside to take calls. Vague about where she's going or where she's been. I haven't seen that behavior since she was a teenager."

"Where does Carl Leaper fit in?" Harriet asked. "Are they close?"

The older woman was taken aback. "I should say not. They used to be friends when they were children, until Carl got in trouble. He's a bad 'un." Meredith snorted. "His uncle thinks he's turned over a new leaf, but I highly doubt it."

"That's too bad," Harriet said sincerely. She swallowed the last of her tea. "Thank you for this. We'll go see if Stacey is still at the manor and call you either way, Meredith. Promise."

Meredith's expression lightened. "Would you do that? I'd appreciate it. Tell her I'll be making her favorite meal tonight, steak and kidney pie."

"That would bring me home," Polly said as she stood. "We'll be in touch."

Harriet was thankful that the drive to Ravenglen Manor was short. She wasn't sure her nerves could take much more excitement. "Stacey is probably out in the field with the horses and didn't hear the phone."

"I hope so," Polly said. "I'm worried."

"So am I." Harriet's stomach churned at the thought that Stacey might be hurt or in danger.

The pillars bracketing Ravenglen Manor's drive appeared, and Harriet hit the brakes, slowing rapidly to make the turn. Nothing like an emergency or two to banish driving nerves. She had more important concerns on her mind.

"She's here." Stacey's little sedan sat near the stables, next to a shiny, newer Land Rover. Harriet pulled up beside it, feeling like the poor country cousin in contrast.

"I'm going to tell Julian we're here," Harriet said as they got out. "Rather than go in unannounced." She was reluctant to roam around a client's property without his knowledge or permission.

She jogged to the back door and knocked. No one came.

"Maybe he's not home," Polly suggested.

"Could be. I want to try one more thing." Harriet gestured. "Come with me."

They followed the path through the garden and around the house. If Julian wasn't in the kitchen, he was probably in his study. If not, she would go ahead and talk to Stacey in the barn and apologize later.

As they drew closer to the study, Harriet noticed the French doors standing open to the soft afternoon air. Julian was probably inside, working.

Then she heard a woman shouting, the words indistinct at this distance.

"What is this, a trend?" Polly muttered.

Harriet put up a hand, indicating they should slow down. She wanted to get the lay of the land before barging in.

Climbing clematis in containers framed the door, providing cover as they crept closer. A quick peek inside revealed a shocking sight.

Julian sat in a chair, his wrists and feet tied, while Yvonne Ellerby stood over him, rage twisting her lovely features. "Tell me where it is!" she shouted. "I know you have it."

"Yvonne, please." His voice was placating. "I've told you over and over. I don't have it. It was stolen."

Harriet bit back a gasp. Had Yvonne hired Damien to find the emerald and diamond necklace? Judging by the scene she'd made at Aunt Jinny's, she still believed it should be hers.

Yvonne clenched her fists. "So you say. Very convenient that you wanted to keep it for *cleaning*. I know the truth, Julian." She stomped one well-shod foot. "You lied to me."

Harriet touched Polly's elbow. "Let's go." She didn't need to stand there and listen any further. Even though Julian was restrained, he didn't appear to be in any danger. They should call Van and have him come over rather than confront Yvonne themselves. One confrontation in a day was enough.

Harriet breathed more easily once they were away from the house.

"That woman is mad," Polly said.

"Agreed," Harriet replied. "The injustice of it all has obviously been festering for decades." She pulled out her phone and called the police. The dispatcher again promised to send an officer right away.

Before going into the stables, Harriet stopped beside the new Land Rover, which had to be Yvonne's, judging by the expensive handbag tossed on the passenger seat. The keys were still in the ignition.

Harriet opened the door and grabbed the keys. "This will slow her down if she tries to leave before the police arrive." She tucked them into her pocket.

The stables were dark and quiet. Through the open doors at the end, Harriet saw the horses grazing in the pasture beyond. Lady appeared well, tail flicking as she cropped grass.

Harriet looked around. Where could Stacey be? Then she saw light coming from the open door of the tack room. "This way."

Their footsteps fell softly on the old wooden boards, and Stacey came into view as they approached. Busy unscrewing a riding trophy from the base, she didn't even glance up when they reached the doorway of the windowless room. She tossed the cup portion aside then poured a glittering heap of jewelry from the base into a leather train case.

Harriet knew beyond a shadow of a doubt that they'd found the missing portion of the Ravenglen Manor collection.

Stacey tossed the base onto the floor and reached for another trophy, repeating her actions.

Harriet's mouth went dry. Maybe they should step away and wait. Van was on his way. He could deal with Stacey. As if reading her mind, Polly stepped behind the doorframe, where Stacey couldn't see her.

Before Harriet could do the same, Stacey raised her head and made eye contact. Her mouth fell open. "It's not what it looks like."

"What is it then?" Harriet asked, keeping her voice level. She didn't want to escalate the situation.

The stable hand's face flushed a deep red as she poured the jewelry into the case. She retrieved the cup half of the trophy, holding it in both hands.

"Julian paid a man to harass my grandmother. This is payback."

So, Stacey knew about Damien—and Julian had hired Damien after all. "He's been arrested. Damien, I mean. Your grandmother is safe. In fact, she's eager for you to come home for dinner. She says steak and kidney pie is your favorite."

Stacey's gaze wavered. "I had the opportunity for a really posh job, working for a relative of the royal family. Julian wouldn't write me a reference, even though he knows them."

"That's awful," Harriet said. Polly stayed quiet, tapping on her phone. Stacey obviously hadn't seen her yet. Harriet guessed Polly was texting Van. "He was wrong for that."

"Yes, he was." Stacey inhaled a deep breath. "Nana told me everything. Julian planned the heist. He had my grandfather steal the jewelry. After he put in the insurance claim, it all came right back here to Ravenglen Manor."

"He paid them off, didn't he?" Harriet said. "With a house, a ring, even a Royal Dux figurine, maybe?"

Stacey grunted in agreement. "All kinds of things. Nothing extremely valuable, of course. He kept the good stuff for himself, even though my grandparents were the ones who took the risk. Not that it did him any good. He hasn't been able to display any of it since, and he loves to show off."

"Did your grandmother know where he kept the jewelry?" Harriet was curious.

Stacey shook her head. "He had it very well hidden in the cellars. Carl helped me find it."

"The chest was Carl's share," Harriet guessed. It made sense. Carl had stolen the jewelry from Julian's cellar and buried it in the dog yard, and Julian had hired Damien to track it down. Stacey had hidden her share of the jewels in the trophies. Huntley and Harriet's discovery of the chest was a random happenstance.

Stacey nodded. "The police are getting too close. That's why I have to get out of here."

As if they could let her leave with stolen goods.

They had to stall until the police arrived, which should be any minute. Van would be thrilled to make the arrest and recover the missing jewels.

"Once I'm done here," Stacey said, "I'm going to go pick up Nana, and we'll head out. Soon we'll be living in our own place, away from Julian and everyone else."

Harriet started to wonder why Stacey would tell her all this. Surely she was aware Harriet would send the police after her. If they weren't already on their way.

Then she had the answer. Stacey suddenly flung the heavy cup at Harriet. "Don't think you're going to stop me," she yelled.

Harriet barely had time to dodge away from the heavy object, which glanced off her shoulder and thumped to the floor.

Polly pounced, grabbed Harriet's arm, and pulled her out of the doorway. She pushed the tack room door shut, trapping Stacey inside, and twisted the key still in the lock. "There. That should keep her."

Stacey began to hammer on the door. "Let me out."

"No way," Harriet shouted back. She rubbed her shoulder. "Ouch."

"I'm glad it wasn't your head," Polly said, ever practical.

Running footsteps sounded in the main aisle of the stable. Harriet whirled, expecting to see Van.

Instead, Yvonne charged toward them. "Someone stole my keys," she screeched. "Was it you?"

Harriet wasn't about to answer that before the police arrived.

"We can help you search for them," Polly said, her voice all innocence.

Stacey pounded on the tack room door. "Help! Let me out."

Yvonne startled. "What's going on?" She went to the door and tried to open it. "It's locked."

"We know," Harriet said. "Stacey Bennett and Carl Evans stole the jewelry from Ravenglen Manor."

The vet's wife rocked back on her high heels. "They did? How? When? They're not old enough." Understanding dawned in her eyes. "From Julian, you mean. I was right. He had the jewelry all along, didn't he? An insurance dodge. He blamed a crime ring and said we'd never see any of it again." Her laugh was bitter. "I knew it."

"That's about the size of it," Harriet said. "We think," she added, wanting to be cautious.

Yvonne tugged on the door again. "Is my necklace in there?"

"Let me out, and I'll tell you," Stacey replied.

Harriet and Polly rolled their eyes at each other. "She's not getting out, and you're not touching the jewelry," Harriet said. "If the necklace hasn't been sold, you can try to make a claim."

"That's not fair," Yvonne whined. "It was a gift. Dozens of people saw him give it to me."

Harriet had seen the photographs, but there was also the matter of Yvonne tying up her former fiancé. Harriet thought that might hurt her claim.

"Did you see the key?" Yvonne demanded.

"To the tack room?" Polly asked, once again all innocence.

Harriet suppressed a grin. She'd seen Polly put the key in her pocket.

Yvonne began scanning the floor. "Where is it?" She ran back and forth.

Leaving her to it, Harriet and Polly made their way to the front entrance.

"Van should be here any minute," Harriet said, squinting toward the road.

"Good," Polly murmured. "The key is burning a hole in my pocket."

Harriet patted her jeans. "And the car keys in mine."

A siren blipped once, and tires crunched on the gravel.

"There he is." Overcome by a rush of relief, Harriet gave Polly a big hug. "We did it. We solved the case." It felt like a huge dark cloud hovering over her head had finally lifted.

Polly squeezed her in return. "We make a great team, don't we? You, me, Van, and Dr. Garrett."

Letting go, Harriet waved at the police car as Van rolled to a stop. "Yes, we do, Polly. And I couldn't be happier."

CHAPTER TWENTY-FOUR

arriet?" Aunt Jinny called up the stairs. "Are you ready to go?"

"Almost," Harriet called back. She stood in front of the full-length mirror, trying to decide whether she liked her outfit. What did one wear to a church fete? Jeans and a T-shirt were far too informal, so she'd dug out a floral sundress. Then she'd had to iron it and find something to cover her bare shoulders.

Her cropped, lacy white cardigan would work, she decided as she tweaked it into place.

Footsteps sounded, and Aunt Jinny appeared in the doorway. She also wore a dress and had added a pink boater, tipped at an angle and trimmed with flowers. "You are lovely." She glanced at Harriet's feet in sandals. "I'll drive."

Harriet laughed, remembering the last time she'd traversed the cliff path wearing inadequate footwear. "Great. Thank you." She indicated her aunt's hat. "Do I need something on my head? I don't think I have a suitable hat."

Aunt Jinny shook her head. "No, you're fine without." She touched the hat brim. "I like an excuse to wear this."

Now that Julian Montcliff doesn't have parties anymore. Last Harriet had heard, he had been charged with insurance fraud. If ordered to repay the claim, he'd be selling the jewelry collection or the manor for real this time.

Harriet picked up the clutch that held her phone and keys. "I'm ready."

She had also learned the answer to her last remaining question. After the jewels disappeared from his cellar, Julian had charged Damien with keeping an eye on activity in the village. He was to watch for anything of interest, such as an attempt to sell stolen goods reported to the police. The day the chest was found, Damien had witnessed Van's rapid response to a call and followed him to Cobble Hill. He'd hidden and watched Van, Harriet, and Aunt Jinny through binoculars. When he saw the telltale sparkle of jewels, he had called Julian, who then rushed to Cobble Hill.

Stacey and Carl had also been charged with theft. More details had come out regarding their discovery of Julian's hidden safe in the cellar. After hearing her grandmother's confession about the heist, Stacey had made it her mission to search the manor whenever she had a chance. When she'd found the safe, she'd alerted Carl, who often worked on the plumbing down there and was able to break in.

Julian couldn't do anything if they took the jewels, Stacey had reasoned. He'd already reported them stolen and had benefited from his deception. He couldn't report them stolen again.

Since he could no longer afford to keep them, his horses were being adopted, with the assistance of Harriet and the other vets. They'd go to good homes where they would continue to be cared for.

Meredith was fully cooperating with the investigation. According to Van, she would likely receive a suspended sentence due to her age. She had told the police that she'd had the milkmaid figurine from the collection and used it to pay her vet bill.

Damien Vitty faced breaking and entering and assault charges. Julian claimed to be appalled by his hired hand's actions, saying he'd merely wanted information. The truth of that statement was for the courts to sort out.

Harold Bailey and all the residents of Cobble Hill were well and truly cleared. As Harriet had suspected, Carl had buried the chest in the dog yard while the clinic was shut down. Because neither Stacey nor Carl was an experienced thief, they each hid their portion of the loot until they could figure out how to sell it. And when Stacey saw Yvonne Ellerby at Ravenglen Manor, she figured she should take the part she'd stolen and run. Unfortunately for Carl, Huntley had found his before he could retrieve it.

As for Yvonne, Julian had declined to press charges. It was still unknown whether she would be able to claim the necklace gifted to her so many decades before. The last Harriet had heard, it had been found intact. That would be quite the belated birthday gift if Yvonne was allowed to keep it.

The church parking lot was already filling up when they arrived. "A good turnout," Aunt Jinny commented. "We should raise a lot of money today." Funds from church events supported repairs to the building and other local charities.

Harriet's stomach clenched with anxiety. A lot of people attending meant many ears listening when she gave her little speech. She hastily opened her bag to make sure she'd brought her notes. Yes, there they were, a slip of folded paper tucked in the corner. Imagining the scene, her anxiety went up a notch. Why on earth had she agreed to a public welcome? Wasn't it enough that her name had been in the paper in connection with the chest and then the solving of the case?

"I'm nervous," she confessed as Aunt Jinny slid into a parking spot.

"About your speech?" Aunt Jinny shut off the car. "You'll do fine."

"I hope so." Harriet would be glad when the ordeal was over. Until then, she'd try not to think about it.

The fete was on the church grounds, with white canopies set on the lawn under huge shade trees and more activities inside the church hall. People milled about, sampling food, buying crafts, and playing games. Laughter, chatter, and instrumental folk music filled the air.

"Hello, Harriet, Dr. Garrett." Polly joined them, Van beside her. She wore a pretty dress, and her dark hair flowed over her shoulders in graceful waves. Van was out of uniform, handsome in a blue button-down shirt and pressed slacks.

The foursome exchanged greetings as they strolled toward the fete. "What a gorgeous day," Polly said. "Couldn't ask for better weather."

Harriet tipped her head back to study the deep blue sky. "No, you couldn't."

"Want me to try my luck at the coconut shy?" Van asked Polly, motioning to a nearby game. He flexed one arm. "I'll win you a prize."

Polly laughed. "Sure. I'd like the teddy bear." The stuffed bear was adorable with his bow tie and friendly smile.

The point of the game was to toss wooden balls at coconuts balanced on posts and try to knock them off. Harriet glanced around, noticing several other traditional games. She'd hopped along in many a sack race in her childhood.

Van took aim, winding up as though to throw a cricket ball.

"Good morning, Harriet," Will called as he approached them. "What do you think of our little event?"

"I love it," Harriet said. "It reminds me of my visits as a child. The fete was always on the agenda."

"We do have the best cake," Will said. "You'll have to try a slice."

"I will later." Harriet's stomach was still queasy with anticipation. Polly clapped and cheered when Van knocked off a coconut.

"He's good. I've seen him in action before." Will faced Harriet. "I was thinking of moving up your welcome."

Harriet's stomach churned. "To when?"

He glanced at his watch. "Right now? Then I'll say the grace for lunch."

"Okay," Harriet said. "Show me where to go." At least she'd be getting it over with and could enjoy the fete sooner. Not to mention a piece of cake.

Harriet heard Polly cheer again then walked away with Will. Van would win that teddy bear yet.

Will led Harriet to the main tent, right in the middle of the grounds. This was where the luncheon would be served. Volunteers hurried around, putting out platters of sandwiches and bowls of salads and large vats of soup.

At one end, a microphone stood on a podium. Will took his position there and picked up a large bell. He rang it then said into the microphone, "May I have your attention, everyone?" He waited until the crowd quieted, many people moving closer to the tent or right under it.

Polly and Van slipped in, the teddy bear in Polly's arms and huge smiles on both of their faces. Aunt Jinny stood with them, along with Anthony and his family. There were the Danbys, and Harriet recognized other faces in the crowd. Her heart warmed when she also spotted the group of vets, touched they'd made the effort after her involvement with getting one of their wives arrested.

Agnes, resplendent in a wide-brimmed hat, replaced Will at the microphone. "Good morning, everyone." Her voice rang out over the grounds. "Welcome to our summer fete. We're so glad to have you all here with us. Thank you to our planning committee for their masterful work." She reeled off a list of names. "And to our wonderful minister, Pastor Will."

She clapped for the people she'd mentioned, and everyone followed suit.

Once the applause died down, she went on. "Today I have a very special guest, a newcomer to our community, though she's hardly a stranger. Dr. Harriet Bailey spent many of her childhood summers visiting her grandfather, our beloved Dr. Harold Bailey. Even more special is that Harriet is following in his large footsteps, having taken over Cobble Hill Vet Clinic. Early indications are that she is every bit as competent, skilled, and sure to be beloved as her grandfather. Everyone, please give a hearty welcome to our very own Dr. Harriet Bailey."

The applause was thunderous, and Barry Tweedy bellowed, "Hear, hear," as Agnes moved aside to let Harriet take the microphone.

Once it died down, Harriet said, "What a wonderful welcome, Agnes and the rest of you." She ignored her notes and spoke from her heart. "I'm so glad to be here in White Church Bay, to have the opportunity to serve you as your veterinarian. I see a lot of old friends—and I hope many new ones as well. Some of my most cherished memories occurred right here growing up, and I look forward to creating many more. I know my grandad would be delighted but not surprised that you've welcomed me so warmly. He always spoke of his community with pride and hoped I would join it someday. Thank you for making that possible. I can't wait to serve you and your pets to the best of my ability. Now let's eat."

Everyone laughed as Will returned to the microphone to lead grace.

As Harriet bowed her head, she added under her breath, "Thank You, Lord, for Your guidance and for making my paths straight. I am so grateful. Amen."

As she raised her head, her eyes met Will's. He extended an elbow. "May I escort you to the buffet table? Fine dining awaits."

Laughing, she took his arm. "Thank you, kind sir."

Harriet's heart soared as they stepped across the grass to get in line. She was home at last.

FROM THE AUTHOR

Dear Reader,

Welcome to our beautiful setting of White Church Bay, a (fictional) historic Yorkshire village on the coast of England! I was especially excited to write in this series due to my own family history. Like our main character, Harriet Bailey, I'm an American with British roots.

My mother hails from King's Lynn, Norfolk, about one hundred and fifty miles directly south of where White Church Bay would be located. Her hometown is also on the coast, and farming plays a prominent role in the economy there as well. I've never had such good root vegetables than are grown in England's rich soil! My grandmother worked the land all her life, and she rode a bicycle well into her eighties. Mum met Dad in King's Lynn, at a historical hotel and gathering place. The man she was waiting for never arrived—and soon my beautiful mother was being chatted up by a handsome US Air Force officer from Queens, New York. The rest, as they say, is history.

While all of England is beautiful and picturesque, there is something special about Yorkshire with its dramatic coastline, quaint villages, and sweeping moors. This region is also rich in history and natural wonders, and having a veterinarian as our main character is especially interesting and heartwarming. As the author of the first book in the Mysteries of Cobble Hill Farm series, I'm thrilled to present *Digging Up Secrets*. I hope you love this series as much as I do.

Signed,

Elizabeth Penney

ABOUT THE AUTHOR

Elizabeth Penney is the Mary Higgins Clark–nominated author of more than three dozen mysteries, women's fiction, and romantic suspense novels.

Raised in Maine, Elizabeth spent her early years in England and France. She now lives in the mountains of New Hampshire, where she enjoys walking in the woods, kayaking on quiet ponds, trying new recipes, and feeding family and friends. Oh, and trying to grow things in the frozen North.

TRUTH BEHIND THE FICTION

A real crime inspired the plot of *Digging Up Secrets*. When I'm plotting a book, I do a ton of research. Not only do I want to get the details right about the locale, but I want the crime to be plausible.

This crime never happened. But it could have.

In 1946, the Duke and Duchess of Windsor, who had been living in Europe, returned to England for a visit. They stayed with the Earl of Dudley at Ednam Lodge in Berkshire. While they were on an overnight trip to London, jewelry and other valuables were stolen from their quarters. A maid discovered the theft, and it was believed that the culprits had entered the house through an open window. Some of the items were found scattered around the green of a nearby golf course.

Rumors abounded regarding the heist, with suspects ranging from the household servants, professional thieves, other members of the royal family, and the Duke of Windsor himself. Why weren't the valuables stored in one of Ednam Lodge's two safes? Why were the royals' quarters left unlocked? Some felt that the Windsors were all but asking to be robbed.

The insurance company paid out without quibbling. Over eighty years later, the crime remains unsolved. The present-day value of the stolen items is over ten million dollars.

Lucky for us, the Ravenglen Manor heist has been solved by our intrepid sleuth, Dr. Harriet Bailey.

Doreen Danby's Apricot Scones

Doreen Danby's apricot scones are a White Church Bay favorite. She makes classic cream scones, which makes them light, tender, and delicious.

Ingredients:

2 cups flour

¼ cup sugar

2½ teaspoons baking powder

¼ teaspoon salt

4 tablespoons salted butter, cut into pieces

½ cup dried apricots, chopped

½ cup heavy cream, plus a tablespoon to glaze the top

Directions:

1. Preheat oven to 425 degrees. Line pan with parchment paper, if preferred, to help with cleanup.
2. Whisk flour, sugar, baking powder, and salt in bowl.
3. Use pastry cutter to cut in butter pieces until mixture resembles large crumbs.
4. Stir in apricot pieces, mix well, and then add cream a little at a time until mixture is moist. If still crumbly and dry, add more cream a spoonful at a time.

5. With clean hands, gather dough and place on lightly floured surface. Knead half a dozen times then pat out and use round cutter or place in pie pan to shape and then cut wedges.

6. Place cut pieces on baking sheet (ungreased if not using parchment paper). Brush tops with cream. Bake for 12 to 15 minutes or until lightly golden. Let cool for ten minutes and serve either warm or at room temperature.

7. Enjoy with clotted cream and your choice of jam or jelly.

*Read on for a sneak peek of another exciting book
in the* Mysteries of Cobble Hill Farm *series!*

Hide and Seek

BY BETH ADAMS

Harriet Bailey slowed and steered the old Land Rover into the driveway. She bumped over the dirt and veered toward the entrance to Cobble Hill Vet Clinic, which was attached to the side of the house. Surrounded by lush gardens and sweeping views over the moors, the stately brick estate in the Yorkshire countryside had belonged to her grandfather, and Harriet still couldn't believe she got to live there now. The late Monday afternoon sunshine gilded the roses, delphinium, and foxglove in the garden, creating a riot of colors behind the low garden wall. She'd moved to England to take over her grandfather's veterinary practice, and it all still felt like a dream.

Harriet parked the Land Rover next to the clinic entrance. She paused to thank the Lord for bringing her to White Church Bay, as she had hundreds of times since her move. Then she hoisted her bag from the back, climbed out of the vehicle, and stepped inside the clinic. Two people sat in the waiting area and she greeted them with a smile. She recognized the woman, and there was also a man she didn't know with a beautiful bloodhound at his feet. She didn't recall a bloodhound on the schedule today, so maybe he was a walk-in.

"How did it go?" Polly Thatcher asked from behind the receptionist's desk. In her midtwenties, Polly had gray eyes and dark hair, and had worked for Harriet's grandfather before her. Harriet didn't know where she'd be without her energetic assistant. Charlie, the calico office cat, perched on the counter.

"A strained ligament," Harriet said. "The horse needs to rest. No jumping for a month or so, and I left some other instructions as well." She stroked Charlie's head as she walked past.

"I bet Mr. Phillips didn't love that."

"I think he realized that, all things considered, a few weeks off is a pretty good outcome. It could have been much worse, even permanent. And he knows that if he pushes it, he's likely to be dealing with that," Harriet said. She loved animals of all kinds, and Angel the Hanoverian horse was beautiful and well-tempered. Angel had done well at horse shows, judging by the ribbons Mr. Phillips displayed along the back wall of the stable. "She should be fine as long as Mr. Phillips follows my instructions. And she's important to him, so I think he will."

"I'm glad to hear that." Polly beckoned to the man with the bloodhound. "Mr. Osbourne, if you'll follow me, I'll get you set up in a room."

The man who stood was probably in his midfifties, with salt-and-pepper hair and a black T-shirt over his dirty jeans. "Come on," he said to the bloodhound, and the dog obeyed and followed him toward the door Polly held open. Harriet noticed the dog wasn't on a leash. He didn't even have a collar, actually.

Polly closed the door behind them, and Harriet smiled at Sahaana Mehta. She had glasses and long dark hair threaded with gray, and she wore a baggy cardigan over her long, flowered sari.

"I'll be with you in a moment, Mrs. Mehta," Harriet said, stepping forward to pet the woman's black lab, Pitch. He licked her hand. "How's this guy doing?"

"Poorly," Sahaana said, her brow creased with concern. "He's been sick and sluggish lately. I think he ate something that disagrees with him."

"Well, we'll bring you back and get it worked out in a few minutes," Harriet promised. According to what Polly had told her, Pitch regularly ate things that made him sick. "We'll get him fixed up."

"Thank you." Sahaana patted the dog's head. "I appreciate it."

"It's what we're here for," Harriet said. She stepped through the door and into the rear of the clinic. Maxwell, the clinic's resident long-haired dachshund, rushed over to greet her, the wheels of his prosthesis squealing.

"Hey, buddy." Maxwell gazed up at her, his tail wagging as his tongue hung out, and she reached down to pet him.

"Mr. Osbourne is in Room Two," Polly said.

"Thank you," said Harriet. "What's the dog's name?"

"He doesn't know."

"What?"

"He'll explain." Polly pressed her lips together. "I'm pretty sure it's Coleridge though."

"Coleridge?"

Polly flapped a hand at her. "I'm getting ahead of myself. I'll let Mr. Osbourne tell you what's going on."

"Okay." Harriet didn't know what to make of the exchange, as it wasn't like Polly to be cryptic. But she stepped inside the exam room and smiled at the man who sat in the wooden chair kept for clients, the dog at his feet. "Good morning. I'm Dr. Bailey."

"Archie Osbourne." He stood and offered his hand to shake, even as he ducked his head shyly. "You're Old Doc Bailey's grand-daughter, is that right?"

Harriet shook his hand. "That's right. Did you know my grandfather?"

"Everybody knew him. He was a wonderful man."

"Thank you," Harriet said. "He really was one of a kind. I've got some big shoes to fill."

"We're glad you're here," Mr. Osbourne told her.

"And who's this?" Harriet bent down and held out her hand so the dog could sniff her and then stroked his head.

"I don't actually know," Mr. Osbourne said. "I'm a gardener, and I was working in Miss Birtwhistle's rose beds when this guy came wandering down the street."

There were several things that were surprising about this, not the least of which was the fact that Miss Jane Birtwhistle, a local cat lover Harriet had become acquainted with, had a gardener help her with her famous roses. But why would a dog like this be wandering the streets alone? If she was right in guessing that he was a purebred bloodhound, he was worth quite a bit. He was in good health, with no signs of contusions or dehydration. He couldn't have been on his own for too long, and he looked well cared for.

"He didn't have a collar, and there was no one with him," Mr. Osbourne continued. "I worried he was lost, so I brought him here to see if he had a microchip."

"That was good thinking," Harriet said. "Let's check it out." She opened a cabinet, took out the handheld scanner, and then reached for the loose skin on the dog's neck. The dog shifted his weight but otherwise didn't seem fazed as she felt along his skin. "I'm afraid I'm not feeling a chip."

"Oh dear," he said. "Well, I'm not really sure what to do with him, in that case."

"Hang on. Polly thought she recognized him. Let's see what she thinks." Harriet opened the door and called for Polly, who came quickly. "I didn't find a chip," Harriet said. "But you thought you recognized the dog, didn't you?"

"It's Coleridge," Polly said. "Liam Beresford's dog. He's been bringing Coleridge here since he was a puppy."

Harriet wasn't sure if she imagined the way Mr. Osbourne's eyes widened when he heard the name. She had never heard of Liam Beresford, but she was sure he would want his dog back.

"That makes it easy," Harriet said. "Why don't we call him and let him know we've got his dog here?"

"Sure thing," Polly said. "I'll do that now." She hurried away.

"Thank you for bringing him in," Harriet said to Mr. Osbourne. "I'm grateful you took the time to do it, and I think Mr. Beresford will be as well."

"I didn't want anything to happen to him," Mr. Osbourne said, scuffing the toe of his boot against the floor. "I feel sort of responsible for the dog until his owner's been notified."

They chatted for a few moments. Mr. Osbourne told Harriet how her grandfather, an esteemed artist as well as veterinarian, had taught his son to paint a decade before. Harriet loved hearing such stories about Grandad's influence on those around him.

Polly returned and poked her head into the exam room. "There was no answer at the Beresford place. I left a message."

"Does Liam have a cell phone?" Harriet asked.

"If he does, the number isn't in our records," Polly said. "So hopefully he'll return our call soon. I've put Mrs. Mehta in Room One."

"Guess I should get back to Miss Birtwhistle's roses," Mr. Osbourne said, gazing down at Coleridge. "Will you be all right, buddy?"

"He's safe here, Mr. Osbourne. We'll get him home," Harriet assured him.

"Thanks, Doc," he replied.

"No problem. I need to go check on Pitch. Polly, would you walk Mr. Osbourne out?"

Harriet walked to the other exam room and chatted with Sahaana while she examined Pitch. Sahaana had noticed something was off that morning when he didn't bound out the door and then refused to eat his breakfast.

"He chewed on some crab shells down at the beach yesterday," Sahaana said. "So it could have been that. Then again, he was also nosing around in the garden, and he could have found anything there."

"I'll give you some antinausea pills, which will get him right back on his feet," Harriet said.

"Thank you." Sahaana peered up at Harriet through glasses that made her eyes appear larger than they were. "You know, I was worried when I heard how young you were. I thought there was no way someone in their early thirties could hold a candle to Old Doc Bailey, but you're every bit as good as he was."

"Thank you." Harriet smiled at the backhanded compliment. "My grandfather was a great man and a great veterinarian. So that means a lot."

A parade of dogs and cats and a pet parakeet kept Harriet busy, and when it was time to close late that afternoon, she found Coleridge behind the desk, next to Maxwell. The clinic's resident pup was delighted to have a friend, but Coleridge was pointedly ignoring the little dog. Charlie was perched on the counter, her tail swishing back and forth.

"Did Coleridge's owner call?" Harriet asked Polly.

"Not yet," Polly said.

Harriet could board him in the kennels on the property if needed, but she would prefer to reunite the dog with his owner, who no doubt missed him. In fact, it was entirely possible that they hadn't heard from Mr. Beresford because he was out searching for Coleridge and hadn't been home to check his messages. "I assume we have Mr. Beresford's address in our records, right? Maybe I'll go drop Coleridge off."

"I bet he would appreciate that," Polly said. "And you should check his house out anyway. Your place here is really nice, but his is something else entirely."

"What do you mean?"

"It's the Beresford house," Polly said, as if that would mean something to Harriet.

"Yes," Harriet replied. "I assumed that was where Liam Beresford would live."

Polly shook her head. "No, it's Beresford Manor. As in, the home of Lord Beresford. The Baron Beresford, formally."

Why was she using his last name so much? "You mean, he's, like, royalty?"

"Not exactly." Polly laughed. "Sometimes I forget you're American, but then sometimes it's so hilariously obvious. He's a baron. That's a title of nobility. It's just below viscount."

"Oh. Okay."

Polly looked like she was about to explain but then shook her head and said, "The point is, he lives at Beresford Manor, which is the house that accompanies the title. It passes down from one baron to the next, along with the money made from the land, to whoever inherits that title. The place is huge and old, literally from another time. And if you haven't seen it yet, you really should check it out. If you thought Ravenglen Manor was something, wait till you get a look at this place."

Ravenglen Manor was the estate of Julian Montcliff, who had recently been charged with insurance fraud by staging a jewel heist of his own collection decades ago.

"Where is it?" Harriet asked, wondering if she'd passed by it at some point without knowing it.

"Outside of town a little ways, to the north, opposite direction of Ravenglen Manor, and perched on top of a cliff. It's set back a bit, so you can't see it from town, but it's there."

"Can you get me the address?"

"Sure, but you won't need it. Just drive north from town until you get to the stop sign and turn right. You'll drive for a while before the road curves around some sheep in a field, past the old elm, and it's there. You can't miss it."

It sounded simple enough, but she still programmed the address listed in the clinic's computers into her phone. She'd learned that what seemed like simple directions to the people who'd grown up in White Church Bay didn't necessarily end up being simple to someone new to driving on the left side of the road.

She brought Charlie and Maxwell through the door to her house and filled their bowls, and then she led Coleridge out of the clinic and to the van. She'd been worried he wouldn't follow without a leash, but the dog walked behind her obediently. She opened the side door of the Land Rover and settled the dog inside, put the Beast in gear, looked both ways, and pulled out onto the road.

Cobble Hill Farm, the property her grandfather had called home, was a beautiful estate, holding not only the house Harriet had inherited and the veterinary practice, but the dower cottage and grounds that her aunt Jinny had inherited from her father and where she lived and saw patients as a general practitioner.

And just across the vet clinic's parking area sat the old outbuilding that Grandad had turned into his art studio and gallery. In his later years, he'd become known for his paintings nearly as much as his veterinary practice.

The low stone wall that separated the estate from the road was covered with spots of green lichen and bits of moss that only made it look more charming. Oaks and hawthorns arched over the roadway, and the neighboring houses quickly gave way to pastoral farmland as she drove north, away from the village of White Church Bay.

Harriet turned right at the stop sign and followed the curve, past woolly sheep grazing on the hills. Sure enough, a huge old elm tree with a thick, knotty trunk and strong arms that spread a green canopy over the road was just up ahead. She drove past the elm and kept going for a few miles before she came to a long driveway off to the right.

She'd been past the place a few times since she'd moved to White Church Bay but had never really noticed it. The property wasn't as easy to spot as Polly had promised. But once she turned into the driveway, she saw that it was lined on both sides with more elms and wound around a gently sloping hillside, past a pond, until eventually the house came into view. Coleridge began to thump his tail and howl when he saw the house. He knew he was home.

And what a home it was. She'd been expecting a big house, based on Polly's description, but this was next-level. The three-story manor was built in gold-colored stone with peaked gables on both sides of the facade and dozens of mullioned windows. Half a dozen stout chimneys rose from the roof, and a circular driveway fronted the house, which was surrounded by rolling green fields. Harriet could see formal gardens and several outbuildings beyond the house, and sweet peas and phlox and delphinium bloomed in the beds surrounding the driveway.

She parked in the section of the driveway that bowed a bit and stepped out uncertainly. There were two other cars there, a compact sedan with several dents and dings, and a sleek black Bentley. They looked incongruous, side by side, and her battered old Land Rover only added to the discord. She let Coleridge out and headed for the front entrance. The massive door—painted a dark blue and framed by a stone pediment—was imposing, which she supposed was probably the intent. There was a doorbell, so she pushed the button and waited. She didn't hear anything inside the house and had started to wonder if she should ring again when the door flew open. An older woman in jeans and a flowered top stood there, staring back at her.

"Oh. Hello," the woman said. As Coleridge pushed his way inside, she added, "Coleridge? Where have you been?"

"I'm Harriet Bailey," Harriet said to the woman, who looked thoroughly confused by what was happening. "I'm the new vet in town. I took over the practice from my grandfather, Harold Bailey." The woman nodded, but Harriet could tell it wasn't entirely registering.

"Someone found this dog in the village and brought him to me, hoping I could find the owner," Harriet continued. "Polly, who works with me, recognized him and said he lives here."

"He does indeed," the woman said. "But where's Lord Beresford?"

"Excuse me?"

"Lord Beresford. He wasn't with the dog?"

"No," Harriet said. "At least, not since I've had him."

"That's very strange," the woman said. She seemed to be in something of a daze.

"I assume that means he's not at home?" Harriet said. Coleridge sniffed about the foyer.

"Oh, yes. I'm sorry. This is all very confusing, but I—" She shook her head. "Please, come in." She gestured for Harriet to step inside and then closed the door behind her. They stood in a soaring hall, with black-and-white tile floors and a massive mahogany staircase that turned at a landing as it rose to the gallery along the second floor. The walls were paneled in matching mahogany, and portraits of men dressed in clothing from various periods of the past were hung in long rows. To the left and to the right, enormous doorways led to large rooms, both of which appeared to be filled with more artwork and antique furniture.

"I'm Mrs. Lewis," the woman said. The dog trotted off, clearly comfortable in this house. Harriet guessed he was looking for his owner. "I come here a few days a week to cook and clean for Lord Beresford. He's 'most always here, you see. He doesn't go out much, except to take Coleridge for walks, and if he has an appointment, I always know about it. But today when I came in, he wasn't here, and there's nothing in his diary about an appointment. He always writes his appointments in his diary."

"Perhaps he was called away unexpectedly?" Harriet hoped the words would soothe the woman, who seemed to be getting worked up, but Mrs. Lewis shook her head.

"The thing is, I don't think he's been here for several days. When I left Friday at noon, everything was fine. I had to pick up my grandson from school, you see. My daughter Marian was out of town for the weekend, a hen's trip with her school friends, and we got to keep little Grant, and we had so much fun with him. He's only five, and he's such a doll."

Just as Harriet was trying to figure out how to get her back on topic, she seemed to remember what she was saying. "Anyway, I left here around noon, and he didn't say anything about plans to go out, but when I showed up today, the mail had piled up, and so had the newspaper."

"No one else took it in?" Harriet asked.

Mrs. Lewis blinked and narrowed her eyes. "Who would have done so?"

"I'm sorry." Harriet could see she'd upset the woman. "I don't mean—I just thought, surely he doesn't live in this big house all alone?"

She nodded. "Lord Beresford is the only resident since his wife passed. There's no one else who would have collected the mail and the like. The gardeners and the men who deal with the estate don't come into the house. I'm the only one who works inside. Have been, since Beatrice passed."

Harriet assumed Beatrice was the baron's late wife.

"Well, maybe he decided to go away for the weekend?" she suggested. "A holiday, like your daughter?"

Mrs. Lewis narrowed her eyes, but then she shook her head. "You're new here, of course. The thing is, Lord Beresford doesn't really go on holiday. He doesn't like to leave the house much at all."

If Harriet lived in a place like this, she wouldn't want to leave it either.

"He's something of a recluse," Mrs. Lewis continued. "Aside from his walks along the cliffs with Coleridge, he pretty much doesn't leave. So for him to vanish like this is totally out of character."

"Have you tried calling him?"

"He doesn't have a cell phone," she said. "Old-fashioned that way. Well, in most ways. Says he doesn't need one because he never goes anywhere, which, okay, that's not unfair. I've tried to convince him he needs one for safety, for when he's walking Coleridge, but he always says he's walking with a giant dog and he couldn't be safer if he was walking with a member of M15."

Harriet wouldn't have gone as far as saying the dog was as good at protection as the British Security Service, but it was true that the sheer size of the bloodhound would deter most anyone with bad intentions.

"And now that I know Coleridge was found wandering the streets…"

"That's unusual too?" Harriet guessed.

"Very," Mrs. Lewis said. "Lord Beresford loves that dog. He would never let him roam free like that. And then there's the study."

"The study?"

Mrs. Lewis nodded. "I'll show you."

Harriet was bewildered, but she followed the housekeeper, drawn both by a sense of obligation and, she had to admit, curiosity. She wanted to see more of this incredible house and to learn more about its reclusive owner.

Mrs. Lewis led her to the left, into a formal drawing room of some kind. The coffered ceilings soared above the marble floors, which were partially covered by several thick area rugs. The walls were covered with the same wood inlaid panels, and two distinct seating areas sat on either side of a massive fireplace with an intricately carved marble mantel. Long velvet curtains framed the windows, and more artwork dotted the walls—moody landscapes, serene still lifes, triumphant battle scenes, representations of Greek and Roman mythology mixed with Impressionist pastoral scenes, and more modern abstract paintings. Harriet wanted to stop and study them, but Mrs. Lewis walked across the parlor and through a doorway on the far side of the room.

Harriet followed her through the doorway and into a room that was smaller, but no less grand. A vast wooden desk was framed by picture windows that looked out over the formal gardens behind the house. A leather-bound book and a sleek silver laptop sat closed on the top, and a leather-covered desk chair sat behind it, a wool cardigan draped over the back. Two leather club chairs sat across from the desk, with a matching couch nearby. More artwork hung on the walls, and Harriet immediately spotted a small painting of a dog. Coleridge, she was pretty sure, and she recognized it right away as one of her grandfather's pieces.

These observations took a back seat in her mind when she saw that the rug had been pushed up, caught by one of the club chairs as if it had been shoved aside. A round wooden table between the club chairs was on its side.

"See the glass there?" Mrs. Lewis said, pointing. Harriet stepped farther into the room and saw what she was pointing at. On the far side of the desk, a smashed glass decanter lay in a dark spot on the rug. "There's something that looks like blood on it."

Harriet bent down and saw that she was right—there was a smear of something dark red on several shards of broken glass.

"That is very strange," Harriet said, straightening up. She suddenly got the sense that she shouldn't touch or disturb anything in the room.

"Do you think something has happened to him?" Mrs. Lewis said. She seemed flustered, overwhelmed, and at a loss as to what to do. Harriet supposed it was no doubt a shock to find the room like this.

"I wouldn't know," Harriet said, just as Coleridge wandered into the room. He sniffed around and then settled on the rug in front of the fireplace, resting his head on his front paws. "But this does seem like a bad sign. I can't really imagine how anything good could have led to this." She looked again at the overturned table, the disturbed rug, and the broken glass smeared with something that resembled blood. "If he doesn't typically leave the house—"

"Not like this, he doesn't."

"And with Coleridge left to wander the streets..." As she said it out loud, she realized how bad it all sounded. "If his behavior seems unusual to you, I think it might be worth reporting it to the police."

Mrs. Lewis nodded. "That's what I thought too. I'll give them a call now. I'll let them know that Lord Beresford is missing."

While Mrs. Lewis placed the call, Harriet stepped forward to study the painting her grandfather had made. She recognized his distinctive realistic style, the soft-edged lines and warm light that always infused his paintings. Many of his paintings had featured animals, so she was sure it was his even before she spotted his signature in the corner of the canvas.

The painting showed a much younger and smaller Coleridge, splayed across a rug in front of the fireplace in this very room. Behind him, a fire burned in the hearth and cast a warm glow over the scene. The dog wore a leather collar studded with bits of metal, which gaped around his puppy-size neck. It was a good likeness of the dog, and a charming image overall.

"I don't know how long he's been gone," Mrs. Lewis was saying into the phone. "The last time I saw him was Friday around noon."

Harriet listened as Mrs. Lewis explained the situation to the person on the other end of the line. "The new lady vet brought his dog back. She said he'd been found on the streets. Lord Beresford would never let Coleridge wander free like that."

Mrs. Lewis was quiet for a moment, and then her tone sharpened. "I've been working at this house since you were in diapers, Van Worthington. I know when something's wrong. You come out here and see for yourself." She hung up and informed Harriet, "Detective Constable Worthington is on his way. Have you met him?"

Harriet nodded. "I have." She'd gotten to know Van when she got caught up in helping to solve the mystery of the Ravenglen Manor jewel heist.

"His mother is an old friend. Anyway, I don't suppose you need to stick around until he shows up. But I don't know what to do about him." She gestured toward Coleridge.

Harriet turned to the dog. His eyes were big, his posture and face forlorn. "I can take him for now, until Lord Beresford comes back. We have boarding facilities at the clinic."

"Would you?" Mrs. Lewis asked. "I'm sure you'd take better care of him than I could. My husband doesn't like dogs."

Harriet would never understand how someone could dislike dogs, but she kept that to herself. "Of course. Could I grab his things? Like his leash, bed, and food? Familiar things often help a dog feel settled in a new place."

"Come with me." Mrs. Lewis took one last glance around the study then led Harriet through another doorway and into a large room lined with bookshelves and scattered with overstuffed chairs, Coleridge on their heels.

They stepped into a hall and toward a small room that led to what appeared to be a back door. This entryway was far less grand than the front, with chipped tile floors, scuffed white beadboard walls, and hooks holding various coats and hats. Coleridge sat down in the doorway.

"Here's a leash," Mrs. Lewis said, pulling one from a bin. "It's not the one Lord Beresford usually uses though." She dug through the bin but apparently didn't find the leash she was hunting for.

"Is there a collar in there?" Harriet asked.

"Again, not the one he usually uses, but there's this old one." She pulled out a leather collar, and Harriet recognized it right away as the one she'd seen in the picture of puppy Coleridge. "It might be too small."

Harriet took it and moved to Coleridge, who sat still while she fastened the collar around his neck. It still fit, and it didn't seem to make him uncomfortable. She got it fastened and then stroked his head. He was a sweet dog.

"His food is through here," Mrs. Lewis said, leading Harriet and Coleridge out of the mudroom.

They made their way through a narrow room lined with old sinks—a scullery, perhaps—and into a large kitchen that bore some evidence of having been updated decades ago. Oak cabinets were stained dark to enhance the grain, and the floor and counter were both made up of tan square tiles. A busy floral wallpaper and valences over the windows made Harriet feel as if she'd stepped back in time, but in a different way from the rest of the house.

Mrs. Lewis opened a cabinet and loaded cans of food from it into a tote bag. It was a brand Harriet knew and recommended to her patients.

"Does he sleep in a crate?" Harriet asked. "Or a dog bed?"

"No," Mrs. Lewis said. "Lord Beresford usually lets him share his bed. He spoils that dog, I tell you."

No matter how sweet he was, Harriet was not about to let the dog sleep on her bed, but she wouldn't try to get him to sleep in a crate either. He would probably be fine with a dog bed.

"I think that's about it," Mrs. Lewis said, handing the bag to Harriet. "Thank you for taking care of him. I know Lord Beresford will be grateful."

"Hopefully it will only be for a little while," Harriet said. "I'm sure he'll turn up soon."

"Let's hope so."

Harriet and Mrs. Lewis exchanged numbers so the housekeeper could let her know when the dog's master returned, and then Harriet followed the older woman back through the grand rooms to the front of the house again.

She took her leave and walked to the Land Rover, her feet crunching over the crushed shell drive, and opened the door. She got Coleridge settled inside then climbed into the driver's seat and started the engine as a police car pulled into the parking area. Harriet held up a hand in greeting as she passed Van Worthington, and then she cast one last glance at the manor before starting down the long driveway. She kept expecting Mr. Darcy or Lord Grantham to step out, but apparently it was a real lord who lived in that great big house.

Back at Cobble Hill Farm, she took Coleridge into the house, where she let him off the leash and let him wander around sniffing as he inspected each room.

"You're going to be staying with me for a little while," she explained as she led him into the kitchen and set his food on the counter. Some people thought it was silly to talk to animals, but Harriet knew they could understand the tone and emotion of a person's voice, if not the words themselves. She did her best to sound calm and confident. "I'm sure you're confused about where your owner is, but he'll be back soon. And I'll take good care of you in the meantime."

She got a bowl, filled it with canned food, and set it on the floor beside a bowl of water. Coleridge quickly wolfed down the entire bowl and then got a drink. Maxwell hurried over, his little wheels squeaking, and Harriet laughed and refilled the bowl.

"You were hungry, weren't you?" She patted Coleridge on the head.

Harriet glanced at the clock on the wall. It was nearly six. She was supposed to have dinner with Aunt Jinny tonight and was due to be over at her place shortly, but she wanted to take Coleridge out for a few minutes before she left. She led him out the back door toward the fenced area behind the barn, where she unclipped him.

"Go on. Check it out."

Coleridge sniffed his way tentatively around the yard, and after a few minutes of exploring, she called him back in.

"I'm going to go have my dinner now," she said to the dog as she led him inside. "Make yourself at home. Maxwell and Charlie will show you around, and I'll return in a little while for a walk."

As if he understood, Coleridge moseyed through the house and settled down in front of the fireplace in the living room. Maxwell rushed over to sit near him. Harriet went to the kitchen to wash her hands. She tossed a salad to take to Aunt Jinny's, and then she put on a sweater—even though it was July, Yorkshire would never get as hot as the summers she was used to—and walked across the yard to the dower cottage.

"Hello," Aunt Jinny said when she opened the door. "You know, you don't need to knock or anything. You're family. You can simply come in, especially when I'm already expecting you." She took the salad bowl from Harriet and pulled her into a hug.

"I'll work on it," Harriet said. She was struck once again by how much her aunt reminded her of Dad. They had the same nose, the same chin, the same light-colored hair. It was like looking at a female version of her father. "How are you?"

"I'm good. Busy day seeing patients. With the nicer weather, everyone seems to be getting outside and hurting themselves. I had two sprained ankles and a burn from a grilling incident today."

"I'm sorry to hear that, though I'm glad you're getting business."

"True. And I'm always happy to help." She smiled and led Harriet into her kitchen, a cozy room with ceiling beams, white cabinets, and a tera-cotta tile floor. An large range and worn dining table took up most of the space in the room, and it had the air of a place that had seen many cups of tea and family meals. A pan of something that smelled delicious sizzled on the stovetop. "Anyway, how was your day?"

"Fine until the end, and then it got kind of strange," Harriet said. "Do you know who Liam Beresford is?"

"The baron, right?" Aunt Jinny set the salad on the table and moved toward the range. "He's a part of the landed gentry, if you care about that kind of thing." Her tone of voice made it clear she didn't. "I knew his younger brother, Peter, years ago. Why?"

"Someone brought his dog into the clinic today. It was running around loose." Harriet told Aunt Jinny about what had happened and about her visit to the manor house.

"So the baron is missing?" Aunt Jinny took the pan off the stove and brought it to the table.

"I don't really know," Harriet said. "Mrs. Lewis thinks it's suspicious and called the police. Van showed up to investigate as I was leaving. Mrs. Lewis couldn't take the dog, so I brought him home."

"Liam does love that dog," Aunt Jinny said. "And I suppose that makes sense. He's pretty much Liam's sole companion these days."

"What's his story?" Harriet asked.

"Lord Beresford's?" Aunt Jinny set a pitcher of water and the bowl of salad on the table.

"Yes. I don't really understand what a baron is."

Aunt Jinny chuckled. "Why don't we sit down and pray, and then I'll explain?"

They took their places at the table, and Aunt Jinny asked the Lord to bless the food and their time together. After the prayer, she raised her head. "So, you know about titles, right? The peerage system?"

"I know that in Regency novels everyone wants to marry a duke. I assume that means that's the highest?" Harriet guessed.

"Short of the royal family, which is a whole nother ball of wax, I suppose it is. It goes, from highest to lowest, duke, marquess, earl, viscount, baron, baronet."

"So baron's not that high."

"To be included in the peerage at all is meant to be a big deal. Whether it actually is or not is up for debate," Aunt Jinny said.

"And those titles are inherited, right? That's why everyone in the movies is so anxious to have an heir to take over the title and land and such."

"Correct. Some of the titles have been passed down for hundreds of years, while others have been created or died out in that time," Aunt Jinny said.

"It all seems a bit undemocratic. To be handed a ticket to wealth and privilege—or not, based entirely on the circumstances of your birth, which no one can control."

"It isn't all that different from how it works across the pond, is it?" Aunt Jinny countered. "The difference is that instead of titles, it's generational wealth. You all get rich through business or a profession and pass wealth along that way. Some are born into luxury while others aren't."

Harriet couldn't argue with that.

"Besides, not all of them inherit wealth along with the title," Aunt Jinny continued. "Many inherit a pile of crushing debt, as well as the weight of the responsibility of keeping a crumbling estate running."

Harriet picked up her fork and lit into the dish she'd learned was called "bubble and squeak." It was made of whatever was left over from Sunday's meal, which today was cabbage, potatoes, carrots, and roast.

"The Baron Beresford is a title that's been around for hundreds of years," Aunt Jinny said. "The original baron was loyal to the crown and was granted the title and the land after Charles II returned to the throne when Cromwell was defeated in the seventeenth century. The first baron built a house on that land, though it's been rebuilt more than once since that time. The house, land, title, and living has been passed down through the generations. The current Baron Beresford inherited it about thirty years ago, after the death of his father."

"Mrs. Lewis told me he's kind of a recluse."

"That's true. He does mostly keep to himself. I think Dad was one of the few people who really spent time with him."

"Grandad was friends with him?"

"Yes, they were friends for many years. From what I understand, the baron was very interested in art and architecture and things of that sort, so he and Dad had that in common. But Dad is so much older, and Liam was never particularly extroverted. Peter, the younger brother, was always much more friendly and outgoing, but even as a boy, Liam seemed standoffish almost to the point of being rude. But I guess he and Dad saw something in each other."

"Grandad always did like to take in strays," Harriet said.

"Isn't that the truth?" Aunt Jinny chuckled.

"Mrs. Lewis mentioned that his wife passed away," Harriet said. "Does he have children?"

"Two sons, I believe. An heir and a spare, as they say."

Harriet speared a potato. "So the eldest will inherit the title and house someday?"

"I suppose he will. Though I believe he lives in London and isn't around much. I haven't heard or seen anything of him in quite a while."

"Would you have interacted with him much anyway?" Aunt Jinny had attended parties at Ravenglen Manor, but Harriet couldn't imagine her down-to-earth aunt enjoying cocktail parties and polo matches with members of the aristocracy.

"Probably not, but typically the heir stays close and is active in the community. Gets involved, shows he cares about the locals, that kind of thing. Raises funds for charity, ingratiates himself."

"It sounds like his father doesn't do a lot of that either." Harriet took another bite.

"True enough. And I suppose he'll inherit either way."

"What if the eldest was a daughter? Would she inherit the title?"

"In some cases, women can inherit titles, and in others, they can't. They changed the law a few years ago to make it easier for women to inherit the crown, but that didn't affect every title. It depended on how they were created back in the day. It's all very steeped in history. I believe this one would pass to the nearest male heir if the baron didn't have a son."

"Are we still living in a world where women don't have the same rights as men? It's so archaic and unfair," Harriet said.

"You aren't the first to say so. There are plenty of people who would like to abolish the peerage system altogether."

"I imagine there's a small but strong minority who are fighting that tooth and nail?"

Aunt Jinny nodded. "I'm sure it'll come as no surprise to you that the people who profit from the system don't want to see it abolished."

Harriet wiped her hands on a napkin. "Do you think there's any chance they would ever abolish it?"

"Who can say? I don't really think about it. It doesn't have much of an impact on my life, nor the lives of most people in England."

The conversation moved on to a funny incident that had happened at Aunt Jinny's clinic that day, and while Harriet enjoyed the rest of the meal, part of her kept thinking about the tradition of inherited titles.

After she'd helped Aunt Jinny clean up from dinner, Harriet said, "I need to take Coleridge for a walk before it gets dark. Any chance you want to come with me?"

"Sure. I could use some exercise. Let me grab a sweater."

A few minutes later they walked back to the big house and Harriet clipped the leash onto Coleridge's collar. Together they started off toward the footpath that led to the cliffs over White Church Bay. As they passed the clinic's parking area, Coleridge started barking. The deep, sonorous sound startled Harriet.

Harriet followed his gaze. "Who's that?" There was a man by the gallery. He had curly brown hair, and he froze when he saw her.

"Who?"

"Over there." Harriet pointed as the man hopped into a little silver car. Coleridge barked again and strained against the leash. "Hello?" Harriet called. "Can I help you?"

The car zoomed backward. She rushed toward it, hoping to—to what? Hoping to stop the man? In his car? She didn't know. But she was certain something wasn't right.

Regardless of how fast she moved, the car was faster. By the time she and Coleridge got to the gallery, all she saw was a cloud of dust as the car disappeared down the driveway.

A NOTE FROM THE EDITORS

We hope you enjoyed the first volume in the Mysteries of Cobble Hill Farm series, published by Guideposts. For over seventy-five years, Guideposts, a nonprofit organization, has been driven by a vision of a world filled with hope. We aspire to be the voice of a trusted friend, a friend who makes you feel more hopeful and connected.

By making a purchase from Guideposts, you join our community in touching millions of lives, inspiring them to believe that all things are possible through faith, hope, and prayer. Your continued support allows us to provide uplifting resources to those in need. Whether through our communities, websites, apps, or publications, we inspire our audiences, bring them together, and comfort, uplift, entertain, and guide them. Visit us at guideposts.org to learn more.

We would love to hear from you. Write us at Guideposts, P.O. Box 5815, Harlan, Iowa 51593 or call us at (800) 932-2145. Did you love *Digging Up Secrets*? Leave a review for this product on guideposts.org/shop. Your feedback helps others in our community find relevant products.

Find inspiration, find faith, find Guideposts.

Shop our best sellers and favorites at
guideposts.org/shop

Or scan the QR code to go directly to our Shop

Find more inspiring stories in these best-loved Guideposts fiction series!

Mysteries of Lancaster County

Follow the Classen sisters as they unravel clues and uncover hidden secrets in Mysteries of Lancaster County. As you get to know these women and their friends, you'll see how God brings each of them together for a fresh start in life.

Secrets of Wayfarers Inn

Retired schoolteachers find themselves owners of an old warehouse-turned-inn that is filled with hidden passages, buried secrets, and stunning surprises that will set them on a course to puzzling mysteries from the Underground Railroad.

Tearoom Mysteries Series

Mix one stately Victorian home, a charming lakeside town in Maine, and two adventurous cousins with a passion for tea and hospitality. Add a large scoop of intriguing mystery, and sprinkle generously with faith, family, and friends, and you have the recipe for *Tearoom Mysteries*.

Ordinary Women of the Bible

Richly imagined stories—based on facts from the Bible—have all the plot twists and suspense of a great mystery, while bringing you fascinating insights on what it was like to be a woman living in the ancient world.

To learn more about these books, visit Guideposts.org/Shop